Visual C++ For Visual Basic Programmers

Bill Locke

Addison-Wesley

Boston • San Francisco • New York • Toronto • Montreal
London • Munich • Paris • Madrid
Capetown • Sydney • Tokyo • Singapore • Mexico City

Many of the designations used by manufacturers and sellers to distinguish their products are claimed as trademarks. Where those designations appear in this book, and Addison-Wesley were aware of a trademark claim, the designations have been printed in initial capital letters or in all capitals.

The author and publisher have taken care in the preparation of this book, but make no expressed or implied warranty of any kind and assume no responsibility for errors or omissions. No liability is assumed for incidental or consequential damages in connection with or arising out of the use of the information or programs contained herein.

The publisher offers discounts on this book when ordered in quantity for special sales.

For more information, please contact:

Pearson Education Corporate Sales Division

201 W. 103rd Street

Indianapolis, IN 46290

(800) 428-5331

corpsales@pearsoned.com

Visit AW on the Web: www.awl.com/cseng/

ISBN **0672322188**

Text printed on recycled paper

1 2 3 4 5 6 7 8 9 10—CRS—05 04 03 02

First printing, March 2002

ASSOCIATE PUBLISHER
Linda Engelman

ACQUISITIONS EDITORS
Karen Wachs
Jenny Watson

DEVELOPMENT EDITOR
Karen Wachs

MANAGING EDITOR
Charlotte Clapp

PROJECT EDITOR
Linda Seifert

COPY EDITOR
Pat Kinyon

INDEXER
Sandra Henselmeier

PROOFREADER
Jody Larsen

TECHNICAL EDITORS
Lyle Bryant
Randy Cornish

TEAM COORDINATOR
Lynne Williams

INTERIOR DESIGNER
Gary Adair

PAGE LAYOUT
Susan Geiselman

Contents at a Glance

Contents

About the Author

Bill Locke is a consultant with Oakwood Systems Group (http://www.oakwoodsys.com), a leading consulting firm based in St Louis. Bill works in Oakwood's Nashville, TN office.

Bill has been involved in the development of tools and add-ons for Visual Basic for as many years as Visual Basic has existed. The original author of VBTools, one of the first custom control packages for Visual Basic, he has developed Visual Basic tools in C and C++ for the past ten years. In that time, he has more than 100 commercially sold custom controls to his credit.

During many of those years, Bill worked as lead developer at MicroHelp Inc., once a leading tools vendor. He is currently a partner in BeCubed Inc (http://www.becubed.com), also a producer of add-on tools.

Bill has spoken at VBITS and other conferences around the United States and the world about the complexities and virtues of using the C++ language to enhance Visual Basic programming.

Dedication

To my family, my wife Lori and our children Christine, Alex, Katie Lou, and William.

To "Granny Lou," our children's great grandmother, who passed away while I was writing this book.
We miss you.

Acknowledgments

There are always many people to thank when doing a project of this type. Invariably you forget to mention someone, and for that I apologize.

First, I thank my entire family—in particular, my wife who takes care of me and our children. Without her support, I would have undoubtedly quit before completing this book. My eight-year-old daughter Christine, who is always first at the door with a hug when I get home. My five-year-old son Alex, who is always first in the car if we're going flying. My daughter Katie Lou, who has been in charge of the house since she turned two, six months ago. My one-year-old son William, who thinks the lights and switches on my computer equipment are for his sole amusement.

To all the people at Sams who worked on the book. In particular, Karen Wachs whose encouragement helped all the way through the project and Lyle Bryant for the technical editing.

Thanks to Bob Flickinger at BeCubed Software for providing code and technical assistance.

Thanks to Oakwood Systems Group for providing a way to make a living so that I was able to choose to write this book in my spare time.

Thanks to you, the reader for buying the book and spending your valuable time reading it.

And finally and most important, I acknowledge our Lord. Proverbs 3:6 says it best, "In all thy ways acknowledge him, and he shall direct thy paths."

Introduction

This book was written for intermediate to advanced Visual Basic programmers. It is not for advanced C and C++ programmers, although intermediate level C programmers might find the book beneficial. Many chapters would be tedious for someone who does not know Visual Basic, because of all the comparisons that are drawn to Visual Basic code.

So now that I have the Visual Basic programmer's attention, I want to ask a simple question. Do you want to program in C, C++, or C#? Are these languages that you want on your tool belt? This question may be more difficult to answer than you might expect.

Why should you care about these languages? The short answer is that the C family of languages is the consummate choice of programmers who want to program without restrictions. You can think of anything you want to do in programming and there is a way to get it done in C, C++, and C#. There are very few language families that can make that claim. Given that, isn't C a language that you would like to know?

The longer answer has to do with the evolution of Basic and C. In the past, Visual Basic had definite advantages in designing user interfaces. It was much simpler to do in Visual Basic than in C or C++. Now, C# and Visual Basic (and a number of other languages, for that matter) use the same designer and share the same user interface design capabilities. The advantage has slipped away from Visual Basic in this department.

Visual Basic had some other qualities that made it easier to develop and use end user programs, especially for fairly inexperienced programmers. This advantage has slipped away too. The latest Visual Basic is a magnitude more complicated than previous versions and much harder to get your arms around. Moving to the latest Visual Basic language from Visual Basic 6 may be just as difficult as making the move to C#.

Microsoft says choosing a language is a lifestyle choice now. I think the choice carries more implications than that. C has always been the internal development language at Microsoft—well, C or a derivative of C. First was C, then C++, and now C# is being used extensively at Microsoft. What affect does this have on the language? Just the effect you might expect. If a Microsoft programmer needs a feature in C, C++, or C# to get his job done, he or she typically gets that feature. So now you are faced with a situation where C# is actually more capable than Visual Basic but, because of the designer, it's just as easy to use.

For example, C# can be used to write unmanaged code; Visual Basic cannot. C# can override operators; Visual Basic cannot. C# can access memory directly; Visual Basic cannot. We could go on with this list and we will later, but the point I want to make now is that Microsoft uses C# as the premier development language in the .NET technologies.

Am I advocating that you switch to C# now? I am advocating that you learn a language that is and has been at the top of this game for many years. This book will concentrate on components and about the differences in Visual Basic and C. I will show you how to write routines and objects that you can use to augment your Visual Basic skills. At the same time, there is enough information in this book to shift to C# completely if you want. My main point remains that you will want to know enough about these languages to augment your Visual Basic skills. If you decide to shift to the C family altogether, this is a good way to begin your transition.

The following summary should introduce you to the main aspects of this book.

- Chapter 1: "How Did We Get Here?"—This chapter will take you on a short history lesson. If you've been in Visual Basic from the start, it may be a review for you. I think, however, that it is good to know where you came from, so you can better understand where you are going.

- Chapter 2: C Basics"—This chapter talks about "bare" C (C language without the C++ extensions), how the language is structured, and the differences between C and Basic code. Samples will be used to demonstrate the differences. This chapter will be a basis for both C++ and C#, because both of these languages are built on the C concept.

- Chapter 3: "C Programming"—This chapter continues the discussion on bare C programming. This chapter lays the foundation for understanding variable types in C and C++. It also covers common programming constructs in C, such as decisions and looping.

- Chapter 4: "C++ Basics"—This chapter will talk about C++ and the basic differences between C and C++. The C++ compiler added features to the language that are not necessarily directly related to classes. We'll cover those changes and prepare you for understanding C++ classes.

- Chapter 5: "C++ Classes"—This chapter focuses on C++ classes. C++ classes are the most common way for a programmer to get introduced to implementation inheritance, and we'll spend a little time understanding this. Inheritance is something that you'll want to understand if you intend to program in C++ or C# technologies.

- Chapter 6: "C++ and Windows"—This chapter is an introduction to the underlying components in a WIN32 program and contains some sample C code that shows how to interact with those components. If you intend to do much work in C or C++ in WIN32, these basics are good to know.

- Chapter 7: "C DLL Basics"—This chapter will take you back a little bit to an older, but still useful technology, a function-based DLL. Many of the features that more modern technologies rely on are implemented in simple DLLs. You'll learn how to write them in this chapter. This chapter also covers basic type conversions between Visual Basic and C.

- Chapter 8: "C DLL Practical Examples"—This chapter contains the samples for the preceding C DLL chapter. It includes samples on subclassing and callbacks. It also provides a discussion about using a type library to simplify access to your DLL.

- Chapter 9: "Components and Controls"—This chapter talks briefly about creating components in different technologies. It discusses the differences between COM technologies and .NET technologies. Then it moves into control technology in depth. It addresses ActiveX control development in detail.

- Chapter 10: "C# Basics"—This chapter will lead you through the differences of the most modern language offerings from Microsoft. We'll discuss the basics of C#. C# was designed from the ground up to do the job that Microsoft has outlined for the .NET technologies and will likely become the premier MS development language.

- Chapter 11: "Applying C#"—In this last chapter, you'll take a deeper look into C# and build a component with it. We'll demonstrate some of the practical differences between C# and the previous development languages.

If you've been thinking about learning to program in C, now is the time to start the journey. You have a steep hill to climb moving from Visual Basic to .NET technologies, and it just might afford you the opportunity to expand your language choice.

How Did We Get We Here?

IN THIS CHAPTER

To learn about C programming is the obvious answer. To take that further, you are really learning to program in C, C++, and C# to support Visual Basic. As such, my view of the history of Visual Basic is slanted very much towards tool development. So, as you begin the task of exploring C, let's talk about what brought you to this point. You learn a lot from history. For example, one thing I've learned is that no matter what the development environment is today, expect it to change. Program in the lowest common denominator when possible.

For me, that has meant bare C code. I have bare C code running in 32-bit controls today that was written back in Visual Basic 1 and 2 timeframes. It runs in this environment, maybe with small changes, just as well as it did in 16 bit.

For example, look at the number of ways that you can write Graphics Device Interface (GDI) code—bare C, MFC, WFC, Visual Basic drawing routines, and now .NET classes and I'm sure many that I've left out.

Many of these technologies abstract the underlying technologies. Why? Typically we abstract a technology to make it easier to use or to allow us to change the underlying technology without having to modify programs that utilize the abstracted layer.

However, if you continually change the abstraction layer, you defeat one of the purposes of abstraction. I am certain that at some point the underlying technology (Windows) will have to change enough to require major changes to legacy code. But I'm here to tell you that the abstraction layer changes a lot more than the underlying system.

I wrote GDI code in bare C for 16-bit VBX controls. When OLE controls came along, there was a lot of pressure to change to MFC for the GDI code (and many other aspects of the code for that matter). For some of it, I did make the change. Then, when ATL became the best option for writing controls, it had to change again.

In most of those cases for ATL, I went back to the 16-bit C code and converted it. It was easier and more applicable than the MFC code. I am not looking forward to writing it in yet another wrapper (.NET). I will probably continue to use the C code.

NOTE

.NET refers to the latest development environment from Microsoft. The code from this system runs "on top of" a common language runtime (CLR). The functionality from the underlying platform is encapsulated in class libraries that are programmed from a choice of languages (usually C#, VB.NET, or C++) that use the CLR.

Yes, I understand that I would give up any chance for cross platform execution of the code by doing this. Maybe more importantly, I would give up advantages provided by managed code in .NET. Those advantages will have to be weighed against the cost of the rewrite.

The CLR may give programmers a better shot at cross platform programming, but what will probably happen is that there will be limited success in cross platform ports, just like there is now. Programmers will probably continue to program for the platform that the code will run on to take advantage of the services provided by that platform, just like they do now. So my C code is probably pretty safe for now.

The Internet has placed a new twist on this cross platform issue. When programming on the Internet, you are delivering most of your code to browsers that are (or should be) providing that platform independence for you. The server-side code that you write (to deliver this UI to users through a browser) doesn't really need to be platform independent, does it? It runs on a dedicated server that is either NT based or UNIX or some flavor of UNIX. You program to the platform on the server and generate generic HTML (ideally).

Of course, in practice, most of us work with more than just straight HTML. We end up using DHTML, script, or some client-side control to get the desired result. In many cases, we limit the types of browsers that can access our site and get 100 percent functionality out of it. It's quite a tangled web (pun intended) to walk though.

We are in the middle of an evolution and revolution. There is a lot of work going on in Internet technologies, but there is still a lot of coding to be done in WIN32 as well. This is where most of us have our roots and it will continue to be an important technology.

A History of Visual Basic and C++

The history of these languages goes back a long way. Well, we're not talking biblical time frames here, but for computers, it was a while back. VB and C++ have their roots in the DOS world. (Most of my own experience in the DOS world was with Basic, I've written very little DOS C code.)

The battle lines between these two languages were drawn back in this environment. C was a professional's language, Basic was for kids playing at programming. A lot of this sentiment came about because of interpreted Basic, GWBasic being one of the more prevalent flavors. We used to call it Gee Wiz Basic and that described it pretty well. Basic has been fighting an uphill battle to gain respect since then.

When Windows came along, this again was a domicile for C programmers. No Basic programmers allowed, until Visual Basic. Enter Visual Basic 1.

16 Bit

We need to start with 16-bit systems because this is where Visual Basic began. Visual Basic 1 through 3 ran on 16-bit systems. Visual Basic 4 was the first 32-bit version to come along.

Thunder—Visual Basic 1

Thunder (the code name for the Visual Basic 1 project) took a big step. I remember listening to people talking about a fad, a toy, and other similar comments. It turns out that the product wasn't a toy or a fad at all. At the time, I worked at MicroHelp, and we turned out some of the first libraries for Visual Basic. It was so new at the time, people thought that we were the ones that integrated the tools into the toolbar!

Visual Basic 1 had a lot of shortcomings—P-code only, limited toolset, forms were saved in binary format, no add-ins. But it was an important first step. The concept of custom controls was born with that product; it was the birth of component programming as we know it today.

I remember some of the more popular controls in MicroHelp's first package. A multi-select list box, Visual Basic's first list box was single select only. A set of scrollbars that had continuous feedback, Visual Basic's scrollbars changed the value on mouse release only. How times change.

This component programming concept has spawned the largest "compiler add-on" segment that has ever been experienced with compilers.

In addition to component programming, Visual Basic 1 also introduced Basic programmers to the idea of event-driven programming. Up to this point in time, unless you were a C/SDK programmer, there wasn't much opportunity to do event-driven programming.

Event-driven programming was a new concept for programmers coming in to the world of Windows from DOS. And because of Visual Basic, the numbers migrating to this programming environment were substantial. All of a sudden, programmers who had never dreamed of programming in Windows were now doing it. What a revolution.

VBXs were the first components. Primitive in nature compared to today's components, but there was still a lot of good things to say about VBXs. They were fairly easy to write. They provided instance data. They provided shared data. VBXs were the first programming element to provide custom properties and events. VBXs were a DLL and carried all the advantages and disadvantages of a 16-bit DLL.

In today's 32-bit world, DLLs load into the executable's program space. Of course, 16-bit DLLs only loaded once. There were complications with Data Segments (DS) and Stack Segments (SS), but they had their advantages. You could use them as a very fast sort-of interprocess communication. You could optimize your code by knowing that only one instance of the code was loaded and that you actually had a data space that was shared between programs.

16-bit DLLs actually came the closest to delivering on what DLLs were originally designed for. The driving thought behind DLLs was to save space, be it in memory or on the disk. In today's environment, we've continually increased the complexity of handling DLLs (whether we call them VBXs, OCXs, COM objects, or whatever). It's to the point now where Microsoft's .NET initiative is cycling back to the days where the libraries were not registered but reside with the EXE.

There have been several complexities introduced in the name of solving "DLL Hell." Most of these complexities were really unnecessary. All that it took to solve the problem in the first place was to install your private DLLs in the directory with the EXE that used them. In 16-bit, this didn't actually solve the DLL hell problem. Because only one copy of a DLL was loaded into memory, it followed that only one copy could exist there. This had the phenomenon of causing programs to fail only while certain other programs were running.

For example, a 16-bit program would load a DLL that a second program uses. But perhaps the DLL was an earlier version of the DLL and was incompatible with the second program. If the second program tried to load while the first program was running, it would not have the proper DLL in memory, because the first program had loaded this other version. 32-bit programs didn't have this problem at all, because the DLLs loaded into the program's code space so both versions could coexist, as long as they were stored on the disk in such a way that each program loaded the proper version of the DLL.

In 32-bit, placing the DLLs with the EXE program would have worked. Because the DLL is loaded into the EXE's code space, different versioned DLLs would not conflict with each other. The registry and the complexities and problems it introduced was a solution to a problem that no longer existed.

But before we get to 32-bit code, we still have some 16-bit experiences to live through.

Visual Basic 2

Visual Basic 2 did not improve on Visual Basic 1.0 dramatically, but it did provide for some unique opportunities to break controls. The DLL-hell situation I have already described started biting control developers really hard, and I believe that it was about this time that Microsoft decided everything should go in the registry, there would be one copy of any DLL, and it should go in the system directory. Things were beginning to get ugly.

On the plus side, Visual Basic 2 added the capability for handling high-color densities within your controls. At the time, we called it 256-color support, but what it actually provided was a way to handle a palette for a control that contained a picture. This, of course, would handle more than 256 colors. We still could only use bitmaps, icons, and metafiles, and that would be true for a long time to come.

Visual Basic 2 also added light controls. All the messages for these controls actually went through the form or control on which that the light control was placed. The fact that the light controls didn't have window handles made management of them somewhat tricky. They had their place, but I chose not to write any of them.

VBFormat became available in Visual Basic 2, callable from your C code within the VBX. This would allow you to format strings using the Visual Basic string formatting "engine." This was quite useful in many controls, but it worked only in Visual Basic.

Getting back to the changes that gave you the ability to break your controls, if your control used any of the Visual Basic 2 functions, it had to check Visual Basic versions and somehow degrade if you were running under Visual Basic 1. This seems fairly trivial, but it depended on what the control was doing at the time as to how trivial this was.

In addition, there were properties that would be associated with VB2-only features. Again, not a big deal, except if a few months later you wanted to add a property to the control and make that property work in any version of Visual Basic. But those Visual Basic 2-only properties in the way. You had to "dummy" those properties in Visual Basic 1 to make it work.

Visual C++ 1

The development of controls for Visual Basic 1 and 2 was done with a DOS editor and a DOS C++ compiler (at least for me). I compiled from the command line and debugged with CodeView. Visual C++ 1.5 changed all of that.

I want to mention Visual C++ 1.52 and its support (although meager) for custom controls here because it is very relevant to the discussion of component programming. It's worth a mention if only because it's kept the original Visual Basic 1.0 custom control specification alive, even today. C++ 1.52 can be found on current MSDN distribution CDs as the current 16-bit C++.

After a few years, you tended to forget about the routines that weren't Visual Basic 1 compatible. Shouldn't be a big deal, right? Visual Basic 1.0 is long gone right? Not exactly! When Visual Basic 2 came out, Visual Basic 1 was still very prevalent. About the same time, Microsoft decided to add VBX support to C++. They decided that it would handle only the Visual Basic 1.0 specification. Who knew at that time it would be the last Visual C++ version done for 16-bit. So the Visual Basic 1 control specification lives on in VC 1.52. I've fixed a problem in a VBX concerning Visual C++ 1.52 this year. I can still write that code, but the entertainment value is pretty small. This is the first Visual C++ and the last 16-bit one.

Visual Basic 3

Visual Basic 3 took a step forward by adding database support. It wasn't really complete support, compared to SQL Server or any advanced database engine, but many people used it anyway.

As far as custom controls were concerned, we got our first taste of data binding. It was rather primitive, and most people who wrote serious code for Visual Basic 3 did not use data binding, but we wrote the code for the controls anyway.

Most people programming in Visual Basic 3 still used fairly heavy support from third-party tools. I can remember UnInstaller, an end user utility produced by MicroHelp. The 16-bit version of that utility used some 13 custom VBXs and a few DLLs written in C. The 32-bit version was a different matter, because more tools were delivered with the development environment.

In my opinion, Visual Basic 3 is the best 16-bit version of Visual Basic ever done. If you have to program in 16-bit, this is the best version of Visual Basic to use. Until Windows 2000, it even ran on multiple platforms (WIN9X/NT) better than some 32-bit code would. This was due to the fact that 16-bit emulation in NT was pretty good, but there were some real differences on the 32-bit side between WIN9X and NT that created some compatibility problems in 32-bit programs.

Visual Basic 4

Visual Basic 4 took a step back in terms of 16-bit programming. It did add support for 16-bit OLE, but I'm not sure why Microsoft bothered. Because Microsoft was basically leaving the 16-bit platform behind, the 16-bit Visual Basic 4, and especially the tools that supported it, were never tested very extensively.

So, Visual Basic 4 was never a serious tool for 16-bit development. Because it was recoded and placed on top of OLE, it was significantly slower in many instances than comparable Visual Basic 3 code.

Visual Basic 4 16-bit supported VBXs. It also supported 16-bit OLE Controls (OCXs). This is a technology that was born with and is still dieing with VB4-16. The VBX specification was not modified with Visual Basic 4, so the last VBX specification was the version for Visual Basic 3.

Because this is the "current" 16-bit Visual Basic, both VBXs from Visual Basic 3 and 16-bit OCXs are current technology for 16-bit. So the only 16-bit Visual Basic control specification that managed to get completely phased out was version 2 VBXs. All the rest of the add-on specifications are alive today. VBX version 1.0 is used in Visual C++ 1.52. VBX version 3.0 is used in Visual Basic 4. 16-bit OCX is used in Visual Basic 4.

Visual Basic 4—First Try

The software of importance in version 4 of Visual Basic ran in the 32-bit environment. It had its problems and so did the supporting 32 bit OCXs. However, it was the serious effort in version 4, which is the only version of Visual Basic that had both 16- and 32-bit versions.

I'm not sure why Microsoft decided to do that—build both 16- and 32-bit versions in the same release. It was difficult for Microsoft, and it was difficult for third-party add-on vendors. Two versions of everything had to be built and tested. It made the 16-bit versions suffer very badly, and even the 32-bit versions suffered some.

Microsoft made it clear that its path would be 32-bit. This made me wonder why they bothered with the 16-bit version of this compiler at all. Visual Basic 3 was a very capable 16-bit environment, and I prefer it over Visual Basic 4-16 even today. There were a few things that you could do with Visual Basic 4-16 that you could not do with Visual Basic 3. This was the only real reason to use VB4.

One of these items was OLE automation. Visual Basic 3 did not have this built in, but Visual Basic 4 did. If you needed an OLE-automated executable in 16 bit, VB4 would deliver that for you. One of the things that you were able to do with 16-bit automation is construct sort of a "poor man's" thunker (a way to call 16-bit DLL routines from 32 bit). The system did not care if automated executables were 16- or 32-bit, so you could use a 16-bit OLE automated executable from 32-bit.

If you had 16-bit code that you just had to access from 32 bit, it could be wrapped in a Visual Basic 4 OLE automated executable and used from a 32-bit program. This was not the fastest way to call routines of course, so if you could use actual thunking, that would be better. However, thunking is very platform dependant, while OLE automation is not.

You could find reasons to use Visual Basic 4-16, but they weren't very prevalent and the platform had more than its share of problems. I always recommended that people not move VB3 programs to VB4-16 unless they had very good reasons, like the one I've already talked about. Otherwise, I recommended people port directly to 32-bit.

32 Bit

The WIN 32 programming environment is the one that most of us are familiar with today. Very little work remains in Visual Basic 16-bit technologies.

Visual Basic 4

As I said earlier, the software of importance in version 4 of Visual Basic ran in the 32-bit environment. This compiler was rather unremarkable compared to the advances made in version 3.

Although VB4 managed to move us to 32-bit code, this was the first attempt for Visual Basic in 32-bit. It was still a P-code compiler with very few features outside of this fact to make you want to use it.

Visual Basic 5—Visual Studio 5

With Visual Basic 5 came a very serious tool. The ability to compile to native code and enough tools to support the environment without purchasing additional tools, added up to a very complete development system. ActiveX control development was introduced with this version of Visual Basic. For the first time, a Visual Basic programmer could write ActiveX controls.

Writing ActiveX controls in Visual Basic never caught on in a big way, something difficult to understand. It is a wonderful way to encapsulate the code whether you are delivering commercial code or writing code "in-house." Since Visual Basic 5, I have not done a significant custom project without writing custom controls. It may be that the practice of writing controls in the .NET technologies might finally catch on.

With the introduction of Visual Basic 5, Microsoft bundled several development products together. Visual Studio 5 is the first system that delivered a complete solution, including a C++ compiler. This was the start of a C++ compiler in every garage. Because you have the tool, why not use it? Visual C++ 2.0 was the first 32-bit C++ compiler, but version 4 was the first one that I used aggressively. You can tell from the version numbers in four that there were still some teething problems with 32 bit. Version 5 is the first one that was bundled into the new Visual Studio suite.

There were some very mild ways to use the Visual C++ 5 compiler or development environment, and there were some very aggressive ways.

Some of the milder ways of using the Visual C++ environment were things like the Find in Files feature (searching for a word or phrases in a file). It would be worth loading the Visual C++ 5 editor just for this feature. This will search files for text strings. It can restrict the search to selected file types. It can traverse subdirectories in the search. It provides a list of lines from files where the hits occur. You can double-click a line to load the file in the editor positioned on that line.

The macro recording capabilities of the editor for advanced editing is something that Visual Basic didn't have until the latest version. You can even debug a Visual Basic program in Visual C++, if it is compiled with the correct switches.

Some of the more aggressive ways to use C and C++ are the subject matter in this book. Visual Studio 5 is the first system that made all of this practical, because most programmers had all the compilers with this version. Of course, most Visual Basic programmers still didn't use the C++ compiler.

Visual Studio 6

Visual Basic 6 was data access revisited. It also added some controls and some tools in the form of wizards. But overall, the development environment did not change all that much from Visual Studio 5.

The reporting capability was added in Visual Basic 6. That was pretty underwhelming, and the proof is that Microsoft went back to Crystal for reporting in the .NET technologies. Adding hierarchical structure to record sets and the flex grid was pretty neat. I found a lot of uses for the hierarchical record sets.

Creating data sources was also useful. Disconnected recordsets and the ability to pass a record-set through a procedure call, even across processes, was a big improvement. This allowed the simple construction of multi-tier code.

The most welcome change for me in Visual Studio 6 was version 3 of ATL. This made the development of controls in this technology practical and much easier than earlier versions of ATL.

There were plenty of other changes in Visual Studio 6, but there were certainly no revelations. A recompile of your Visual Basic 5 project, and then it was pretty much business as usual.

.NET

The latest technology from Microsoft changes all the rules. Only Visual C/C++ will work essentially like they did before. Visual J++ is gone, Visual Interdev is gone, and Visual Basic is now based on a class model (as are all .NET languages). This is not your Grandma's Visual Basic. It requires a level of understanding not required for Visual Basic before. It also requires a port or rewrite for most code to work.

When Microsoft reported that Visual Basic would use implementation inheritance, I assumed they meant like in Visual C++, where it is optional. You can code in C or C++. Not so in .NET languages, they are class based, and this is the only way that they can work.

C# is the same way. Migrating from Visual Basic 6 to Visual Basic .NET will be difficult, possibly just as difficult as just going directly to C#. I think a lot of programmers will do just that, move directly to C#.

When we talk about writing code in languages that support the Common Runtime Language (CLR), we talk about writing managed code as compared to unmanaged code. Managed code runs on top of the CLR and is so named because objects are garbage collected for the programmer. Unmanaged code is any code that does not run on top of the CLR. C and C++ are unmanaged code (although C++ has managed extensions available), Visual Basic and C# in this new technology are managed code.

Visual Basic's Contribution

Visual Basic revolutionized the way we write Windows programs. The ease with which a user interface can be generated and the simplicity of placing code behind that interface has not been matched in any tool, except for possibly the managed code within .NET. VB is a wonderful environment, but don't get caught up doing things in it that you shouldn't. I have watched so many people try to make Visual Basic do things for which it was never designed. And to what end? Typically, when you hack something, it's unstable, hard to code, and difficult to debug. This describes some of the Visual Basic code I've seen written simply because it could be done.

You wouldn't use a rake to dig a hole. Using the right tool will usually always result in better code. Sometimes, the choice of tool will not make that big of a difference, sometimes it will. Don't be afraid to use C or C++ if the situation dictates that. This is the objective of this book, to put those tools to work for you.

Strengths of Visual Basic

The managed code in the .NET system has leveled the playing field for a lot of languages. To compare features, you have to lump most of the managed code languages together. For example, C# is more like Visual Basic than it is like C++ in terms of the features it provides. The design environment in .NET has grown out of the Visual Basic versions that preceded it.

Absolute Best Ever Interface Design Tool

Visual Basic is probably the strongest WIN32 RAD design tool there is. Visual Basic has always been the choice of programmers for the simple fact that you can design an interface in it in just a few minutes. .NET makes that available to many languages, but C and C++ are still pretty much the same.

Strong Typing

Visual Basic has always provided strong typing for variables. This eliminates mishandling of pointers because there are none and also eliminates the problems of incorrect casting, again because there is no casting.

Visual Basic does have conversions; intrinsic conversions will convert certain variables to other types when it believes that this is appropriate. Because these conversions introduce inadvertent bugs, you are much better off to convert explicitly. Don't confuse Variants, and variable conversions with loose typing, this isn't loose typing. The conversions and the Variants have a very strong set of rules as to what can be converted, loose typing doesn't.

Interactive Debugging Environment

In conjunction with the interface design capabilities of Visual Basic, the interactive environment has made Visual Basic what it is today. Programmers choose it and use it because you can write, run, debug, and change code on-the-fly, all without leaving the environment. Nothing compares to it.

Support from Tools Vendors

Visual Basic has always had great support from third-party vendors. This has grown from 8-10 vendors to literally hundreds of vendors. The choice of add-in tools for Visual Basic is staggering, and this will continue into the .NET system.

This only makes a Visual Basic programmer's job easier. You can use well-written, well-debugged, C code written by specialists tailored to do a specific job.

Weaknesses of Visual Basic

Although Visual Basic is a great RAD tool, this focus makes VB inappropriate for some programming requirements. Visual Basic does a great job helping programmers work efficiently and quickly. To do this, VB insulates the programmer from the underlying system, making access to the underlying system more difficult. That's the idea of this book—to show you those weaknesses and how to use C/C++ to close the gaps.

Speed and Efficiency

Forever we've talked about the speed of Basic code. Basic has never shaken the image it earned of being a toy, through interpreted Basic that ran in DOS on the original PC. Of course, early versions of Visual Basic helped support the idea that Basic is indeed slower. Running P-code instead of compiling to executable code slowed the earlier versions of Visual Basic.

With version 5, you could finally compile to code that would execute directly. Visual Basic 5 and 6 actually used the same compiler as Visual C. The speed (obviously) was very comparable. The only differences that really remained were the things that were being done in the Visual Basic runtime. Some things were still quite slow, string handling for example.

One of the biggest inefficiencies with Visual Basic, starting with version 4 had to do with Unicode strings. Visual Basic used Unicode strings internally, but because it interacted with ANSI systems, Microsoft decided that all calls out of Visual Basic to APIs would result in strings being translated to ANSI. Of course, the opposite conversion was made when the routine returned.

The .NET technologies return to the concept of an intermediate code (IL). Microsoft has taken steps to make sure that the IL Just in Time (JIT) compiler will run efficiently. However, if you want true compiled code, you can direct the JIT compiler to compile the entire project at installation.

Strong Typing

Visual Basic has always provided strong variable typing. This, along with the lack of pointers, creates a language that cannot elegantly handle some situations where the type of data may not be known until runtime. A classic example of this would be the SendMessage API where the lp parameter could contain almost any type of variable. This includes a pointer to any data type (structs and strings included), an int or long value directly in lp, or a combination of values, twp word values for example.

This type of data is pretty common in message systems that must handle various types of data. So while strong typing has its advantages, it also has disadvantages.

While Visual Basic supports a Variant data type, this does not address the issue of strong typing. A variant internally can contain many different types of data. Externally, however, it is still a variant and must be addressed as such. A Variant in VB will not understand a C string, nor will it handle a user-defined type. Both of these are quite common in the previous SendMessage sample.

Property Values Not in Code

Visual Basic has always been a joy to work with while designing interfaces. My only long-time beef with the design environment has been the way that control property values have been stored and the design of many controls with design-time only properties.

What I mean is that property values are written to the form file (.frm), with binary data going to the .frx file. It's usually not possible to tell when properties have been changed from their defaults. This makes debugging difficult with a control whose properties have been manipulated in design mode. Visual Basic has forced this kind of behavior by providing controls with properties that can only be changed in design mode. This effectively kills my workaround, which has always been to put property changes in code during the form load.

If property settings are in code, you have clear indications of what properties have been changed. .NET changes this for the better. There are no property storage mechanisms that cause the property values to be written to a property bag. The property setting goes in the code, right where I like it.

C++'s Contribution

C++ has always worked better for code that is closer to the system. Certainly user interface code has been written many times in C and C++, but that is not where its strengths are.

When we examine what has traditionally been coded in C++ compared to Visual Basic, the differences are strong. C and C++ are typically used for production-level code, while VB is used for RAD projects. For example, Visual Basic itself is written in C++. Most of the third-party controls that support Visual Basic are written in C++. Most of the Microsoft Office products are written in C/C++.

While most of us are not involved with production code at that level, there have to be reasons for the choices that have been made. It is usually possible to write more efficient code in C++ because you simply have more choices in the way you handle memory and the way you interact with the system. You are able to tailor the code to the specific process to make it faster or smaller. Even with .NET, there will be time that C/C++ is still the better or only choice.

Strengths of C++

Visual C++ really does have some qualities that make it a better choice for many programming jobs. Some of these differences are now mitigated in the .NET technologies, but many still remain. As we list these, we'll discuss the relationship to .NET technologies.

Implementation Inheritance

Implementation inheritance is an important programming strategy allowing common code to reside in base classes that can be used by classes that derive from those base classes. Inheritance makes it much easier to reuse your work.

Implementation inheritance has always been a strength of Visual C over Visual Basic. The .NET technologies have changed that, introducing implementation inheritance to Visual Basic programmers for the first time since the existence of Visual Basic.

Weaker Typing, Type Casting Possible

Weaker typing in C and C++ make type casting possible. C and C++ also use variable pointers. These two things combine to make C/C++ very flexible in the way that data is handled by the compiler. If you want a long value to become a pointer to a string, you can simply type cast it and poof—it's a string. You certainly should make sure that the long value contains a valid pointer to a string, but the point is that you can do this.

This makes C ideal for handling data passed around by a messaging system like Windows. It doesn't matter what that long value really is; it can be cast correctly with very little overhead and correctly handled by the code. Visual Basic has to jump through some real hoops to get this same thing done, usually resorting to memory copies into variables of the correct type.

Most Anything Is Possible

You can do many things in C++ that make the tool very flexible. C/C++ can handle pointers and manipulate memory directly. It works at a closer level with the Windows API. This API was designed to be called from C programs and, as such, the data and structures fit with writing bare C or C++ code.

C or C++ is also the tool that you would use to write "low-level" code, such as drivers and services.

More sample code is available in C and C++ than any other language. There is certainly a litany of sample code available in Visual Basic, but many areas that C sample code covers aren't even programmed in Visual Basic.

Weaknesses of C++

The very things that give C and C++ their strengths also contribute to their weaknesses. Simply because the language is lower level in nature and can access the system at that level results in the following shortcomings:

- *Nothing is really easy*—For all this flexibility, there is a price. C and C++ are harder to program than comparable code in Visual Basic. Handling pointers and typecasting are troublesome at best. Using classes results in better coding techniques, but these techniques are more difficult to grasp.

- *UI Design is tedious to say the least*—Writing user interface code in C or C++ is archaic compared to the way we do it in Visual Basic. C and C++ do not have designers like Visual Basic has always had. Classes make the C++ code easier than bare C code, but still more difficult than VB code. In fact, I think many people will find VB.NET code more difficult to write than traditional VB code because of the classes.

- *Weaker typing*—Of course weaker typing has its downside too. Pointers and casting are difficult concepts to grasp and hard to implement. There is plenty of room to make mistakes, and these mistakes are usually catastrophic to the program.

C#

C# is the latest offering from Microsoft in the C family. It is not a "traditional" C offering because of the fact that it is based on the CLR, just like all of the language in the .NET technology.

I find it slightly odd that Microsoft continued its unmanaged code option in C and C++ and did not provide that option in Visual Basic. I believe some people are going to like the "old" Basic and, without it in the new languages, this will stop some people from moving up.

Where does C# fit into our task of learning C and C++? I think that many people that make the move from Visual Basic to .NET technologies will move right to C#. Why? Because there is no real advantage in remaining with Visual Basic any longer. The class syntax in C# is easier and more logical than VB.NET, and some things are possible in C# that just aren't possible in Visual Basic .NET.

C# compared to VB.NET will have similar strengths. C# will have the same designer as Visual Basic, and the language runtime is the same for both languages. The largest difference in .NET will be the syntax.

C# shares many of the same strengths and weaknesses as C++. The biggest difference is that C# sits on top of a very large runtime (the CLR). This will affect its performance and certainly will affect the ease of distribution.

I feel very strongly that C# will be the future of Microsoft development products. This will be the premier .NET language and the one that will be used most often internally at Microsoft.

C Basics

IN THIS CHAPTER

You are probably wondering why you should learn bare C when there is so much to-do about C# and C++. Bare C is the most basic of the C language family and it's important to know it. C is the basis of the other languages (C++ and C#) and knowing C makes it easier to understand those languages.

A vast amount of sample code is available in C. Understanding C allows you read, use, and even convert that code to other languages like C++, C#, or even Visual Basic.

Using C is sometimes the only way to get small, independent DLLs or executables. C++, C#, and Visual Basic rely on a lot of support code—C does not. As a result, I have written useful DLLs in C that were as small as 4KB.

Remember too, that much of what can be done in any language depends on the system it is running on. Many Windows APIs can be used more effectively from C or C++ and this is one advantage to using those languages.

The idea of this chapter is to introduce you to the lowest common denominator and show you those statements as they are compared to Visual Basic. Whether you are writing code in C, C++, or C#, the basics of the languages are the same. In this chapter, we explore these basic language elements and how to use them. The chapters on C++ and C# will build on this chapter.

The sections in this chapter will cover the following topics:

- Tokens and Elements—This section includes keywords, identifiers, constants, and literals. These are the most basic elements of the language.
- Structure—This section talks about how to use the elements of the language. It discusses compiler directives, code structure, lifetime, scope, and visibility.
- Functions—This section explains how to create and use functions.

Earlier versions of Visual Basic are used for comparisons in most of this chapter. The latest version of Visual Basic in the .NET technologies is less illustrative of the differences because it is based on implementation inheritance and has little correlation to bare C.

Tokens and Elements

This section sets the foundation for learning C by looking at the smallest identifiable elements of code. Tokens and elements refer to those portions of the source code that will not be parsed by the compiler. These include things like keywords, identifiers, constants, and literals. The compiler breaks down the code to these elements to turn it into executable code. This is true of all compilers, including Visual Basic.

This section covers the following programming elements:

- Keywords contain many differences from Visual Basic. I'll map the C and VB keywords so that you can easily compare the two sets.
- Identifiers are quite similar in either language. Some definite differences exist and I'll point them out in this section.
- Constants are handled quite differently in the two languages. Some things can be done in C that aren't even possible in VB, such as macros. On the other hand, some things in Visual Basic that were true constants are handled as constant variables in C, such as strings.
- Literals do not exist in Visual Basic. Visual basic has string constants. In C, you must use string literals, which function similarly to string constants.
- Predefined constants exist in both languages. In VB, they are quite prevalent. There are very few in C and they are not often used.

Keywords

Keywords define a language and its capability. Table 2.1 lists the keywords in C, a brief description of each, and the Visual Basic counterparts.

TABLE 2.1 List of C Keywords

Keyword	Fundamental Use	Visual Basic Equivalent
auto	Variable scope	None (is the default)
break	Loop, decision	exit for, exit do
case	Decision	Case
char	Variable type	string (similar)
const	Variable modifier	None
continue	Loop	Next
default	Decision construct	Case Else
do	Loop	Do—Loop
double	Variable type	Double
else	Decision	Else
enum	Variable type	Enum
extern	Variable scope	Public (similar)
float	Variable type	Single
for	Loop	For
goto	Jump	Goto
if	Decision	If

TABLE 2.1   Continued

Keyword	Fundamental Use	Visual Basic Equivalent
int	Variable type	Long
long	Variable type	Long
register	Variable scope	None
return	Function return	Exit Function (similar)
short	Variable type	Integer
signed	Variable qualifier	None
sizeof	Variable size	Len (similar)
static	Variable scope	Static
struct	User-defined type	Type
switch	Decision	Select Case
typedef	New variable type	None
union	Type of structure	Simulate with types
unsigned	Variable qualifier	None
void	Empty return value	None, use Sub
volatile	Variable scope	None
while	Loop	While—Wend

Identifiers

Identifiers are similar in nature no matter what language they come from. This section explores the differences.

Identifiers, of course, are the names you give to variables, labels, functions, and types; which are later turned into tokens by the compiler.

Variable names in C++ work similarly to variable names in Visual Basic, in that A–Z, a–z, 0–9, and an underscore are legal characters to use in an identifier. However, a variable name cannot begin with a numeric. You must avoid reserved words, and of course the reserved word list is somewhat different than the one for Visual Basic. The keyword list in Table 2.1 demonstrates this.

> **TIP**
>
> There are some ANSI–Microsoft specific issues concerning leading underscores. To avoid these issues, it is best not to begin an identifier with an underscore.

One special identifier, which also exists in Visual Basic, is a statement label, more commonly referred to in Visual Basic as a line label. This label is used in conjunction with a goto to transfer control from one place in a program to another. (Yes, C allows the same bad form as Visual Basic in terms of the goto.) VB uses the line labels for error handling as well, so there is a noble purpose in VB for a line label. In C, though, it exists solely as a target for a goto.

> **NOTE**
>
> ANSI C and Microsoft C compilers differ in a few ways. One is the number of significant characters in the identifier name. ANSI C has 31 significant characters for an internal name and only six characters for an identifier that has extern scope. Microsoft C allows 247 significant characters in any identifier. If you are not worried about ANSI C compatibility (you might be if you want your code to compile in a different compiler or on a different platform), you don't have to worry about the length of your identifier names. Two hundred and forty-seven characters are more than enough.

C also differs from Visual Basic in case sensitivity. C treats uppercase and lowercase letters as different characters within identifiers, whereas Visual Basic considers the uppercase and lowercase representations of a character to be the same for purposes of an identifier. For example, consider This, this, and THIS. These are three separate variables in C, but they would represent the same variable within a Visual Basic program.

Later versions of Visual Basic actually change the case of variables to match the declaration if there is one. If there is no declaration, VB typically changes the case to match the other uses of the variable name. Of course none of us program without declaring variables, because that would be bad form. In C, it's not just bad form, it isn't allowed.

> **TIP**
>
> In Visual Basic you can actually use this feature (automatically changing case) to your advantage to check variable name spelling if you've used some uppercase letters and you type your variables after the declaration all lowercase as you write code. When you move the cursor off the line, the variable changes case to match the declaration and you know you've spelled the variable correctly. C, on the other hand, is not going to be that helpful. It's important to develop a personal coding style so that you do not have to constantly refer to a variable declaration to see how to spell and capitalize it.

Constants

You'll find several fundamental differences between the understanding of what constants are in Visual Basic, versus how they are defined in C. Unlike VB, where constants can be of any intrinsic type, constants in C are numbers or characters.

> **NOTE**
>
> In reality, even the char data type is a numeric type. C doesn't really have an intrinsic type that is a string. Character arrays are commonly referred to as a string in C, but actually are just a char array.

A *character string* is termed a literal and is different than a constant. We'll talk more about string literals in that section.

In Visual Basic, the const statement produces a true constant. Unlike VB, the const modifier in C produces a variable that cannot be modified. While a const variable in C cannot be modified, in every other respect a const variable in C is handled by the compiler like it is a variable.

> **NOTE**
>
> There are some differences in the way the C compiler and the C++ compiler handle variables modified by the const modifier. In C you *cannot* use a const variable every-where you can a constant, but in C++, you can.

Finally, although an identifier can be declared to represent a constant as it is in Visual Basic, the syntax is quite different. In C, a preprocessor directive is used to define constants. This is done with the #define preprocessor directive.

In the following sections you'll find an exploration of the more specific differences in identifier syntax, covering numeric and then character constants.

Numeric Constants

Let's talk about numeric constants first. These take the form of long, float, or double. Longs can be signed or unsigned; signed constants can be positive or negative in value. The floating point numbers can also contain exponents.

Several letters can be combined with a numeric constant. When using these letters with constants, case is not significant. The following letters may appear in a numeric constant:

- E—Exponent portion of the number follows. This can be used in Visual Basic, but VB converts the number and removes the exponent if it is reasonable to do that.
- D—D at the end signifies a double type. This is the default, so this could be left off. This corresponds to a # type declaration tag in Visual Basic.
- L—At the end, L signifies a long type. Avoid using the lowercase letter l. It is easy to confuse it with the numeral 1. This corresponds to the & type declaration tag in Visual Basic.
- L—At the beginning, L signifies a wide character constant. This is only used in conjunction with character constants.
- F—At the end, F signifies a float type. This corresponds to a ! type declaration tag in Visual Basic.
- U—Used in combination with L, U forms an unsigned constant. There are no unsigned numbers in Visual Basic, so there is nothing that corresponds to this.
- X—At the start of the number, X signifies that this number is hexadecimal format. As such, the number can contain valid hexadecimal numbers and letters—0–9 and A–F. This corresponds to the &H syntax in Visual Basic.

These are samples of floating point constant definitions, followed by their Visual Basic counterparts:

```
#define cnst_dNum -22453e-2        /* C double -224.54 */
Public Const cnst_dNum = -224.54#     'VB double -224.54

#define cnst_fNum 325.22f          /* C float 325.22 */
Public Const cnst_fNum = 325.22    'VB single 325.22

#define cnst_lNum 3224F            /* C float 3,224 */
Public Const cnst_lNum = 3224!     'VB single 3,224

#define cnst_dNum1 1032.45d        /* C double 1,032.45 */
Public Const cnst_dNum1 1032.45#   'VB double 1,032.45
```

Floating-point numbers are expressed in base 10; however, integral numeric types can be expressed in hexadecimal or octal in addition to base 10. Integral types can also be signed or unsigned. Following are samples of integral constant definitions, followed by the Visual Basic expressions:

```
#define cnst_lNum -22453L          /* C long -22,454 */
Public Const cnst_lNum = -22454&    'VB long -22,454

#define cnst_lNum1 0XB5FUL          /* C unsigned long hex B5F or 2,911 dec */
Public Const cnst_lNum1 = &HB5F&    'VB long hex B5F or 2,911 dec
➥   VB has no unsigned
```

The limits imposed on numeric constants in C are similar to the limits in Visual Basic. The largest differences have to do with unsigned integral types. (I'll summarize those limits later in this chapter.)

Character Constants

As mentioned before, character constants are single character constants. A *character constant* is formed by enclosing a character inside a set of single quotation marks. Any character may be placed inside the single quote except for a single quote ('), a backslash (\), or a newline character.

A character constant can also be an *escape sequence*. An escape sequence is a backslash (\) followed by another character. These escape sequences are recognized as a single character by the compiler so they are legal for a character constant. Most of the escape sequences have special meanings. Table 2.2 summarizes the ANSI escape sequences recognized by the C compiler.

TABLE 2.2   List of ANSI Escape Sequences

Escape Sequence	Represents
\a	Bell (alert)
\b	Backspace
\f	Formfeed
\n	New line (also known as line feed)
\r	Carriage return
\t	Horizontal tab
\v	Vertical tab
\'	Single quotation mark
\"	Double quotation mark
\\	Backslash
\?	Literal question mark
\ooo	ASCII character in octal notation
\xhhh	ASCII character in hexadecimal notation

Note that the backslash (\)is also the line continuation character in C. If a newline follows a backslash, C assumes the next line is part of the current line. It is also possible to place the line continuation anywhere, even within string literals.

> **NOTE**
>
> The backslash line continuation character maps to the underscore (_) in Visual Basic. In Visual Basic you can continue a string literal on the next line, but you must close the string literal with a double quote on the line with the continuation character and reopen the it with the double quote on the next.

In C, the octal and hexadecimal notations used in escape sequences allow nonprintable characters that are not a part of the simple escape sequences to be placed in character constants and literals. You can also specify simple escape sequences with them and many times there are multiple ways to get the same character into the constant. For example the backspace character can be specified in the following ways: \b, \010, \x8, \x08, and \x008.

The octal or hexadecimal values must be in the range of valid char values in the case of type char and in the range of wide characters in the case of a wchar.

Literals

A *string literal* is the closest that C can get to a string constant. In practice a string literal works more like a constant, but in storage it is more like a variable.

Character constants are the closest things in Visual Basic to string literals in C. In use, these two are similar; they differ only in their implementation.

String literals are similar to constants in that their value cannot be changed after the program is compiled. A string literal has a constant value, but a literal is actually handled like a variable in memory.

You need to understand the distinction between a character and a character string. A character constant represents a single character. A character string literal represents an array of characters. The syntax for these two items differs. The biggest difference is that the character constant is truly a constant, while the string literal really is not a constant. Constants are handled in the precompiler step. The string literal is not handled by the precompiler and consequently is not a constant. So whereas Visual Basic has the concept of a string constant, C doesn't.

String Literal Characteristics

You can concatenate literals, but if you try to change one, that action is undefined. Also literals that are the same may be grouped together in memory, so two different literals may point to the same location.

Some of the things discussed in character constants apply to string literals. Escape sequences work in string literals the same as character constants. You will find this out if you ever try to put a pathname into a program in the form of a literal. All the backslashes must be doubled up. One exception is that single quotes do not need to be an escape sequence. They can appear in a literal string normally.

String Literal Use

String literals are typically assigned to a variable when that variable is declared. The string literal determines the size of the char array (or wchar_t array in the case of wide characters). For wide characters, the literal should be prefaced with an L. This again is the same as a character constant.

These lines demonstrate ways to fill an array with characters. The first line demonstrates a string literal. The second line is the way you may have accomplished the same thing with constants.

```
char ctest[] = "Some string";
char ctest[] = {'S','o','m','e',' ','s','t','r','i','n','g','\0' };
```

When working with string literals, adjacent strings are concatenated. For example, the first declaration following is the same as the second one:

```
char cStr[] = "12" "34";
char cStr[] = "1234";
```

String Literal Splicing

String splicing makes it easier to specify long strings across multiple lines. The first three lines following are an example of string slicing. This string can also be specified using line splicing as shown in the last three lines following:

```
char cStr[] = "This is the first line. "
"This is the second line. "
"This is the third line.";

char cStr[] = "This is the first line. \
This is the second line. \
This is the third line.";
```

A null character, \0, is appended at the end of each string literal to provide an end-of-string marker for C string-handling functions. This is required in order to know where strings end in memory since C does not keep track of this for you.

When the first string contains an escape character, string splicing can yield surprising results. Consider the two declarations following:

```
char cStrA[] = "\01" "23"
char cStrB[] = "\0123"
```

Although it appears that cStrA and cStrB contain the same values, the values they actually contain are as follows:

cStrA contains \01,2,3,\0

cStrB contains \012,3,\0

This is because the escape sequence is evaluated differently in these two statements. In the string splicing example (CstrA) the escape sequence is evaluated before the string slicing takes effect. In the second example, (CStrB) the first three numbers are evaluated after the slash, so the strings end up containing different values.

> **NOTE**
>
> The maximum length of a string literal is around 2,048 bytes. There are some sub-tleties going on in the Microsoft compiler that allow the string to use a little less space if you use line splicing as opposed to string splicing as described above. The savings are about one byte per line.

There can be some confusion and ambiguity when using escape sequences, because the escape code terminates at the first character that is not a hexadecimal digit. The following example is intended to create a string literal containing ASCII 6, followed by the string done:

```
"\x06done"
```

The actual result is a hexadecimal 6D, which is the ASCII code for a lowercase *m*, followed by the string one. The following examples produce the desired results:

```
"\x006done"    //use an extra 0
 "\006done"    //use octal
"\x06" "done"    //use string splicing
```

Predefined Constants and Macros

Visual Basic offers many predefined constants and macros that are provided by the compiler and are always available. There are no real counterparts in C or C++. Most of the constants and macros that you use in C programming are provided by header files or possibly the #import directive. There are a few predefined ones and Tables 2.3 and 2.4 summarize those constants.

> **NOTE**
>
> ANSI constants are provided by any ANSI compatible C compiler (including Visual C). Microsoft specific constants are only found in Microsoft compilers.

TABLE 2.3   ANSI-Compatible Predefined Constants

Macro	Description
__DATE__	The compilation date of the current source file. The date is a string literal of the form *Mmm dd yyyy*.
__FILE__	The name of the current source file. __FILE__ expands to a string surrounded by double quotation marks.
__LINE__	The line number in the current source file. The line number is a decimal integer constant. It can be altered with a #line directive, see that section in this chapter for more information.
__STDC__	Indicates full conformance with the ANSI C standard. Defined as the integer constant 1 only if the /Za compiler option is given and you are not compiling C++ code; otherwise is undefined.
__TIME__	The most recent compilation time of the current source file. The time is a string literal of the form *hh:mm:ss*.
__TIMESTAMP__	The date and time of the last modification of the current source file, expressed as a string literal in the form *Ddd Mmm Date hh:mm:ss yyyy*.

TABLE 2.4   ANSI-Compatible Predefined Constants

Macro	Description
_CHAR_UNSIGNED	Default char type is unsigned.
__cplusplus	Defined for C++ programs only. This will be defined in Visual C if the file being compiled has a CPP extension.
_CPPRTTI	Defined for code compiled with Run-Time Type Information.
_CPPUNWIND	Defined for code compiled with Exception Handling enabled.
_DLL	Defined when Multithread DLL is specified.
_M_ALPHA	Defined for DEC ALPHA platforms.
_M_IX86	Defined for x86 processors.
_M_MPPC	Defined for Power Macintosh platforms.
_M_MRX000	Defined for MIPS platforms. Default is 4000.
_M_PPC	Defined for PowerPC platforms. Default is 604.
_MFC_VER	Defines the MFC version. For example this is defined as 0x0421 for Microsoft Foundation Class Library 4.21. It is always defined.
_MSC_EXTENSIONS	This macro is defined when compiling with the /Ze compiler option (the default). Its value, when defined, is 1.

TABLE 2.4   Continued

Macro	Description
_MSC_VER	Defines the compiler version. Defined as 1200 for Microsoft Visual C++ 6.0. Always defined.
_MT	Defined when Multithreaded DLL or Multithreaded is specified.
_WIN32	Defined for applications for Win32®. Always defined.

Structure

The previous section looked at the elements of the C language. This section explains the structure of C source code using those elements and how this structure affects the source and compiler. The code structure of C is where some of the biggest differences between Visual Basic and C are located. Compiler directives and code structure are quite different.

This section covers the following topics:

- Directives—Precompiler instructions, such as conditional compiling.
- Code structure—There's semicolons all over the place.
- Lifetime—About automatic and static variables.
- Scope and visibility—About global and local variables.

Directives

Preprocessor directives instruct a compiler how to handle the source code and are carried out by the preprocessor before the actual compilation of the program. Visual Basic has conditional compiling and it is quite useful in certain circumstances; this is about the extent of its preprocessor directives. In C, preprocessor directives perform a wide range of services for us, from including other source files to conditionally compiling code.

You can recognize a compiler directive from the leading #. The # must be the first non–white space character on the line. Continuation lines may be used in the directive.

This section covers the following compiler directives:

- #include—Includes other source files in the compilation unit.
- #define—Defines a constant.
- #if, #else, #elif, #endif—Conditionally includes lines of code in the compilation unit.
- #ifdef, #ifndef, #else, #endif—Conditionally includes lines of code in the compilation unit based on the definition of a constant.

- #line—Sets an internally stored line number and filename.
- #error—Generates a compile time error.
- #pragma—An environment specific action, like ignoring a warning in the compiler.

#include

#include is a compiler directive I've always missed in Visual Basic. It's not absolutely necessary because of the way that VB modules can be constructed and used, but I still miss it.

The #include directive tells the compiler to insert the contents of the specified file at the location of the include statement.

```
#include "sourcefile.h"
#include <sourcefile.h>
```

The bracketed form instructs the compiler to first look at the /I compiler setting for include directories and then in the directories in the INCLUDE environment variable setting.

The "quoted form" tells the compiler to first look for the include file in the current directory. Then it follows the bracketed form's search path (/I and INCLUDE environment variable) to attempt to find the include file. Include files are typically used for declarations and the like, but they are not restricted to containing declarations. Include files can contain functional code as well as declarations.

> **NOTE**
>
> There is no counterpart in Visual Basic to the include statement. This is something that I've always felt Visual Basic needed. We had include directives in older DOS versions of Basic and there are times when this feature would be helpful to a VB programmer.

#define, #undef

The #define directive in its simplest form defines a constant. In this capacity it is very much like Visual Basic's Const statement. Any identifier in the source file that matches the defined identifier is replaced with the constant token-string. If the constant is defined with no token-string, then the constant is removed from the source code.

Syntax:

```
#define identifier token-string
```

It is possible to use the #define directive for a macro, which is sort of an in-line routine. The identifier portion can contain parameters that are used within the token-string portion of the directive to produce a result. (This is not, strictly speaking, a constant.)

For example, the following macro demonstrates this in a very simple manner. It takes two numbers and multiplies them. This is not a very useful macro, but it's simple enough so that it's not confusing. The use of the macro is shown following the declaration:

```
#define MULT(x, y) (x*y)
float f1=10.2;
float f2=4;
float f3=MULT(f1,f2);
```

Note that because this is a macro and not a function, the variable types used can be any type where the operation is valid. In this case, any type that can be multiplied together may be used.

2

C BASICS

> **TIP**
>
> Personally, I don't make extensive use of macros. Sometimes they can enhance the readability of code, but many times, they don't. Use them wisely, if at all.

The #undef directive gets rid of the define for a particular identifier. Seldom used but possibly helpful in complex include files.

#if, #elif, #else, #endif

Conditional compilation directives are more similar to Visual Basic syntax than any C syntax. The #if, #elif, #else, and #endif directives are used for conditional compilation. They follow normal #if, #elseif, #else, and #endif syntax. You can have an #if block, optional #elif blocks (there could be several of these), and an optional #else block just before the #endif (multiple else statements aren't allowed). The #endif closes the #if block. You need one #endif for every #if directive. #if directives may be nested.

The #if directive tests a condition and if it is true, then the lines of code within the if block are included in the compilation, as following:

```
#define DEBUG 1
#if DEBUG==1
    //these lines of code are included when DEBUG=1
#elif DEBUG==2
    //these lines of code are included when DEBUG=2
#elif DEBUG==3
    //these lines of code are included when DEBUG=3
#else
    //these lines of code are included when DEBUG is not equal to either 1,2 or 3
#endif
```

Notice that there are multiple #elifs and they follow the #if directive. There is only one #else and it precedes the #endif directive. When the code is included, it takes the lines up to the next #elif, #else, or #endif within the applicable #if block.

Within any #if directive, only one block of code will be included. Even if multiple #elif statements evaluate to true, only the first #elif that evaluates to true will be included. For that reason these blocks should be constructed in a way that makes them mutually exclusive.

The #if directive condition is an integer constant expression with some additional restrictions. It can contain only integral constants, character constants, and the defined operator. You cannot use sizeof or any cast operator. The expression should not perform any environmental inquiries and must be insulated from the operating environment.

TIP

The defined operator may be used within #if or #elif directives. If the defined operator is used within an #if directive, the directive functions exactly like the #ifdef directive.

There may be some advantage to using the defined operator within #if, because it can also be used within the #elif statement. However, most statements requiring this test can be constructed with #ifdef or #ifndef.

The syntax of the defined operator is

```
#if defined(identifier)
```

or

```
#if defined identifier
```

#ifdef, #ifndef, #else, #endif

The directives #else and #endif can also be used with the #ifdef and #ifndef directives. The structure and usage is very similar to the #if directive when used with the defined operator.

#ifdef tests the existence of a constant. If the constant has been defined then the expression evaluates to true. The #ifndef statement does the opposite. It evaluates to true if the constant has not been defined.

Note that the constant does not have to contain anything, it just has to be defined. For example:

```
#define TEST
```

Defining TEST in this way is sufficient to define the TEST constant for purposes of these directives. This type of define is used quite often in conjunction with the #ifdef directive.

One of the most common uses for the #ifndef directive is to make sure an include file gets included only once. This is done by checking for a constant and then defining the constant within the #ifndef block:

```
#ifndef MYHFILE
#define MYHFILE
//content of h file goes here
#endif
```

If the include file appears in several other source files and because of this ends up being compiled in your source code several times, these directives will solve the errors generated by the multiple references. The first include will cause the source lines to be drawn into the compilation unit and define MYHFILE. The source code will not be used again because the #ifndef directive will cause the source lines to be skipped.

With the Microsoft compiler the constant can also be passed from the compiler's command line with the /D option. This constant can be tested like any other. For example, try using the command line to turn on a debug mode:

```
#ifdef DEBUG
    //debugging stuff here
#else
    //release stuff here
#endif
```

The following compile line defines the DEBUG constant and causes the debug lines to be included in the compile.

```
CL /DDEBUG testprog.cpp
```

#line

The #line directive sets the compiler's internally stored line number and source filename. This allows control over the reported line numbers from the compiler and in asserts.

Syntax:

```
#line line-number "filename"
```

Note that the filename should be enclosed in double quotes. The line number can be any integer constant. You could use defined constants or macros, but the final form must fit this syntax. There are two predefined macros that can access the line number and the filename. __LINE__ and __FILE__ macros return the line number and filename.

2

C BASICS

NOTE

The only counterpart to the line directive in Visual Basic is the `Erl` function; nothing can return the source filename for you. Even the `Erl` function requires numbering the lines by hand.

#error

The `#error` directive allows you to generate your own compile time error. There is no counterpart in Visual Basic for this useful directive.

For example, suppose you've written some source code that absolutely requires C++ to compile properly. You could write the following set of directives to keep it from being compiled in bare C.

```
#ifndef __cplusplus

    #error Requires C++

#endif
```

If the `#error` directive is encountered, the compilation process terminates.

#pragma

Pragmas are used to make the compiler perform some environment specific action. You can think of pragmas as handling special cases in the compiler.

Visual Basic doesn't have an equivalent to pragmas, because its compiler doesn't have much of the flexibility that the C compiler has built in. Visual Basic controls the environment enough that pragmas aren't required.

Pragmas are typically different for different compilers. As such, the pragmas listed here are for the Microsoft compiler. I'll list a reference and description for each pragma, but will offer detailed descriptions only for pragmas that you might commonly use.

NOTE

In reality, you will seldom use a pragma. The most useful in my estimation are the intrinsic and the warning pragmas. The intrinsic pragma allows the programmer to take advantage of intrinsic functions in the system.

The warning pragma is used to turn off warning and error messages in the compiler. This is done on lines of code that generate these messages, but the programmer has determined that the code functions properly, so he just wants the warnings turned off.

`alloc_text`—Names a code section.

`auto_inline`—Turns inline expansion on or off.

`bss_seg`—Specifies the default segment for uninitialized data.

`check_stack`—Turns stack probes on or off.

`code_seg`—Specifies a code section where functions are stored.

`const_seg`—Specifies the default section for constant data.

`comment`—Places a comment into an object file or executable file. The comment is one of five types: `compiler`, `exestr`, `lib`, `linker`, or `user`.

`component`—Controls browser information.

`data_seg`—Specifies the default section for data.

`function`—Forces functions to be called, as opposed to being inline.

`hdrstop`—Controls the way precompiled headers work.

`include_alias`—Specifies a short filename that is substituted for the long filename.

`inline_depth`—Sets the number of times inline expansion can occur.

`inline_recursion`—Controls the inline expansion direct inline calls.

`intrinsic`—Intrinsic is a more common pragma, so I'll provide more specifics for this pragma. This pragma affects some C runtime routines that have intrinsic forms. This pragma specifies that calls to functions specified in the pragma's argument list are intrinsic.

> **NOTE**
>
> The pragma takes effect at the first function specified within the pragma. It continues to the end of the file or until another function pragma is specified with the same function. This pragma must be used at the global level. Programs that use intrinsic functions are faster, but larger.
>
> Functions that have intrinsic forms are `_disable`, `_enable`, `_inp`, `_inpw`, `_lrotl`, `_lrotr`, `_outp`, `_outpw`, `_rotl`, `_rotr`, `_strset`, `abs`, `fabs`, `labs`, `memcmp`, `memcpy`, `memset`, `strcat`, `strcmp`, `strcpy`, and `strlen`.
>
> Functions that are not really intrinsic but can call directly into the math chip are `acos`, `asin`, `cosh`, `fmod`, `pow`, `sinh`, and `tanh`.
>
> Functions that have true intrinsic forms when using the `/Oi` and `/Og` compiler options are `atan`, `atan2`, `cos`, `exp`, `log`, `log10`, `sin`, `sqrt`, and `tan`.

`message`—Sends a string literal to the standard output. The compilation will continue.

`once`—Indicates that the file that this pragma appears in will be included only once.

`pack`—Specifies structure packing alignment

`setlocale`—Defines the target locale (country and language) at compile time.

`warning`—This pragma allows selective modification to the behavior of warning messages. It is another common pragma, so we'll spend a little effort on this one.

The syntax is as follows:

```
#pragma warning (warning specifier: number list)
#pragma warning (push)
#pragma warning (pop)
```

Table 2.5 shows the different values that the specifier can have.

TABLE 2.5   Warning Specifier

Warning-specifier	Meaning
Once	Display the specified message(s) only once.
default	Apply the default compiler behavior to the specified message(s).
1, 2, 3, 4	Apply the given warning level to the specified warning message(s).
disable	Do not issue the specified warning message(s).
Error	Report the specified warnings as errors.

The list can contain any warning numbers. Multiple warning numbers, as well as multiple options, can be included together.

For example:

```
#pragma warning (disable: 4509 38; once: 4454; error: 155)
```

For warning numbers associated with code generation (greater than 4699), the pragma must be placed outside any function declarations.

TIP

The most common use for the `#pragma` warning directive is to "clean up" a compile and get rid of the warning messages. The example in Listing 2.1 shows how to disable a warning message, then enable it after the suspect code. Use with caution, and only when absolutely sure.

Listing 2.1   Pragma Warning

```
int i;
#pragma warning(disable:4705)
void func()
{
    i;
}
#pragma warning(default:4705)
```

The push and pop syntax is supported in warning pragmas. These routines make it simple to restore the pragma warning state. The pop restores to the warning state when the previous push was executed.

```
#pragma warning( push[, n] )
```

```
#pragma warning ( pop )
```

Where n sets the warning level.

Any changes made to the warning level between push and pop are undone when pop is executed.

As I have stated before, pragmas are seldom used, but it is useful to know what they are in case you see them.

Code Structure

There are several important differences between C and Visual Basic in terms of program structure. Here I'll discuss statements, code blocks, functions, and function prototypes in reference to how they affect program structure. Functions and function prototypes are discussed later in this chapter in their own section.

You probably already know that most code lines end with a semicolon, but not all. You probably have seen the curly braces in program code as well.

C code typically follows a statement with a semicolon or the start of a block (refer to Listing 2.2); an if statement typically begins a block. What happens if you don't need multiple statements? You still don't use a semicolon here, as shown in the second part of Listing 2.2.

Listing 2.2   if Statements Begin a Block

```
if (expression)
{
    //multiple statements
}
if (expression)
    //single statement
```

Looping or flow control statements begin a block. Expression and assignment statements do not start a block and so require semicolons on the end of a line. An example of a statement that requires a semicolon would be an assignment statement.

```
i = 5;
```

Function prototypes do not begin a block and so are followed with a semicolon. Functions themselves are blocks and so the header of a function is not followed by a semicolon. The following code demonstrates this:

```
int MyFunction(void);
int MyFunction(void)
{
    //function body
}
```

Lifetime

The lifetime of variables, functions, and objects in a program is a pretty common concept both in Visual Basic and C compilers.

The broadest lifetime is one that spans the entire program. Functions have a lifetime that spans the entire program. Global variables are variables that are declared outside the scope of any function and span the entire program.

The narrowest lifetime is one that exists for the duration of a block of code (this is code within a set of matching braces). These are automatic variables, so called because they go away automatically. Most variables used within a function have automatic storage. That means that the variables exist within the scope of the function and their lifetime applies only to the execution time of the function. Function parameters also have automatic storage. They exist during the execution of the function.

A variable that is declared static has a lifetime that exists for the entire execution of the program. As a matter of fact in C, that's the term we apply to global variables as well. In other words, if the variable has a lifetime that is the same as the program, then that variable is static.

You can declare static variables within functions. In this case, the scope and visibility may only apply to that function, but the lifetime is still the same as the program.

Scope and Visibility

Visibility and scope refer to the same thing, but from the opposite viewpoints and both are related to lifetime. From the variable's viewpoint, a variable has scope, what parts of the code can the variable participate in.

Visibility is from the code's viewpoint. Can a particular variable be seen from this section of the code? The scope of an identifier determines its visibility. Scope may be limited to the file, function, block, or prototype in which it appears.

Lifetime can affect scope. Obviously if the variable doesn't exist at a particular place in the code, it can't have visibility at that spot.

Identifiers, except for labels, have their scope determined by the location at which the declaration occurs. The only exception to this rule is `extern` variables. This section discusses variable scope including prototype, block, function, file, and `extern` and how a variable of each scope is created.

Function Prototype Scope

This is the most limited scope and is hardly worth mentioning because the scope is limited to one line of code. What this scope entails is a function prototype (declaration) and it means that the variable names used within a function prototype are not visible anywhere else in the program. Visual Basic has the same type of scope for a variable that appears in a declaration.

Block Scope

Block scope applies to blocks and curly braces. A set of braces (a matching open and close) form a block. Variables may be declared within these blocks and if they are, their scope is limited to that block. These types of variables are called *local variables*. Visual Basic does not have block scope, because there is no concept of a block in VB.

An example may do more good to let you see how block scope works.

```
//Function Header
{
    int ifunc;
    for (ifunc=1;infunc<2;ifunc++)
    {
        int iblock;
    }
}
```

In this sample, the `ifunc` variable will be visible in the entire function. However the `iblock` variable is visible only within the braces that define the `for` loop.

Function Scope

Although in Visual Basic, variables can have function scope, in C, only labels have function scope. They must be unique within the function and are not visible outside of it. You can cause a variable to have what *effectively* is function scope, but this is more properly termed block scope.

File Scope

File scope is analogous to module level variables in Visual Basic. Because these declarations in C may be in include files, this is more properly termed as a translation unit rather than a file. The variable's scope begins at the point that it is declared and goes to the end of the translation unit.

extern Scope

Extern scope applies to an identifier declared at the file level (outside any function) and qualified with the extern modifier. You must declare the variable in every file that will use it or it will not be visible in that file.

Using extern is roughly analogous to the Public and Global modifiers in a standard module in Visual Basic. Declaring a Public variable in every file is not necessary in Visual Basic, because the Public identifier will be visible to any module included in the program.

The default for any variable declared at the file level without using the static modifier works the same as if extern were used explicitly. I like to say that any variable defined at the file level with the static keyword has internal linkage. Any other variable declared at the file level has external linkage.

Namespaces

The term *namespaces* as it applies to C refers to the compiler setting up different areas to handle the different type of identifiers; this is not to be confused with C++'s namespace feature. What this means is that these namespaces are different from each other and that the same identifier will not be a duplicate as long as they reside in different namespaces. For example, it is possible to have a statement label and a variable named the same, because they are in different namespaces.

This section explains the different namespaces and what is included in each one.

- Statement labels or line labels—These are followed by a colon. Case labels do not qualify as statement labels.
- Structure, Union, and Enumeration tags—These immediately follow the words struct, union, or enum. They must be distinct from all other tags of these types, but need not be distinct from other identifiers.
- Members of structures or unions—Definitions of member names always occur within the structure or union type specifiers and must be distinct from other names within that same structure or union. They do not have to be distinct from other identifiers.
- Ordinary identifiers—All other names fall into the namespace that include variables, functions, and enumeration constants.
- Typedef Names—Cannot be used as identifiers within the same scope.

Functions

C functions work very much like Visual Basic functions. C does not have the concept of Subs as compared to Functions, but does have functions with void returns, which accomplish the same thing.

Because you are already familiar with the concept of functions, I will not go into detail here. Chapter 7, "DLLs," deals with functions.

In this section I'll cover the following topics:

- Prototypes—Function declarations.
- Definitions—Function body and implementation.
- Invoking functions—The syntax of calling functions.
- DllMain—Where execution begins.

Prototypes

Before a function can be used in C, it must be prototyped or the definition must appear in code before the call is made. In C, the prototype typically looks just like the definition, except that it is terminated with a semicolon.

```
int myFunction(int var1, int *var2);
```

You don't have to include variable names within the parameters, although it is good practice to make sure you keep the parameters ordered properly. A prototype in C is only used for type checking. That is why the parameter names are not required. The function definition (discussed in the next section) will have the parameter names that will be used within the function.

```
int myFunction(int,  int*);
```

> **NOTE**
>
> The Visual Basic form of a prototype (a Declare) is used to call functions that are in DLLs. You don't have to declare functions that are written right in your VB code. Whereas a prototype in C does not require the variable names, in VB the variable names are required even though they are not used for anything.

Definitions

Function definitions also include the function body. This is where the function implementation is located. Braces are used to define the boundary of the function body.

Function parameters pass information to the function. Parameters are passed by value. In C, you pass either the variable or the pointer to the variable. The way the parameters are passed affect the way you can work with the variables in the routine. In C, you must know if you are working with a pointer and access the contents of the variable differently if you have a pointer, than if you have the variable value.

In C, you typically say that you have the value of the variable or have the address. If you have the value, you can work directly with that value, but you cannot change it. Why not? All this has to do with the way the parameters are passed. It depends on whether the parameter value is on the stack or the address of the variable is on the stack. If the value is on the stack and you were to change it, it would simply be discarded when the function returns. If the address is on the stack, we can change the original variable through that address.

Let's take a look at this using the myFunction routine introduced in the previous section.

```
int myFunction(int var1, int *var2)
{
    *var2 = var1;
    return var1;
}
```

This function is simple, but it demonstrates three concepts very well. The by value parameter (var1) is used as an r-value. You should never use a variable passed as a parameter as an l-value. You can use the contents of a pointer variable as an l-value, as I've done in the sample, but not the variable itself.

Use the indirection operator to assign this value to the var2 variable. This changes the value of the original variable passed to you. You then return the var1 value as the result of the function. This demonstrates the three ways that functions share information with their calling code.

> **NOTE**
>
> Visual Basic programmers are familiar with passing parameters by value or by reference. In C, we pass either the variable (which corresponds with by value in VB) or the pointer to the variable (which corresponds to the by reference in VB). In Visual Basic, the variable is accessed the same way, no matter how it is passed to the routine, whereas in C, the code is very different, depending on whether we have a variable value or a variable address.

Invoking Functions

In Visual Basic you have several choices in the way you call a function. This involves whether or not you place the braces around the parameters. If we use the return value or use the Call syntax, we use the braces, otherwise we do not. In VB, the `myFunction` routine shown later could be called in the following ways:

```
x = myFunction(5, y)

Call myFunction(5,y)

myFunction 5,y
```

In C, the same form is used in all circumstances. From the calling side it is important to again pay attention to whether you are using pointers or not. You can't provide a constant as a value to a parameter that requires an address. We might invoke the `myFunction` routine in the following manner:

```
x = myFunction(5, &y);
```

or simply:

```
myFunction(5, &y);
```

Notice that the first form uses the return value and the second form does not. Chapter 7 goes into much more detail about functions and how they are called.

main, wmain, DllMain

The latest versions of Visual Basic have the concept of a Main function; in C, the main function is where a normal program begins execution.

The `wmain` function is a main function that is Unicode compatible and so can be discussed along with the main function. There is a lot to say about the main Function, but this book focuses on supporting Visual Basic with DLLs and functions. So `DllMain` is more important to us. This is where execution begins in a DLL in Windows.

> **NOTE**
>
> The `DllMain` function is discussed in Chapter 7; here I'll dig just a little more to explain why you might be interested in this function.

It's optional to include this function in your DLL. If you do not, the DLL you create will include a default routine. If you decide to use it there are a couple of things that you can do with the routine.

Syntax:

```
BOOL WINAPI DllMain(HANDLE hinstDLL, DWORD dwReason, LPVOID lpvReserved);
```

The most common use of this routine is to obtain the instance handle (a handle to a running executable). You would need this handle, in order to load reources if your DLL has them. One way to do this is to save the instance handle into a global variable. Refer to Listing 2.3.

LISTING 2.3   Saving the Handle

```
HANDLE     g_hinstDLL;
BOOL WINAPI DllMain(HANDLE hinstDLL, DWORD dwReason, LPVOID lpvReserved)
{
    g_hinstDLL = hinstDLL;
}
```

You could then use the g_hinstDLL variable as the handle to load a resource from any routine in the DLL.

The dwReason parameter holds the reason that this routine was called. The DllMain routine can be called for several reasons, such as when the DLL is attached to a processor or a thread. This routine is also called when a thread is detached and when the DLL is detached from a process.

The values listed in Table 2.6 are possible values for the dwReason parameter.

TABLE 2.6   DllMain dwReason Parameter

Value	Description
DLL_PROCESS_ATTACH	This value is used to indicate that the DLL is being loaded into the process space of an executable.
DLL_THREAD_ATTACH	This value is used to indicate that the current process that has this DLL loaded started a new thread. The call is made in the context of the new thread. The routine will not be called with this value when the DLL is attached to the process.
	The entry point of a DLL is called with this value for threads that are created after the DLL is loaded. Threads created before a call to LoadLibrary will not have the opportunity to call the entry point, so those threads are not seen by the DllMain routine.
DLL_THREAD_DETACH	This value is used to indicate that a thread is exiting cleanly. Do any thread local cleanup.
DLL_PROCESS_DETACH	This value is used to indicate that the DLL is being unloaded from the address space of an executable. This would have been caused by the termination of this program or a call to FreeLibrary. Do any Thread local cleanup.

The `lpvReserved` specifies some other aspects of the DLL initialization and cleanup for a process. During attach, this parameter is NULL for dynamic loads and non-NULL for static loads. During detach, this parameter is NULL if `DllMain` has been called because of a call to `FreeLibrary` and non-NULL if caused by the executable unloading.

Function Pointers

The concept of function pointers is an important one, and it usually comes into play in "call back" functions. This is where the code that you are using needs to call a function that you write; you provide the address of that function and the code calls it when appropriate. Visual Basic has the `AddressOf` operator to provide function pointers to use in this manner. The `AddressOf` functionality is quite limited, however, and C is better suited to tasks where `AddressOf` is employed.

Function pointers can be used in COM objects. The `vtable` in COM objects consists of a group of function pointers that access the methods and properties of the COM object.

You may also use function pointers to call "typical" functions. This might be done when you are not certain that the function will exist. Using a function pointer and testing it to see whether you get a pointer will tell you whether the function is there or not. If it's there you can use it; if not you will use a less desirable method to get the information that you need.

Summary

In this chapter, we looked at the basics of the C language. This is the language that I continue to use and write support code for Visual Basic that runs in 16-bit, 32-bit, and all versions of Visual Basic.

There have been subtle changes, but I can call C code from C# that looks very much like the code I wrote in Version 1.0 VBXs.

2

C BASICS

C Programming

IN THIS CHAPTER

This chapter continues to explore the basic elements of C programming. The idea of this chapter is to build on the information presented in the previous chapter and complete the coverage of the C language. Expressions and statements apply equally well to C++ and C#.

The sections in this chapter cover the following topics:

- "Variables and Data"—This section covers variable storage and data. This includes type specifiers and qualifiers, variables and declarators, and initialization.
- "Expressions"—This section deals with expressions, which are usually assignment or logical operators and operands. This section also covers operators, precedence, conversions, and type casts.
- "Statements"—This section describes statements, which control the flow of the program and use expressions, tokens, and other statements. This section discusses assignment, control, flow, and looping.

Variables and Data

This section introduces variables, as well as how to store access data in C. This section discusses type specifiers and qualifiers, variables, declarators, and initialization.

Type Specifiers and Qualifiers

Type specifiers define the type of a variable or function. The type specifiers include void, char, short, int, long, float, double, signed, and unsigned.

The signed char, signed int, signed short int, signed long int, along with their unsigned counterparts, are termed integral types. When used alone any integral type is assumed to be signed.

> **NOTE**
>
> I would not suggest using the unsigned or signed specifiers by themselves, because this isn't common practice. On the other hand, you will often see the signed modifier left off of type specifiers.

The float, double, and long double are floating point types. Floating-point types are always signed, so you won't see unsigned qualifiers used with them.

The optional keywords, signed and unsigned can precede or follow any of the integral types (except enum) and can also be used alone, in which case int is implicitly combined with them.

Type void has three distinct uses:

- To specify a function with no return value.
- To specify an argument type list for a function that has no arguments.
- To specify a pointer to an unspecified type.

The const modifier is used to modify a variable declaration so that the value of the variable cannot be changed. You can use this modifier on a variable and assign the variable value at the time of declaration. Another common way to use this modifier is with a parameter passed to a routine. This keeps the routine from modifying the variable.

TABLE 3.1   Type Specifiers and Equivalents

Type Specifiers	Equivalents	Visual Basic Equivalents
signed char	char	Byte
signed int	signed, int	Long
signed short int	short, signed short	Integer
signed long int	long, signed long	Long
unsigned char	-	-
unsigned int	unsigned	-
unsigned short int	unsigned short	-
unsigned long int	unsigned long	-
Float	-	Single
double	-	Double
long double	double	Double
void	-	-
const	-	-

Table 3.1 is a cross-reference of the simple types. Obviously, there are other variable types that are worth discussing, but these are the intrinsic types available in C programs.

Variables and Declarators

In this section I'll introduce and discuss variables, as well as discuss how to declare variables. *Declarator* simply refers to the way you declare a variable. You'll use the type specifiers introduced in the previous section.

3

C PROGRAMMING

In Visual Basic, you can declare a variable without declaring its type. The type is a variant if you declare the variable in this manner. C is much stricter about the way variable declarations are done, and you cannot leave off the type completely.

In this section, I'll cover the following variable and declarator subjects:

- "Simple Variables"—This section covers declaring intrinsic non-pointer types such as `int`, `long`, `float`, `char`, and `double`.
- "typedef"—This section covers how you create new names for variable types.
- "Arrays"—Arrays are quite different in C. This section covers declaring and using them.
- "Pointers"—Pointers are usually a dreaded subject for Visual Basic programmers. This section tries to ease your fears.
- "Enumeration Variables"—Enumeration Variables are a type of integer with values restricted to the listed values.
- "Structures"—Structures are user-defined types. This is a large section. In C, there are many ways to declare a structure and you should be able to recognize them.
- "Unions"—Unions are new to you if you haven't been exposed to C. However they are a simple concept and seldom used.

Simple Variables

The simplest form of a declarator specifies the variables `name` and `type`. Storage classes (static or extern) or types (`int`, `long`, and others) are required on variable declarations. This type of declaration can be used on numeric variables, structures, unions, enumerations, void types, and for types "created" by `typedef` names. Pointer, array, and function types require more complicated declarators.

Following are some sample declarations and Visual Basic equivalents:

```
int x;             //C declaration
Dim x As Long      'VB declaration

short y = 1;       //C declaration
Dim y As Integer   'VB declaration
y = 1
```

typedef

`typedef` allows you to declare synonyms for existing types. It is used extensively in Windows to define variable types. While the definition is not really a new type, it is used like one. (There is more discussion of `typedef` in the section on structures, where it is used extensively to define structure types.)

The following code shows a simple variable `typedef`, which just allows you to use a new name for a variable type. In this case ULONG instead of `unsigned long`.

```
typedef unsigned int ULONG;
ULONG var;
```

Using `typedef` with functions is not as common as simple variables, but it is possible to do this.

```
typedef int MyFunc(int, int);
//using the above typedef, this declaration
MyFunc Doit;
//is the same as this declaration
int Doit(int, int);
```

Arrays

An array declaration names the array, and specifies the type and can also specify the number of elements. A variable of array type is a pointer to the memory location of the first element in the array.

If the declaration does not contain the number of elements, this declaration must declare a variable that has been defined elsewhere. This most commonly would refer to an extern array declaration. In these particular cases it's just as easy to declare this as a pointer to whatever type the array contains.

The following code shows some C samples of array declarations followed with the Visual Basic equivalents (the equivalents assume that option base 0 is used).

The following code shows simple arrays, an array of structures, and how to access the array data:

```
short a[10];        //c style
Dim a(9) As Integer     'VB style

char c[2][3];       //c style
Dim c(1, 2) As Byte    'VB style

//c style
struct {
short a, b;
} intarray[50];
'VB style
Type twoint
    Dim a As Integer
    Dim b As Integer
End Type
Dim intarray(49) As twoint
```

```
a[0] = 1;      //C style
a(0) = 1       'VB style

c[0][1] = 2;    //cstyle
c(0,1) = 2     'VB style
```

> **NOTE**
>
> The storage on the VB array is different than the C array. So if you are going to pass the array back and forth, you need to declare multidimensional arrays carefully.

When you use a C array within code, you refer to the array elements using a subscript within a set of square brackets. You can review the above code for a sample of both single and multidimensional arrays.

Pointers

Pointers have traditionally been a dreaded subject in C. There are no real intrinsic equivalents in Visual Basic for pointers, although there are ways to load a pointer into a Visual Basic variable. That variable is still a `long`, however, and just contains a value that is equal to a pointer. You wouldn't expect Visual Basic to be able to manipulate that pointer or use it in the way that C can.

The declaration of pointers is usually fairly simple, but understanding what they do and how to use them can be difficult.

A pointer is a variable (or cast) that holds the memory address of another variable. It "points" to that variable, hence the name.

> **NOTE**
>
> Remember that a pointer must always have a variable or valid location in memory to point to. I've seen code where pointers were used without having anything to point to. It's easy to get lulled into trying to use a pointer like this. Of course the compiler or operating system will let you know, usually in ways you would rather not see.

When you look at a variable that contains the address of another variable, it seems to be simple to understand what is happening. But this simplicity quickly gets lost in the syntax and details of dealing with pointers. Let's get some of the syntax details out of the way and then I'll talk about some of the theory and usage.

The pointer syntax uses an asterisk. By convention, you should use the variable name px to indicate a pointer to x.

3

C PROGRAMMING

> **NOTE**
>
> It isn't mandatory to precede pointer variables with p, but it helps to have a rule and follow it. C programmers usually follow a naming convention known as the Hungarian naming convention.

```
int *px;
```

This is a variable defined as a pointer to an int. Right now the variable has a "bogus" value in it. Unlike Visual Basic variables, C variables do not automatically get initialized. This means that the variable will contain whatever happened to be in the memory of the computer at the point that the memory is allocated for the variable. Variables aren't initialized at creation, mostly for speed purposes. Also, even if you did automatically initialize it, it's a pointer. You don't know what it points to. You could only initialize it to NULL, so that you could understand that it doesn't contain a valid value.

Suppose you wanted this pointer to contain the address of a variable.

```
int x = 10;
int *px = &x;
```

You would introduce a new operator in this code. The & operator, called the address of operator, provides the address of the variable it precedes. So px now contains the address of x. Pretty easy right? How do you refer to the value of x by using x's address, which is stored in px? Although this is a little confusing, you use the asterisk again. This is called the indirection operator.

```
y = *px;
```

This operation says that y equals the value stored at px. This would be equal to 10, if you assume the following code sample, which I introduced earlier:

```
int x = 10;
int *px = &x;
```

Still pretty simple, right?

Let's look at arrays again. Pointers are a pretty common way to look at arrays and actually the array name is a pointer. You can learn several lessons about pointers by looking at arrays and in particular char arrays.

Consider the following declarations:

```
char cArray[20];
char *pArray = cArray;
```

You can refer to elements of the array with either pointer variable and you can use the array syntax on either pointer. So saying cArray[5] is the same as saying pArray[5]. This is another way to refer to the value of a pointer. They both would refer to the same value.

Remember above that you used the asterisk to refer to the value of a pointer and you can use that syntax on these pointers to get the value of the first element in the array. So *cArray provides the same value as saying cArray[0].

There is one big difference between cArray (the array) and pArray (the pointer). pArray can be an lvalue, whereas cArray cannot. You saw earlier that you can set the value of pArray and you do not have to set it to the start of the array. The following code demonstrates this:

```
char cArray[20];
cArray[4] = 7;
char *pArray = cArray + 4;
```

This points pArray at the fifth element in the array. So now *pArray and cArray[4] would be equal, and given the above code, that value would be 7.

You've used a character array for an example, but any simple variable type or array can be manipulated by a pointer variable.

Pointers are used extensively in function call parameters. Using a pointer in a parameter is the only way to allow changes to the variable value. This is because C always passes function arguments by value, so the only way to change the function argument is to pass a pointer to the parameter. In this case, the pointer variable itself is passed by value, but that is okay, because you are only interested in what the pointer points to.

Enumeration Variables

An enumeration consists of a set of named integer constants. The enum type in VB and C work very similarly. The storage in C for an enumeration is the same as an int. You could use an enumeration in place of an int when it serves your purpose to have a defined set of values.

The following rules apply to enumerations:

- The constant values in an enumeration start at 0 and increment by 1 unless otherwise set.
- An enumeration can contain duplicate constant values, but not duplicate identifiers.
- Identifiers within an enumeration must be unique from other identifiers within the same scope. The enum does not "hide" the identifiers from the rest of the program. This is different than structures and unions. See Listing 3.1.

LISTING 3.1   Enumeration

```
enum WEEKDAY
{
en_Sunday = 1,
en_Monday = 2,
en_Tuesday = 3,
en_Wednesday = 4,
en_Thursday = 5,
en_Friday = 6,
en_Saturday = 7
};
```

Any portion of the program that can see the enumeration in Listing 3.1 can use the values inside the enumeration just like it is a constant.

Structures

While structures, or User Defined Types (UDTs) are very similar in nature in both VB and C, their definition and use can be very different in some notable ways. For example, while there is basically one way to define a UDT in Visual Basic, it turns out there are a number of variations for structure definition in C.

Attributes of Structures

The structure consists of named members of any type and these named members are not visible beyond the scope of the structure. So to refer to a structure member you must qualify the named member with the structure variable.

In C you know that you can refer to values with actual by value variables or with pointer variables. You use different syntax to refer to the structure members depending upon whether you are using a by value structure variable or a pointer to a structure. When the variable is a structure variable (by value) the dot syntax is used (`VarName.MemberName`). When the variable is a pointer the pointer syntax is used (`VarName->MemberName`).

> **NOTE**
>
> Syntax variation with pointers can trip you up when you first work with structures. Once you understand, it's easy to deal with. You will end up using the pointer syntax quite a bit, because Windows' messages like to send you pointers to structures in the lp parameter.

3

C PROGRAMMING

Listing 3.2 shows both forms of structure variables. Both variables access the same structure, but because one is a pointer variable it uses the pointer syntax.

LISTING 3.2   Structure Variables and Pointers

```
Struct DOG
{
    char name[25];
    int legs;
    int brains;
};
struct DOG tDog;
struct DOG *pDog = &tDog;    //pDog points to tDog
tDog.legs = 4;         //dot syntax
pDog->brains = 0;   //pointer syntax
```

Notice in Listing 3.2 that the tDog and pDog variables access the same values. Since pDog points to tDog, it can change the values in tDog.

Declaration of Structures

There are several ways to declare structures. Structure definition can be like law: If there is no apparent rule, apply the reasonable person theory.

For example, you may declare an anonymous structure and name a variable. You may name variables at the time that you declare the structure, or declare them later. You may embed structures within structures, either through declaration or direct struct statements.

Listings 3.3 through 3.9 show some variations of structure definition.

Listing 3.3 shows an anonymous definition. This is a structure without a tag. You should include a variable name, this variable can be used within the scope of the structure definition.

LISTING 3.3   Anonymous Structure Definition

```
//anonymous structure declares variable x
struct
{
    int i;
    int y;
}x;
```

Listing 3.4 shows another anonymous definition. The only difference here is that this code also includes a pointer variable definition. Both these variables can be used within the scope of the structure definition.

LISTING 3.4 Anonymous Structure Definition

```
//anonymous structure declares variable x and pointer p
struct
{
    int i;
    int y;
}x, *p;
```

Listing 3.5 shows a more common form of a structure definition. This one includes a tag to use for definition of other variables. The last line demonstrates how to use the tag to define a structure variable based on that `struct`.

LISTING 3.5 Named Structure Definition

```
//named structure declares variable x and pointer p
struct b
{
    int i;
    int y;
}x,*p;
//declaring a variable tVar from a named structure b
struct b tVar;
```

Listing 3.6 shows an embedded structure. The embedded structure is named and defined within the main structure. The structure declared in this manner also exists at file scope level. You can declare a variable based on the embedded structure, as long as it is named.

LISTING 3.6 Embedded Structure Definition

```
//embedded structure
struct b
{
    int i;
    int y;
    struct c
    {
        int z;
    }h;
}x,*p;

//embedded structure c exists at file scope level
struct c tVar1;
```

LISTING 3.6   Continued

```
//accessing embedded structure members
//x is the named variable in struct b above
//h is the named variable of the embedded structure and a member of x
//z is the member in h
x.h.z = 1;
//p is a pointer to structure b
p=&x;
p->h.z = 1;
```

Listing 3.7 shows how to do an embedded structure by using a named structure defined outside the main structure. The results here are as exactly the same as if the structure were defined within the main structure.

LISTING 3.7   Embedded Named Structure Definition

```
//we can also embed named structures
//the following code is the same as the above c struct
struct c
{
    int z;
};
struct b
{
    int i;
    int y;
    struct c h;
}x, *p;
```

Listing 3.8 demonstrates that the embedded structure can be a pointer to a structure as well as the actual structure variable. Remember that the pointer must point to something real. You can't just put the pointer in the structure and start setting values into a variable that isn't there.

LISTING 3.8   Embedded Pointer to a Named Structure

```
struct c
{
    int z;
};
//we could use a pointer to the c struct as well
struct b
{
    int i;
    int y;
    struct c *h;
```

LISTING 3.8   Continued

```
}x,*p;

struct c tVar;
x.h = &tVar;
//remember the pointer must point to something
p=&x;
x.h=&x.c;
//access the value this way
x.c.z=1;
//or
p->h->z = 1;
//or
x.h->z = 1;
```

A structure cannot contain a member that is the type of structure being defined. It can however, contain a member declared as a pointer to the structure in which it appears. This allows construction of linked lists. You'll find a demonstration in Listing 3.9.

LISTING 3.9   Embedded Pointer to the Main Structure

```
//we could use a pointer to the b struct
struct b
{
    int i;
    int y;
    struct b *next;
};
```

> **NOTE**
>
> As you can see, the structure definitions can be complicated and deceptive. Understanding structure definitions ranks with understanding pointers in terms of importance. This is why I'm going to introduce typedef specifically as it's used with the struct key word.

typedef with Structures

Using typedef with the structure definition is a popular thing to do, but it does introduce more complexities into an already complex subject. If you use the typedef in conjunction with the struct keyword, the uses of the struct parts change a little. This will make the definition simpler and more "VB-like" than any other way of doing it.

Specifically, the spot where you would define variables becomes an area to define variable types. The sample in Listing 3.10 might make this clearer.

LISTING 3.10   Using `typedef` with `struct`

```
//typedef with struct
typedef struct tagDOG
{
    int legs;
    int brains;
}DOG, *PDOG;
//you can define the variable with the tag
struct tagDOG var1;
//you can define the variable with the typedef
DOG var2;
PDOG var3 = &var2;
var1.legs = 4;
var1.breains = 0;
var2.legs = 4;
var3->brains = 0;
```

The `typedef` keyword in this situation allows you to get rid of the `struct` keyword in your declarations. This makes the declarations cleaner and, in my opinion, easier to read. You can still include a tag and use the tag, along with the struct keyword to declare a variable.

Using `struct` essentially allows you to define a new variable type. In Visual Basic, you cannot declare variables along with the UDT declaration, instead you define a variable type for the UDT. This is what `typedef` allows you to do. You define a new variable type that is used to declare your variables.

Unions

Unions have no Visual Basic counterpart. Similar to a structure, a union's primary differentiating feature is that it saves memory because you can use only one element of it at a time. In other words, the union members are all stored in the same spot in memory, so when using the union, it is only possible to use one member at a time. This is a useful feature, but not one that you will use often.

The union will take up the amount of space required by its largest member. All members will access the same spot in memory, so you have to be sure what is in the union before you access the member. Many times you will find a union included in a structure along with a structure member that defines the type of variable contained in the union.

Initialization

Initialization is an important factor when programming in C. Visual Basic variables are always initialized to default values; scalar variables are initialized to 0, string variables are initialized to empty strings. In C, variables are not initialized.

Variables can and will contain "garbage" unless the programmer initializes them.

> **CAUTION**
>
> If you don't initialize variables in C bad things can happen. Some C programmers advocate initializing every variable. I don't see that as necessary, but you *do* need to know what you are going to use a variable for and it must be initialized before it is used as an r-value.
>
> A pointer in particular is critical to be initialized. It is simply useless if it is not initialized. Using an uninitialized pointer is a bad error and can crash your program and the system. It is however, a common error.

Scalar Variables

Scalar variables are single value variables, as opposed to aggregate variables and arrays. There are several rules about initializing variables, depending on their scope and storage class:

- File-scope level variables —These can be initialized where they are declared, but they will take on a 0 value if not initialized.

- Global static variables —These variables follow the same rules as for file-scope.

- Automatic variables—These variables are reinitialized each time they come within scope. They do not get a value automatically as global static variables do. They must be initialized if you want them to contain non-garbage values.

- Static variables—Such variables must be initialized with constant expressions. Automatic variables can be initialized with constants or any type of expression, including functions.

Listing 3.11 shows several ways to initialize scalar variables.

LISTING 3.11 Initialize Scalar Variables

```
//initialize i to 10
int i = 10;
//initialize pointer px to a null value
int *px = 0;
```

3

C PROGRAMMING

LISTING 3.11   Continued

```
//initialize pointer pi to address of i
int *pi = &i;
//initialize constant int to 12 * 25, value of x cannot be changed
const int x = (12 * 25);
```

Aggregate Variables

In C aggregate variables (structures and arrays) may be initialized with constants in an initializer-list. Visual Basic has no initializer list, you simply use code to initialize aggregate variables. You can also write code that will initialize aggregate variables in C. Using code to initialize variables is straightforward, you just write the code to put the values into the variable.

In the case of initializer lists, for each list, the constant expressions are assigned, in order, to each item in the list. The list should match the size of the variable that the list is initializing. Remember that static variables initialize themselves if a list is too short, but automatic variables that have members not covered by the initializer list will be undefined. If the list is too long, an error occurs.

The list for a structure has a value for each member in the structure. The initializer for a union is a constant expression, which is assigned to the first member of the union.

If an array has an unknown size, the list defines the array size. There is no way to set values in the middle of an array without setting the items at the first of the array. You can initialize the array with code if this is required.

Listing 3.12 demonstrates some different ways to initialize aggregate variables.

LISTING 3.12   Initialize Aggregate Variables

```
//int array with three items in the array
int i[] = {1,2,3};
//double dimensions
int x[2][3] =
{
    {1,1,1},
    {2,2,2}
};
//structure
struct y
{
    int a,b,c;
    float d;
}var = {1,2,3,4.0};
```

Strings

You may initialize strings with a string literal, or, since a string in C is really an array, you can also initialize it with a list of constants. For a string (which is enclosed in double quotes), the character \0 is assigned to the end of the list for you.

Listing 3.13 demonstrates this.

LISTING 3.13   Initializing Strings

```
//use a string literal - null terminator automatically added
char c[] = "This is one way";
//use constant list - null terminator automatically added
char d[] = {'A','n','o','t','h','e','r',' ','w','a','y'};
//bad thing - results in string that is not terminated
char e[3] = "abcd";
//wide string
w_char w[] = L"This is a wide string.";
```

Expressions

Expressions cover assigning or computing values and use a sequence of operators and operands. The operators and operands are combined in such a way as to obtain the desired results.

There are an unlimited number of ways to build expressions, but there are some basic rules that are fairly easy to follow. Most of these rules in C are similar to those in Visual Basic. C has some "shortcut" operators that make statements shorter, like the ++ operator that can increment a variable.

This section covers the operators, precedence, conversions, and type casts. This gives you the building blocks for expressions.

Operators and Precedence

In this section I discuss operators, their uses, and their precedence. This provides much of the information you need in order to successfully use these operators within expressions.

Unary Operators

The unary operators in C include *, &, sizeof, -, ~, !, ++, and --. You've seen and used the indirection (*) and address-of operators (&) earlier in this chapter in the section on pointers:

- Indirection operator—This is used to assign a value to the variable that a pointer variable is pointing to.

- Address-of operator—This operator is used to assign a variable's address to a pointer. These are demonstrated following:

```
int x=10;
int *px = &x;   //address-of operator to assign pointer
*px = 20;       //indirection to assign value
```

- Sizeof operator—This operator provides the amount of storage required to store the item in the operand. This is expressed in bytes. Len in Visual Basic roughly equates to this operator.

- Negation operator (-)—This operator does what you might expect: It returns the negative of the operand. Visual Basic has the same operator.

- Bitwise not (~)—This operator produces the bitwise complement of the operand. The logical not (!) produces the logical opposite of the operand. Visual Basic uses the NOT keyword for the logical not.

- Increment (++)and decrement (- -)operators—These operators can be used in a couple ways. When used within an expression, it is significant if these operators are used as prefix operators or suffix operators. Basically they increment or decrement the variable they are affixed to. Used creatively they can save code. The code following shows how to use these operators.

```
x = 0;
item[++x] = 1;   //item[1]
x = 0;
item[x++] = 1;   //item[0]
```

Using the increment operator as a prefix changes the value before the assignment. Using it as a suffix operator increments the value after the assignment.

Binary Operators

The binary operators include *, /, %, +, -, <<, >>, <, >, <=, >=, ==, !, =, &, |, ^, &&, ||, and ,; only some of these have counterparts in Visual Basic. And unlike VB, C also allows a combination of the assignment operator and other binary operators.

The multiplicative operators—the multiplication (*), division (/), and remainder (%) —all have counterparts in Visual Basic. Only the remainder operator is different in VB, the Mod operator is used in VB instead of the %. The multiplication and division operators are the same in C and VB. These three operators work pretty much like you'd expect.

The additive operators plus(+) and minus (-) have direct counterparts in Visual Basic and work just as you'd expect.

The bitwise shift operators shift their operand left(<<) or right (>>) by the number of positions specified. Visual Basic can simulate this by multiplying by a number, but the shift still does things a bit differently than a multiplication does and works across the entire unsigned number. Because of signed numbers, bit shifts in Visual Basic are fairly complex issues.

Logical comparison operators are the same as Visual Basic in many cases, but different enough in a couple of cases to be aggravating. The <, >, <=, and >= operators are all the same as VB and work like you would expect them. The equivalent comparison is different (==) in C than in VB (=). Also the not operator in C (!) is different than VB (NOT). A common way of using the not operator (!) in C has a different counterpart in VB: not equal in C is !=, in VB it is <>.

Bitwise operators AND (&), OR (|), and exclusive OR (^) compare to the Visual Basic key-words AND, OR, and XOR. The problem with the Visual Basic operators is that context decides whether they are bit operators or logical operators and this can produce unexpected results in some cases. In addition you have the fact that there are no unsigned types in Visual Basic which hinder the use of bitwise operators.

Logical operators AND (&&) and OR (||) compare to the Visual Basic operators AND and OR. Again in VB, context determines which operation is performed, logical or bitwise.

The == operator is worth further mention. This is an equal comparison operator. In Visual Basic the equal operator does double duty, both as assignment and comparison. Not so in C. This has both good points and bad points and it can be especially troublesome to a VB programmer.

VB programmers are used to using the equal sign for comparison and so typically make the mistake of trying to use it in C. This is a simple thing, but sometimes habit takes over. Many times misuse of this operator will not produce an error, just an unwanted result.

C operators are summarized in Table 3.2.

TABLE 3.2   C Operators

Operator	Basic Use	Visual Basic
Unary		
*	Indirection	None
&	Address of	Varptr
sizeof	Size of	Len(x)—sort of
-	Negation	-
~	Bitwise not	NOT

3

C PROGRAMMING

TABLE 3.2 Continued

Operator	Basic Use	Visual Basic
!	Logical not	NOT
++	Increment	x = x + 1
- -	Decrement	x = x - 1
Binary		
*	Multiplication	*
/	Division	/
%	Remainder	MOD
+	Addition	+
-	Subtraction	-
<<	Left bit shift	None
>>	Right bit shift	None
<	Less than	<
>	Greater then	>
<=	Less then or equal	<=
>=	Greater than or equal	>=
==	Logical equal	=
!	Not	NOT
=	Equal assignment	=
&	Bitwise AND	AND
|	Bitwise inclusive OR	OR
^	Bitwise exclusive or	XOR
&&	Logical AND	AND
||	Logical OR	OR
,	Sequential evaluation	None
? :	Conditional Evaluator	IIF
Assignment		
=	Simple assignment	=
*=	Multiplication assignment	x = x * y
/=	Division assignment	x = x / y
%=	Remainder assignment	x = x MOD y
+=	Addition assignment	x = x + y

TABLE 3.2 Continued

Operator	Basic Use	Visual Basic
`<<=`	Left shift assignment	None
`>>=`	Right shift assignment	None
`&=`	Bit AND assignment	x = x AND y
`|=`	Bit OR assignment	x = x OR y
`^=`	Bit Exclusive OR assignment	x = x XOR y

Precedence

Operators listed at the same level have the same precedence. As in Visual Basic, grouping statement segments within parentheses can alter precedence.

Table 3.3 summarizes operator precedence.

TABLE 3.3 C Operator Precedence

Symbols	Basic Use	Associativity
`[]().-> postfix ++ postfix --`	Expression	Left to Right
`Prefix ++ prefix — sizeof & * - ~ !`	Unary	Right to Left
`Type casts`	Unary	Right to Left
`* / %`	Multiplicative	Left to Right
`+ -`	Additive	Left to Right
`<< >>`	Bitwise shift	Left to Right
`< > <= >=`	Relational	Left to Right
`== !=`	Logical Equality	Left to Right
`&`	Bitwise AND	Left to Right
`^`	Bitwise Exclusive OR	Left to Right
`|`	Bitwise Inclusive OR	Left to Right
`&&`	Logical-AND	Left to Right
`||`	Logical-OR	Left to Right
`?:`	Conditional-expression	Right to Left
`= *= /= %= += -= <<= >>= &= ^= |=`	Assignment	Right to Left
`,`	Sequential evaluation	Left to Right

3

C PROGRAMMING

There are subtle problems that can creep into expressions with multiple operators depending on your compiler and the current compilation flags. For example, logical expressions will often "shortcut" the latter part of the expression if the first part is enough to determine the outcome of the logical expression.

TIP

Precedence is difficult to deal with in complex expressions. My advice is to group your expressions so there will be little ambiguity.

Conversions and Type Casts

Conversions and type casts follow a set of rules. These rules involve a couple of definitions that you need to know to understand the conversions involving numeric data:

- Sign extend—This rule dictates how smaller integral types are converted to larger ones. The number must be represented in a different manner because the bit that denotes the negativity is in a different spot.

- Preserve low order word or byte—This rule describes how a larger integral type is converted to a smaller one. The high order word or byte will be ignored, effectively it is dropped.

- Loss of precision—This rule governs what happens when a number is converted to float and the significant digits are larger than 7. It can also happen with a double after 14 digits.

From Signed Integral Types

When converting from signed integral types, the main point to remember in integral conversions is that there is a loss of the upper bytes when going from a larger integral to a smaller one, like a long to a short. If there is information contained in the upper bytes, it will therefore be lost. Converting from a smaller int to a larger one involves no real problems. Converting a signed integer to an unsigned one doesn't change the data as long as they are the same size. It may change the way the bits are interpreted if the signed number is negative, but the in memory representation will remain unchanged as long as they are the same size.

Converting an integral type to a decimal type (float or double) should leave the number unchanged, unless the number is longer than the decimal type's significant digits, in which case a loss of precision will occur. A summary of signed integral conversions is shown in Table

3.4. Also a floating-point representation has gaps in its coverage of all decimal numbers (which is infinite).

NOTE

Because the long will be converted to a mantissa and an exponent (for example, 1000 becomes 1E+3), you can actually end up with a different number than what you started with. This has nothing to do with loss of precision that results from too few significant digits.

TABLE 3.4 Signed Integral Conversions

From	To	Method
char	short	Sign-extend
char	long	Sign-extend
char	unsigned char	Preserve pattern; high-order bit loses function as sign bit
char	unsigned short	Sign-extend to short; convert short to unsigned short
char	unsigned long	Sign-extend to long; convert long to unsigned long
char	float	Sign-extend to long; convert long to float
char	double	Sign-extend to long; convert long to double
char	long double	Sign-extend to long; convert long to double
short	char	Preserve low-order byte
short	long	Sign-extend
short	unsigned char	Preserve low-order byte
short	unsigned short	Preserve bit pattern; high-order bit loses function as sign bit
short	unsigned long	Sign-extend to long; convert long to unsigned long
short	float	Sign-extend to long; convert long to float
short	double	Sign-extend to long; convert long to double
short	long double	Sign-extend to long; convert long to double
long	char	Preserve low-order byte
long	short	Preserve low-order word
long	unsigned char	Preserve low-order byte
long	unsigned short	Preserve low-order word

3

C PROGRAMMING

TABLE 3.4   Continued

From	To	Method
long	unsigned long	Preserve bit pattern; high-order bit loses function as sign bit
long	float	Represent as float. If long cannot be represented exactly, some precision is lost.
long	double	Represent as double. If long cannot be represented exactly as a double, some precision is lost.
long	long double	Represent as double. If long cannot be represented exactly as a double, some precision is lost.

From Unsigned Integral Types

The concerns with unsigned types are the same as with signed integral types. Again, going from unsigned to signed may change the way the bits are interpreted, but in memory it will still be the same if the types are the same size. A summary of unsigned integral conversions is shown in Table 3.5.

TABLE 3.5   Unsigned Integral Conversions

From	To	Method
unsigned char	char	Preserve bit pattern; high-order bit becomes sign bit
unsigned char	short	Zero-extend
unsigned char	long	Zero-extend
unsigned char	unsigned short	Zero-extend
unsigned char	unsigned long	Zero-extend
unsigned char	float	Convert to long; convert long to float
unsigned char	double	Convert to long; convert long to double
unsigned char	long double	Convert to long; convert long to double
unsigned short	char	Preserve low-order byte
unsigned short	short	Preserve bit pattern; high-order bit becomes sign bit
unsigned short	long	Zero-extend
unsigned short	unsigned char	Preserve low-order byte
unsigned short	unsigned long	Zero-extend
unsigned short	float	Convert to long; convert long to float

TABLE 3.5   Continued

From	To	Method
unsigned short	double	Convert to long; convert long to double
unsigned short	long double	Convert to long; convert long to double
unsigned long	char	Preserve low-order byte
unsigned long	short	Preserve low-order word
unsigned long	long	Preserve bit pattern; high-order bit becomes sign bit
unsigned long	unsigned char	Preserve low-order byte
unsigned long	unsigned short	Preserve low-order word
unsigned long	float	Convert to long; convert long to float
unsigned long	double	Convert directly to double
unsigned long	long double	Convert to long; convert long to double

From Floating Point Types

Floating point conversions can result in loss of precision or can even be undefined if, for example, the float value is converted to a short and the float value is out of the short's range. A summary of floating point conversions is shown in Table 3.6.

TABLE 3.6   Floating Point Conversions

From	To	Method
Float	char	Convert to long; convert long to char
Float	short	Convert to long; convert long to short
Float	Llong	Truncate at decimal point. If result is too large to be represented as long, result is undefined.
Float	unsigned short	Convert to long; convert long to unsigned short
Float	unsigned long	Convert to long; convert long to unsigned long
Float	double	Change internal representation
Float	long double	Change internal representation
Double	char	Convert to float; convert float to char
Double	short	Convert to float; convert float to short
Double	long	Truncate at decimal point. If result is too large to be represented as long, result is undefined.

TABLE 3.6   Continued

From	To	Method
Double	unsigned short	Convert to long; convert long to unsigned short
Double	unsigned long	Convert to long; convert long to unsigned long
double	float	Represent as a float. If double value cannot be represented exactly as float, loss of precision occurs. If value is too large to be represented as float, the result is undefined.
long double	char	Convert to float; convert float to char
long double	short	Convert to float; convert float to short
long double	long	Truncate at decimal point. If result is too large to be represented as long, result is undefined.
long double	unsigned short	Convert to long; convert long to unsigned short
long double	unsigned long	Convert to long; convert long to unsigned long
long double	float	Represent as a float. If double value cannot be represented exactly as float, loss of precision occurs. If value is too large to be represented as float, the result is undefined.
long double	double	The long double value is treated as double.

To and From Pointers

Pointers can be converted to integral types and back to pointers. Here you simply need to be aware of the size of the pointer and the size of the integral, which may be determined by the memory-addressing model of your operating system (for example, 32 bit for WIN32).

Generally speaking pointers can be converted without loss of data or any consequences. However there can be some alignment issues with some types of pointers, as well as other issues with the data.

> **NOTE**
>
> The biggest issue in converting a pointer has to do with accessing the data after the pointer is converted. Usually this is why you convert the pointer, so you can access the data. However, there is no protection in C if you want to convert a pointer to a double to a pointer to a long and then try to use the data like it contains long data. This gives erroneous results, but you can do it.

Other Types

Because an enum is an integer, conversions for it work the same as for an integer. For the Microsoft compiler, an integer is the same as a long.

Void types have no value and cannot be converted—only void pointers may be converted to other pointer types with no loss of information.

Type Casts

Type casts are the way you change one variable type to another. Obviously some type casts are allowable and others are not. The conversion rules you saw in the previous sections apply to type casts as well as implicit conversions. The code following shows a few examples of type casts.

```
//type casts
//int to short
int i=2;
short sval = (short) i;
//long to pointer - common in handling lParam of SendMessage
char *p;
p = (char *)lParam;
```

Table 3.7 summarizes the allowable type casts.

TABLE 3.7   Type Cast Conversions

Destination Types	Potential Sources
Integral types	Any integer type or floating-point type, or pointer to an object
Floating-point	Any arithmetic type
A pointer to an object, or (void *)	Any integer type, (void *), a pointer to an object, or a function pointer
Function pointer	Any integral type, a pointer to an object, or a function pointer
A structure, union, or array	None
Void type	Any type

Statements

You have already been exposed to some of what this section covers. Here you'll look at statements and how they relate to the Visual Basic code with which you are familiar.

This section covers assignment statements, control, flow, and looping statements.

Assignment

Visual Basic offers only the simple assignment; however, in C you have what are termed *simple assignments* (x=1;) and *compound assignments* (x+=1;).

Simple assignments in C are shown here:

```
x = 2;
```

```
y = x;
```

C also offers compound assignments, like the one shown here:

```
x += 2;
```

In Visual Basic, this compound assignment must be expressed in a different way.

```
x = x + 2
```

The Visual Basic form is also allowed in C:

```
x = x + 2;
```

However, x+=2 can more easily be optimized by the C/C++ compiler.

Control and Flow

The C statements involved with flow control include goto, switch, case, default, break, if, and else. These types of statements fall into two general categories, if statements and case statements. Both C and Visual Basic have these two types of statements, but there are some elementary differences between the two languages.

Goto

The goto and label statements fall outside these two general categories (if and case), but a goto is flow control. A goto is also one of the basic constructs of programming.

> **NOTE**
>
> It is well accepted that certain other programming elements do a good job of hiding the ugliness of jumps or goto. Loop constructs and logical constructs make the goto almost extinct. However, all of these programming tasks are constructed by using jumps which is a goto in its rawest form.

The goto in C statement works just like the goto statement in Visual Basic. This statement shouldn't show up in your code very much, if at all. goto makes the code difficult to read and maintain and is considered bad form.

if

Let's take a look at the if statement now. In Visual Basic there are five statements involved with the if construct: If, Then, ElseIf, Else, and End If. Only the if and else exist in C, while the Then and End If statements are implied in the way the language is used. The ElseIf feature is actually lost. The C if statement uses parenthesis to enclose the logical expression used within the if statement.

In C if statements typically use blocks, or compound statements as they are sometimes called. The braces that are used with the if block can impact the way the if statement is evaluated and so these blocks should be constructed with care. Nested if statements can be especially tricky. It is wise to use braces to make sure the statements work as you expect them to work. Look at Listing 3.14.

LISTING 3.14   if Blocks

```
//c nested if
if (x>1)
    if (x<10)
        y=1;
    else
        y=0;

'Equivalent Basic code
If x > 1 Then
    If x < 10 Then
        y = 1
    Else
        y = 0
    End If
End If

//c nested If with braces
if (x>1)
{
    if (x<10)
        y=1;
}
else
    y=0;

'Equivalent Basic code
If x > 1 Then
    If x < 10 Then
        y = 1
    End If
```

3

C PROGRAMMING

LISTING 3.14 Continued

```
Else
    y = 0
End If
```

I've indented the `else` statement to make it clear which `if` statement it goes with; in the first nested `if` statement, the `else` is paired with the nested `if`. Except for the braces, the two C listings are identical. When the braces are added, the `else` is paired with the first `if` statement, completely changing the logic of the statement.

If you use block `If` statements in Visual Basic there is little ambiguity. C is more difficult to read and easier to make mistakes in grouping the statements.

> **TIP**
>
> I recommend giving the braces their own line. It increases the readability. If you are unsure, use the braces to force the code to behave as you want it to. However, a good editor should make the program flow more obvious by auto indenting and brace matching.

Case

The other type of flow control is a case statement. In Visual Basic this consists of `Select Case`, `Case Else`, and `End Select`. C uses `switch`, `case`, and `default`. Again the braces take the place of the closing or `End Select` statement in VB.

There are some differences to look for in the C switch statement. The biggest is that control will fall through the case statements. The break statement must be used to exit a case statement in C. This offers some interesting ways to structure code within the `switch–case` statement. Listing 3.15 shows a `switch–case` statement and the equivalent Visual Basic code.

LISTING 3.15 case Statements

```
switch (x)
{
    case 0:
        y0++;
        break;
    case 1:
        y1++;
```

LISTING 3.15   Continued

```
        break;
    case 2:
        y2++;
    default:
        y++;
}
'Equivalent VB case statement
Select Case x
    case 0:
        y0=y0 + 1
    case 1:
        y1 = y1 + 1
    case 2:
        y2 = y2 + 1
        Y = y + 1
    Case Else:
        y = y + 1
End Select
```

Notice the break statements in the C code. These are required to keep the flow from dropping through to the next case statement.

NOTE

Visual Basic does by default what the break statement adds to a case statement in C.

If you look closer at the case 2 statement, you see that the C code falls through to the default and both y2 and y are incremented.

To get this functionality in Visual Basic, you place the code in both the case 2 and the Case Else in order. This doesn't seem too bad, but it depends upon how much code you are talking about.

Looping

There are three basic types of looping provided within Visual Basic and C: For–Next, Do–Loop and While–Wend. Again C does away with the statement in VB used to close these loop statements, relying instead upon the braces to close the loop statement.

For

For loops share a very similar structure between Visual Basic and C, but as usual the C syntax is somewhat more cryptic. Let's take a look at the for statements in Listing 3.16.

LISTING 3.16   for Loop

```
 'C loop, 1 to 10, but code exits at 5
for (x=1;x<10;x++)
{
    if (1==x)
        continue;
    if (5==x)
        break;
    y++;
}

'VB equivalent
For x=1 To 9 Step 1
    If x = 1 Then
        x = x + 1
    End if
    If x = 5 Then
        Exit For
    End If
    y = y + 1
Next
```

Again you use the braces to define the beginning and end of the set of statements. You should be starting to see a pattern with the braces by now. C typically doesn't use some kind of closing statement like Visual Basic does.

> **NOTE**
>
> I have demonstrated what I consider to be poorly structured code here to demonstrate the continue statement. As a matter of fact, I discourage the use of a continue statement because it destroys the structure of the loop. The Visual Basic code I've written here doesn't really duplicate the continue statement, just allows the code to act the same. As a Visual Basic programmer, you never had the continue statement and you can probably do without it in C.

Notice too in Listing 3.16 that the break statement does the job of the Exit For. You saw the break statement before in the switch case. Break does double and triple duty. Usually the break statement means exit from whatever block statement you are in. It will exit from switch, for, while, and do blocks.

One more thing to notice before you leave this listing is the comparison that you are doing. The if statement compares x to 5 and exits the for if they are equal. The constant is placed first and the x is placed after the double equals. Note that if you place the x first and follow with a single equal sign (x=5) that this is a legal statement, will assign 5 to x and return true. The loop will exit the first time through. Depending on warning levels, the compiler may (but not necessarily) warn you about this. Getting in the habit of placing the constant first will help you guard against this misstep. A constant cannot be an l-value so if you follow the constant with a single equal, you will receive an error during compile.

Do

The other type of loop provided by C is the do–while, or the while by itself. In Visual Basic you typically use While Wend if you test at the front of the loop, or Do–Until if you test at the end. In reality the while or Until will test at either end of the loop in Visual Basic; the Until is just another way to do the test. The Until is not really required and C doesn't have it.

Listing 3.17 shows you both types of loops and the Visual Basic equivalents.

LISTING 3.17   do and while Loops

```
do
{
    x++;
}
while (x < 10);

'VB equivalent
Do
    x = x + 1
Loop While x < 10

while (x < 10)
{
    x++;
}

'VB equivalent
While x < 10
    x = x + 1
Wend
```

What are the differences in these two styles of loops? Mostly, the do loop executes the contents of the loop at least one time. The While loop tests the expression and if the test fails the loop is never executed. Sound familiar? It should, it works the same as Visual Basic and logic dictates that it should.

Remember break? It gets you out of the loop early, just like Exit Do or Exit While. Continue can be used to go to the next iteration of the loop.

Summary

This chapter examined basics of the C language. Most of the C code that you would write finds its basis in this chapter.

You've compared variables, expressions, and statements in C to statements that you use in Visual Basic and by now you should be beginning to have a feel for the C language.

C++ Basics

IN THIS CHAPTER

In some respects C++ can be thought of as a "supercharged" C. It adds some functionality that is related to the base language, and in this vein it is simply an updated and improved C. However, it's impossible to talk about the basics of C++ without also introducing classes. I will introduce some of the technical aspects of writing classes in this chapter and then expand on those technical details in Chapter 5, "C++ Classes."

This chapter begins by exploring the improvements that C++ provides and builds on the things that you learned in the previous two chapters—it isn't going to be possible to understand everything in this chapter without knowing the information in Chapters 2, "C Basics," and 3, "C Programming."

We will follow the chapter structure introduced there, providing new sections where required to cover C++. I will also refer you to those chapters quite often when the material is applicable to the discussion.

This chapter will cover the following topics:

- Tokens and Elements—This section includes keywords, identifiers, constants, and literals.
- Structure—This section talks about how to use the elements of the language. I'll discuss compiler directives, code structure, lifetime, scope, and visibility.
- Functions—This section discusses how to create and use functions. I'll discuss the technicalities of functions in classes.
- Variables and Data—This section covers variable storage and data. This includes type specifiers and qualifiers, variables, declarators, and initialization.
- Expressions—This section deals with expressions, which are usually assignment or logical operators and operands. This section also covers operators in general, conversions, and type casts.
- Statements—Statements control the flow of the program and use expressions, tokens, and other statements. This section talks about assignment, control, flow, and looping.

Tokens and Elements

This section discusses the most basic parts of the language—the tokens and elements. The bulk of this information is covered in the Tokens and Elements section in Chapter 2. I will cover the differences here.

C++ Keywords

It is helpful to see all the keywords together to see what the C++ language is adding for you. A list of the keywords in C++, a brief description of each, and the Visual Basic counterpart is listed in Table 4.1. I'll mark the new keywords in italics so that you can tell them from the C-only keywords.

TABLE 4.1 List of C Keywords

Keyword	Fundamental Use	Visual Basic Equivalent
Auto	variable scope	None (is the default)
bad_cast	*exception*	*None*
bad_typeid	*exception*	*None*
bool	*variable type*	Boolean
break	loop, decision	exit for, exit do
case	Decision	Case
catch	*error handling*	Resume
char	variable type	string (similar)
class	*class declarator*	cls module
const	variable modifier	None
const_cast	*casting*	*None*
continue	loop	Next
default	decision construct	Case Else
delete	*remove objects*	set X = Nothing
do	loop	Do - Loop
double	variable type	Double
dynamic_cast	*casting*	*None*
else	decision	Else
enum	variable type	Enum
except	*error handling*	On Error Label
explicit	*constructors*	None
extern	variable scope	Public (similar)
false	*bool constant*	False
finally	*error handling*	Resume
float	variable type	Single
for	loop	For
friend	*function class*	Friend
goto	jump	Goto
if	decision	If

TABLE 4.1   Continued

Keyword	Fundamental Use	Visual Basic Equivalent
inline	inline functions	None
int	variable type	Long
long	variable type	Long
mutable	class specifier	None
namespace	groups identifiers	None
new	creates objects	New
operator		
private	class specifier	Private
protected	class specifier	None
public	class specifier	Public
register	variable scope	None
reinterpret_cast	casting	None
return	function return	Exit Function (similar)
short	variable type	Integer
signed	variable qualifier	None
sizeof	variable size	Len (similar)
static	variable scope	Static
static_cast	casting	None
struct	User Defined Type	Type
switch	decision	Select Case
template	declares a template	None
this	this pointer	Me
throw	error handling	Err.Raise
true	bool const	True
try	error handling	On Error Goto
type_info	type information	none
typedef	New variable type	none
typeid	type information	none
typename	type information	none
union	type of structure	Simulate with Types
unsigned	variable qualifier	none

TABLE 4.1   Continued

Keyword	Fundamental Use	Visual Basic Equivalent
using	scope	References dialog
virtual	function modifier	None
void	empty return value	none, use Sub
volatile	variable scope	none
while	loop	While - Wend

Identifiers

Identifiers are similar in nature no matter what language they come from. However C++ does add some functionality to C in this area.

Identifiers are the names you give to variables, labels, functions, and types and which are later turned into tokens by the compiler. In C++ identifiers also cover names of classes, class members, and class functions.

Although the classes work somewhat differently in Visual Basic, identifiers also cover classes and class members in that language.

As discussed in Chapter 2, letters, numbers, and underscores can be used to construct identifiers. You cannot use a number to start an identifier, and the use of two leading underscores or a leading underscore followed by a capital letter in any scope is reserved by C++. You should also avoid using a leading underscore followed by a lowercase letter at a file scope level because of possible conflicts with current or future identifiers.

An identifier cannot match a reserved word. It also cannot be longer than 247 characters, which seems pretty generous until you look at the name decoration added by C++. Name decoration is something that C++ compilers do to function names to allow function overloading, which I'll discuss later in this chapter. Name decoration encodes the function parameter types into the name of the function so the compiler can differentiate functions that have the same name, but different parameter types.

Constants and Literals

Constants and literals do not change much from C to C++. Most of the information that you need on them is in the section on Constants and the section on Literals in Chapter 2.

It is worth mentioning though that the type of a character constant in C++ is char and in C it is an int—this could give you some unexpected results if you were using sizeof on constants.

Also in C++ the `const` modifier on a variable will allow it to be used anywhere a "regular" constant is used. In C that is impossible.

Structure

I've discussed C program structure already. In many cases C++ and C structure are similar. When you move to working with classes, you will see much of that similarity collapse though. If you are writing C code, you can think of C++ as a supercharged C compiler. When you start using classes, however, there are some new concepts to learn.

This section discusses directives, scope, visibility, lifetime, and linkage.

Directives

Directives are preprocessor instructions. You explored all but one of the directives in Chapter 2; C++ adds a new directive associated with COM objects.

#import is a directive that incorporates type library information into a source file. The concept is quite simple, but this is one of the most complex directives in C++. The following lines show two forms of the import statement.

```
#import "filename" [attributes]

#import <filename> [attributes]
```

The filename in the previous import statements can be quoted or bracketed. There can be multiple attributes separated by spaces or commas.

The quoted form and the bracketed form work the same as the quoted and bracketed forms of the include directive. The bracketed form will look along the PATH environment list, then the LIB environment list, and then any path specified by the /I compiler option. The quoted form will look in the directory of the file that contains the import statement first, and then use the path specifications listed for the bracketed type.

#import will work on any of the following types of files that contain type library information: A type library file (.TLB or .ODL), an executable file (.EXE), a library file (.DLL or .OCX), a compound document holding a type library, or any other file format that can be read by the LoadTypeLib API. You would most commonly use #import with a .TLB, .DLL, or .OCX.

The #import directive creates two include files that have the type library interfaces constructed in C++ wrapper code. This wrapper code allows the programmer to make calls into the COM component that the import applies to. There is quite a bit of other code in the header files including forward references, type definitions, `Typeinfo` declarations, and GUIDs. These output files' content may be influenced by the attributes that can be set within the #import directive.

This is an example that imports the Microsoft common control's OCX:

```
#import "C:\WINDOWS\SYSTEM\MSCOMCTL.OCX" raw_interfaces_only, raw_native_types,
no_namespace, named_guids
```

As with any set of options with a compiler feature, some of these attributes you will use quite often and others you will probably use rarely. Personally, I use the attributes that begin with raw quite often because the raw attribute provides the interface wrappers I need; I use no_namespace almost every time because I don't need the complication of the namespace defined in the type library. I'll provide a brief description of each available attribute:

- exclude—This attribute can be used to exclude items that might create duplicate definitions. It can take any number of arguments, each being a top-level type library item to be excluded.

- high_method_prefix—This attribute is used to specify a prefix to be used in naming high-level methods.

- high_property_prefixes—This attribute is used to specify alternate prefixes for all three property methods (propget, propput, and propputref).

- implementation_only—This attribute suppresses the generation of the .TLH header file (the primary header file). This file contains all the declarations used to expose the type-library contents. This attribute is intended for use in conjunction with the no_implementation attribute as a way of keeping the implementations out of the precompiled header (PCH) file.

- include(...)—This attribute can be used to disable an automatic exclusion if items have been excluded and they should not have been. #import attempts to avoid multiple definition errors by automatically excluding definitions of items defined in system headers or other type libraries. This attribute can take any number of arguments, each being the name of the type library item to be included.

- inject_statement—This attribute inserts its argument as source text into the type library header. The text is placed at the beginning of the namespace declaration that wraps the type library contents in the header file.

- named_guids—This attribute tells the compiler to define and initialize GUID variables in old style, of the form LIBID_MyLib, CLSID_MyCoClass, IID_MyInterface, and DIID_MyDispInterface.

- no_implementation—This attribute suppresses the generation of the .TLI header, which contains the implementations of the wrapper member functions. This attribute is used in conjunction with implementation_only.

- no_auto_exclude—This attribute provides a more global way of including items that would normally be automatically excluded by #import.

- no_namespace—This attribute excludes the namespace that is normally defined in the type library.

- raw_dispinterfaces—This attribute tells the compiler to generate low-level wrapper functions for dispinterface methods and properties that call IDispatch::Invoke and return the HRESULT error code. Otherwise functions that throw C++ exceptions in case of failure will be generated.

- raw_interfaces_only—This attribute suppresses the generation of error-handling wrapper functions. It also causes the function names to come directly from the type library rather than having a prefix. This attribute allows you to expose the low-level contents of the type library, which is typically what you want to do.

- raw_method_prefix—This attribute causes the low-level properties and methods to be exposed by member functions named with a prefix of your choosing. By default this prefix would be raw_. This attribute is used to avoid name collisions with the high-level error-handling member functions.

> **NOTE**
>
> The raw_method_prefix always takes precedence over raw_interfaces_only in specifying a prefix. If both attributes are used in the same #import statement, the prefix specified by the raw_method_prefix attribute is used.

- raw_native_types—This attribute is used to disable the use of the _bstr_t and _variant_t COM support classes in the high-level wrapper functions, and force the use of low-level data types instead (BSTR and VARIANT data types).

- raw_property_prefixes—By default, low-level propget, propput, and propputref methods are exposed by member functions named with prefixes of get_, put_, and putref_ respectively. These prefixes are compatible with the names used in the header files generated by MIDL. The raw_property_prefixes attribute is used to specify alternate prefixes for all three property methods.

- rename—This attribute is used to work around name collision problems. If this attribute is specified, the compiler replaces all occurrences of the old name in a type library with the user-supplied new name in the resulting header files.

- rename_namespace—This attribute is used to rename the namespace that contains the contents of the type library. To remove the namespace, use the no_namespace attribute.

Scope, Visibility, and Lifetime

The scope, visibility, and lifetime of variables and objects in C++ very much follow the conventions in C discussed in earlier chapters. Automatic storage still makes up the bulk of the variables and objects you work with in C++, just like C. Static variables and objects exist throughout the life of the program. External objects are visible to other translation units.

There is a new scope available, called class scope. Variables, functions, and objects declared within a class have class scope. Their visibility is limited to the class in which they are declared, and their lifetime also depends on that class.

Since classes are self-contained units, you don't declare variables, functions, or objects that can live outside the confines of the class. In other words, it is impossible to define a variable within a class that would have a lifetime equal to the program that the class is used in.

Linkage

Linkage is the way that translation units "see" other translation units. You will spend more time on this topic now than you have in earlier chapters. Linkage is important because it determines how separate translation units access each other; the things that you do to affect linkage will determine how you can access C++ code from Visual Basic.

The keyword `extern` is central to any discussion on linkage. This is the keyword that give items external linkage. There are three basic types of linkage: external, internal, and none. External linkage is usually accomplished with the `extern` keyword, and internal linkage with the `static` keyword. There are certain program elements that have no linkage (like enums).

Linkage at a file scope is internal if the item is explicitly defined as static. Enumerators and typedefs have no linkage. All other items at file scope is external.

Linkage at a class scope is external except for enumerators and typedefs, which have no linkage. Even items with static applied explicitly, have external linkage.

Block scope items have no linkage, unless it is explicitly defined as extern.

The `extern` keyword supports a string parameter that can take either "C" or "C++" as its parameter (this keyword is quite important in Chapter 7, "C DLLs," in which I will talk about DLLs that support Visual Basic). `extern "C"` is the way a C (.c extension) program provides external linkage. `extern "C++"` is the way a C++ program (.cpp extension) supports its external linkage.

Visual Basic can use functions (not data) that are declared external and exported in such a way that the name decoration is removed from the function. If you use `extern "C++"`, there is a lot of name decoration that is added onto the actual name of the exported item. Other C++ modules can deal with the name decoration can access the functions. Visual Basic cannot access functions with C++ linkage. Visual Basic can access functions with C linkage.

To provide linkage for a Visual Basic program in C++ code you must use the extern "C" linkage specification. This along with a definition file will make the functions accessible from Visual Basic. I will go into greater detail on how to do this in Chapter 7.

Functions

Functions in C++ follow C conventions.

This section covers prototypes, variable number of parameters, and overloading. I will also briefly cover some of the complexities that classes add to function declarations; most of those complexities will be more fully explored in Chapter 5, although some will be briefly mentioned here.

Prototype

Function prototypes work essentially the same in C++ as they do in C. In C++ there is an issue of external linkage. If a prototype appears in a .CPP file, the external linkage will be C++, unless you change it with the extern modifier. The extern modifier can take either "C" or "C++" as a parameter and this affects the external linkage of the function. This is applied to the function prototype.

Functions can use the `inline` and the `virtual` modifiers in the function prototype. The `inline` modifier causes the function to be placed "inline" within the code so that at the point of the function call, the code for the function call is actually placed where the call is made. This gets rid of the overhead of the function call. Whether the inlining of the code actually happens is something the compiler determines based on compiler settings and internal optimizations. The virtual modifier is used in conjunction with classes and you will explore it in Chapter 5.

Variable Number of Parameters

Like Visual Basic, C++ can have functions that define and use a variable number of parameters. However, C++ does not have optional parameters in the same way that Visual Basic does—a C++ function can provide default parameters that can be omitted, which is similar to optional parameters in Visual Basic, but parameters with defaults are not quite as flexible as optional parameters. In C++ it is impossible to leave out a parameter without having a default value, as it is in Visual Basic.

C++ cannot leave out an optional parameter when interacting with a Visual Basic object; if C++ and Visual Basic need to interact with optional parameters, C++ makes that happen with Variants. It must use the proper parameter or set up a Variant in a special way.

Both Visual Basic and C++ can have a variable number of parameters at the end of a function. The way that the two languages implement these functions is not compatible. It would be possible to write code between the two languages to handle the variable parameters, because it is essentially arrays that provide the functionality in Visual Basic. If you have variable parameters in a VB function, those are provided through a SAFEARRAY. This is an OLE type. Chapter 7 explains safe arrays. It would be possible to handle a VB function in C++ (if you could deal with name decoration) but there is no real way to write a C++ function with variable parameters and interface it with Visual Basic.

Overloading

Function overloading is a capability provided by C++ that is impossible in Visual Basic. You can use Variants in Visual Basic as parameters and pass different types through those Variant parameters. However, doing this is not the same as overloading a function because the overloaded function provides strong type checking, whereas the variant does not.

Overloading a function is the process of using the same function name with different parameter lists within the same scope. (I'll talk about overloading operators later in this chapter.) Although function overloading is commonly applied to class functions, function overloading will work perfectly well without a class.

Overloaded functions differentiate between argument types that take different initializers. An argument of a given type and a reference to that type are considered the same for the purposes of overloading. They are considered the same because they take the same initializers. For example, foo(double, double) is considered the same as foo(double&, double&). Declaring two such functions causes an error.

For the same reason, function arguments of a type modified by const or volatile are not treated differently than the base type for the purposes of overloading, unless the types are reference types. The function overloading mechanism can distinguish between *references* that are qualified by const and volatile and references to the base type. This makes code such as the following possible:

```
class Test
{
public:
    Test(){cout << "Test default constructor\n";}
    Test(Test &x){cout << "Test&\n";}
    Test(const Test &cx){cout << "const Test&\n";}
    Test(volatile Test &vx){cout << "volatile Test&\n";}
    Test(int) {cout << "int Test\n";}
    Test(double) {cout << "double Test\n";}
    //next line is an error, return not used
    double Test(double) { cout << "double Test\n";}
};
void main()
{
    Test t1;     //default constructor
    Test t2(t1);    //Calls Test(Test&)
    const Test t3;     //default constructor
    Test t4(t3);    //Calls Test(const Test&)
```

```
    volatile Test t5;      //default constructor
    Test t6(t5);     //Calls Test(volatile Test &)
}
```

Table 4.2 summarizes the function declaration elements and their effect on determining function overloading.

TABLE 4.2   List of C Keywords

Function Declaration Element	Used for Overloading?
Function return type	No
Number of arguments	Yes
Type of arguments	Yes
Presence or absence of ellipses	Yes
Use of typedef names	No
Unspecified array bounds	No
const or volatile (in cv-mod-list)	Yes

Overloaded functions are a powerful and useful concept. Using the same function to handle different types of data simplifies function use.

Variables and Data

Variables and data are covered in detail in Chapter 3—in this chapter, you examine some things that affect variables and data as they are modified by C++.

This section covers runtime type information, C++ definitions and declarations, variables, declarators, and namespaces.

Runtime Type Information

RTTI, or *runtime type information*, allows the type of an object to be determined during program execution. Visual Basic has something similar in the Typeof operator that is used in conjunction with an If statement. Both TypeOf and RTTI are only useful for object types and will not work on intrinsic types like Integer, Long, and others. RTTI was added to the C++ language because many vendors of class libraries were implementing this functionality themselves. It became apparent that support for runtime type information could be useful at the language level. This information is typically used for debugging information and during development.

There are three main C++ language elements to runtime type information. The `dynamic_cast` operator is used for conversion of polymorphic types. The `typeid` operator is used for identifying the exact type of an object. The `type_info` class is used to hold results from the `typeid` operator.

The `typeid` operator allows the type of an object to be determined at run time. If the expression is dereferencing a pointer, and that pointer's value is zero, `typeid` throws a `bad_typeid` exception. If the pointer does not point to a valid object, a `__non_rtti_object` exception is thrown.

If the expression is neither a pointer nor a reference to a base class of the object, the result is a `type_info` reference representing the static type of the expression.

The `type_info` class describes type information generated within the program by the compiler. Objects of this class effectively store a pointer to a name for the type. The `type_info` class also stores an encoded value suitable for comparing two types for equality.

As I said above the `dynamic_cast` operator is used for casting polymorphic types. The `dynamic_cast` operator will perform a runtime check of the classes involved and the cast will be safe. A normal C cast or a `static_cast` operator will perform the cast, but it may not be safe.

Type information is generated for polymorphic classes only if the /GR compiler option is specified.

C++ Definitions and Declarations

A definition is a unique specification of an object, variable, function, class, or enumerator. Because definitions must be unique, a program can contain only one definition for a given program element.

Declarations (discussed in Chapter 2) introduce names into a program. Declarations can occur more than once in a program (definitions cannot). Therefore, classes, structures, enumerated types, and other user-defined types can be declared for each compilation unit. The constraint on this multiple declaration is that all declarations must be identical. So, declarations can appear multiple times while definitions cannot. You can think of the definition as being the implementation of a declaration.

Declarations can also serve as a definition, with the following exceptions:

- A function prototype (a function declaration with no function body) is a declaration and not a definition.
- The declaration contains the `extern` specifier but no initializer (objects and variables) or function body (functions). This tells us that the definition is not necessarily in the current translation unit and gives the name external linkage.

- Because static class data members are discrete variables shared by all objects of the class, they must be defined and initialized outside the class declaration. Chapter 5 talks more about static class members.

- A class name declaration with no following definition, such as class t, which is better known as a forward reference.

- A typedef statement is a declaration without a definition.

The following lines of code show the differences between declarations and declarations that are also definitions.

```
//integer variables declared and defined
int iVar;
int iVar1 = 10;
//integer variable declared only
extern int iVar;
//a function can act as a declaration and definition
int Foo(int iVar){return iVar;}
//function declared only
int Foo(int iVar);
```

The point of a declaration is important in name hiding. Names can be hidden in C and in Visual Basic as well. It is worth knowing how this will affect your code. This works essentially the same as it does in Visual Basic, with the caveats of block scope, which does not exist in Visual Basic.

A name is considered to be declared immediately after its declarator but before its (optional) initializer. An enumerator is considered to be declared immediately after the identifier that names it but before its (optional) initializer.

The following lines of code demonstrate this concept:

```
//file scope variable, declared, defined and initialized
int iVar = 5;
void main()
{
  //block variable hides file scope variable
  int iVar = iVar;
}
```

The block scope variable hides the file scope variable, but it does not take on the value of the file scope variable. There is no error, but the value of the block scope variable is undefined. This is because the block variable hides the file scope variable at the point of declaration, which is before the initialization. This is exactly how it would work in VB, except that the local variable in VB would be initialized to 0.

Enumerators hide names in the same manner that block scope can. However, enumerators are exported to the enclosing scope of the enumeration and this generates different results. In the following example because the enumerators are exported to the enclosing scope, they are considered to have global scope. But since those identifiers are already defined in global scope, this generates the error.

```
const int One = 1, Two = 2, Three = 3;
enum Nums
{
  One = 1,   //generates an error
  Two = 2,   //generates an error
  Three = 3 //generates an error
}
```

Because the identifiers in the preceding code are already defined in global scope, an error message is generated.

> **TIP**
>
> Using the same name to refer to more than one program element is considered poor programming practice and should be avoided. In this example, this practice causes an error. Hiding variables is not considered good programming practice either. However, you should understand how it works.

In C++ you can hide a name by declaring it in an enclosed block—something impossible in Visual Basic since there is no concept of a block. In C++ a curly brace can start a new block almost anywhere. The following code demonstrates how you can hide a variable in an inner block that is declared in an outer block. This code also hides a file scoped variable, but it also shows how to access the file scoped variable with the scope resolution operator.

```
//file scope variable,
int iVar = 5;
void main()
{
  //here iVar is file scope value of 5
  //block variable hides file scope variable
  int iVar;
  for (iVar = 1; iVar < 10; i++)
  {
    //here iVar carries the value of the first loop
    int iVar;  //hides iVar from the first loop
    for (iVar = 1; iVar < 10; i++)
    {
      //here iVar carries the value from the second loop
```

4

C++ BASICS

```
    ::iVar = 2; //sets file scoped iVar
  }
}
```

Class names can be hidden by declaring a function, object, variable, or enumerator in the same scope. However, the class name can still be accessed when prefixed by the keyword class. Although doing so is not useful, knowing about the possibility is important because if you do it inadvertently you won't receive an error (on the variable declaration), but probably will receive an error trying to access the class.

Variables and Declarators

C++ has three distinct classifications of types: fundamental types, types derived from fundamental types, and classes.

The fundamental types that were discussed in Chapter 3 apply to C++. There are two additional sets of fundamental types worth mentioning—sized integer and reference.

Sized Integers

C++ supports sized integer types. You can declare 8, 16, 32, or 64-bit integer variables by using the **__int**n type specifier, where n is the size, in bits, of the integer variable. The following lines of code declare one variable for each of these types of sized integers:

```
int8 iSmall;   //Declares 8-bit integer
int16 iMedium;   //Declares 16-bit integer
int32 iLarge;   //Declares 32-bit integer
int64 iHuge;   //Declares 64-bit integer
```

The types __int8, __int16, and __int32 are synonyms for the ANSI types that have the same size, and are useful for writing portable code that behaves identically across multiple platforms.

The __int8 data type is synonymous with type char, __int16 is synonymous with type short, and __int32 is synonymous with type int or long. The __int64 has no ANSI equivalent.

Since these types are considered synonyms by the compiler, you have to be careful when using them as arguments to overloaded function calls. You could overload a function that would be ambiguous.

```
void SomeFunc(__int8) { }
voic SomeFunc( char ) { }
void Main()
{
    __int8    i;
```

```
    char    c;
    SomeFunc(c);    //Ambiguous function calls
    SomeFunc(i);    //char is synonymous with __int8
}
```

Since these names are actually replaced by current compilers, I simply use the current names (char, short and int). However, it could be that using the sized integer type may save you some time and effort on a port in the future.

NOTE

C and C++ have always morphed the size of an integer to match the size of the system that the program is compiled to run on. The idea behind this is that this would benefit the programmer by taking advantage of the increased memory access and, in particular, keeping it the same size as a pointer. This has caused me some grief in the past and as a result I use variable types that do not change size from platform to platform, unless I'm actually working with pointers.

Reference Type

A reference holds the address of an object but behaves syntactically like an object. For example, a reference to a structure allows members of that structure to be accessed using the member-selection operator (.) instead of the pointer member-selection operator (->).

Although arguments passed as reference types observe the syntax of non-pointer types, they are modifiable unless declared as const. Any function prototyped as taking a reference type can accept an actual object of the same type in its place because there is a standard conversion from typename to typename&.

Functions can be declared to return a reference type. There are two reasons to make such a declaration. One, the information being returned is a large enough object that returning a reference is more efficient than returning a copy. Second, the return type of the function must be an l-value.

Namespace

Namespaces have become more important to programmers. With the introduction of C# in .NET, namespaces and the using directive have replaced include files in that language. In .NET #include doesn't exist (in C#), and namespaces are used to group classes into units. Traditional Visual Basic has no concept of namespaces as you use them here.

In C++ a namespace is a declarative region that attaches an additional identifier to any names declared inside it. The additional identifier makes it less likely that a name will conflict with names declared elsewhere in the program. It is possible to use the same name in separate namespaces without conflict even if the names appear in the same translation unit. As long as they appear in separate namespaces, each name will be unique because of the addition of the namespace identifier.

```
namespace mynamespace{int myvar;}
```

```
mynamespace::myvar
```

Declarations in the file scope of a translation unit, outside all namespaces, are still members of the global namespace and can be accessed with the scope operator.

```
::myvar
```

Each unnamed namespace has an identifier that differs from all other identifiers in the entire program. Unnamed namespaces are a superior replacement for the static declaration of variables. They allow variables and functions to be visible within an entire translation unit, yet not visible externally.

A namespace definition must appear either at file scope or immediately within another namespace definition. Unlike other declarative regions, the definition of a namespace can be split over several parts of a single translation unit. In other words, it's possible to have multiple namespace declarations for the same namespace, the regions following the first just add to the namespace. The following lines of code demonstrate this:

```
namespace A
{
    int iVar;
}
namespace B
{
    int iVar2;
}
namespace A
{
    int iVar3;
}
```

The above code generates two namespaces (A and B). Namespace B has one variable in it (iVar2). Namespace A has two variables in it (iVar and iVar3).

You can use an alias with a namespace. This allows you to shorten a long namespace or provide a more descriptive name.

```
namespace a_stupid_name_that_i_dont_want_to_use{...}

namespace asn= a_stupid_name_that_i_dont_want_to_use;
```

A namespace name cannot conflict with any other entity in the same declarative region. In addition, a global namespace name cannot conflict with any other global entity name.

There are several options available to the programmer when using the contents of a namespace in the program. The programmer can always explicitly name the namespace and program element.

```
namespace mynamespace{int myvar;}
mynamespace::myvar
```

Since this can become somewhat bulky to write in your code, the using declaration and the using directive are in the language so that you do not have to qualify the programming element with the namespace every time you use it.

The using declaration introduces a name into the declarative region in which the using declaration appears. The name becomes a synonym for an entity declared elsewhere. It allows an individual name from a specific namespace to be used without explicit qualification. This is in contrast to the using directive, which allows *all* the names in a namespace to be used without qualification.

While the using declaration can refer to classes, you'll use namespaces for the examples here (Chapter 5 will expand on what the using declaration does in reference to classes). The following lines demonstrate a simple using declaration:

```
namespace C
{
   int iVar;
}
void main
{
   using C::iVar;
   iVar = 2;   //references the iVar in namespace C
}
```

A using declaration for a namespace element can appear in another namespace. This causes the programming element in the first name space to be used. The following lines of code demonstrate this:

```
void g_func();
namespace A
```

```
{
  void a_func();
}
namespace B
{
  using ::g_func;  //global function
  using A::a_func; //A's function
}
void main()
{
  B::g_func();  //calls the global function through B's reference
  B::a_func();  //calls A's function through B's reference
}
```

Other programming elements can conflict with using declarations, so you must be careful to avoid errors that can be caused by duplicate definitions.

The using directive allows all of the elements of a namespace to be accessed without explicitly qualifying any of the members. This is in contrast to the using declaration that I just talked about which exposes a single element of the namespace.

The unqualified names can be used from the point of the using directive on. It is very easy to introduce ambiguities with the using directive, especially if you use using directives within namespaces. These ambiguities occur when elements from more than one namespace are named the same. If you have using directives in effect for more than one namespace and these namespaces have programming elements named the same, then an explicit name is required to access those members.

Local variables of the same name of namespace elements that are visible to the program take precedence over those namespace elements. Again, an explicit reference is used to access the namespace member.

Expressions

Expressions cover assigning or computing values, and use a sequence of operators and operands. The operators and operands are combined in such a way as to obtain the desired results. This section discusses operators and casting (the process of taking a variable of a certain type and referring to it as a different type).

Operators

In C you looked at unary operators (one operand), binary operators (two operands), and ternary operators (three operands). C++ adds some extra operators. Table 4.3 lists the operators in C++. The ones in italics are unique to C++.

TABLE 4.3   C Operators

Operator	Name or Meaning	Visual Basic
::	*Scope resolution*	*None*
::	*Global*	*None*
[ ]	Array subscript	( )
( )	Function call	( )
( )	Conversion	None
.	Member selection (object)	.
->	Member selection (pointer)	None
++	Increment	x = x + 1
--	Decrement	x = x - 1
new	*Allocate object*	New
delete	*Deallocate object*	Delete
delete[ ]	*Deallocate object*	Delete
*	Dereference	None
&	Address-of	Address-of
+	Unary plus	None
–	Arithmetic negation (unary)	None
!	Logical NOT	None
~	Bitwise complement	Not
sizeof	Size of object	Len(x)
sizeof ( )	Size of type	Len(x)
typeid( )	*Type name*	*None*
(type)	Type cast (conversion)	None
const_cast	*Type cast (conversion)*	*None*
dynamic_cast	*Type cast (conversion)*	*None*
reinterpret_cast	*Type cast (conversion)*	*None*
static_cast	*Type cast (conversion)*	*None*
.*	*Apply pointer to class member (objects)*	*None*
->*	*Dereference pointer to class member*	*None*
*	Multiplication	*
/	Division	/
%	Remainder (modulus)	MOD

4

C++ BASICS

TABLE 4.3   Continued

Operator	Name or Meaning	Visual Basic
+	Addition	+
–	Subtraction	-
<<	Left bit shift	None
>>	Right bit shift	None
<	Less than	<
>	Greater than	>
<=	Less than or equal to	<=
>=	Greater than or equal to	>=
==	Equality	=
!=	Inequality	<>
&	Bitwise AND	And
^	Bitwise exclusive OR	Xor
|	Bitwise OR	Or
&&	Logical AND	And
||	Logical OR	Or
e1?e2:e3	Conditional	IIf
=	Assignment	=
*=	Multiplication assignment	x = x * y
/=	Division assignment	x = x / y
%=	Modulus assignment	x = x Mod y
+=	Addition assignment	x = x + y
–=	Subtraction assignment	Right to left
<<=	Left-shift assignment	None
>>=	Right-shift assignment	None
&=	Bitwise AND assignment	x = x And y
|=	Bitwise inclusive OR assignment	x = x Or y
^=	Bitwise exclusive OR assignment	x = x Xor y
,	Comma	Left to right

As you can see, many of the C operators apply to C++ as well. The operators added by C++ have to do mostly with C++ classes.

Operator overloading in C++ is very important and can be achieved on most of the operators listed above. Visual Basic does not have this feature, so this will be foreign to most VB programmers. While it is possible to overload operators on a global basis, operator overloading is typically done to provide operators for classes. For example, it you have a point class and wanted to set one point equal to another with a normal addition assignment operator in one statement, you would have to overload the assignment operator.

Consider the following code:

```cpp
#include "stdafx.h"
class Point
{
public:
    Point &operator=( Point & );   // Right side is the argument.
    int x;
    int y;
};


// Define assignment operator.
Point &Point::operator=( Point &pt )
{
    x = pt.x;
    y = pt.y;

    return *this;  // Assignment operator returns left side.
}
int main(int argc, char* argv[])
{
    Point    pt1;
    Point    pt2;

    pt1.x = 4;
    pt1.y = 2;
    pt2 = pt1;

    printf("Hello World!\n");
    return 0;
}
```

Although classes will be discussed more fully in the next chapter, this sample demonstrates operator overloading. You are defining and implementing an assignment operator. This is an assignment operator overload for the Point class.

4

C++ BASICS

The following items define the constraints of operator overloading:

- Operators must either be class member functions or take an argument that is of `class` or `enumerated` type, or arguments that are references to class or enumerated types.
- Operators obey the precedence, grouping, and number of operands dictated by their typical use with built-in types. Therefore, there is no way to express the concept "add 2 and 3 to an object of type `Point`, expecting 2 to be added to the x coordinate and 3 to be added to the y coordinate."
- Unary operators declared as member functions take no arguments, except when declared as global functions—in such cases they take one argument.
- Binary operators declared as member functions take one argument except when declared as global functions—in such cases they take two arguments.
- Overloaded operators cannot have default arguments.
- All overloaded operators except `assignment` are inherited by derived classes.
- The first argument for member-function overloaded operators is always of the class type of the object for which the operator is invoked (the class in which the operator is declared, or a class derived from that class). No conversions are supplied for the first argument.

Casting

As mentioned earlier, casting is the process of taking a variable and referring to it as a different type. This can be dangerous and difficult to apply, but it is a very powerful concept. Essentially you are changing a variable's type.

There are several casting operators specific to the C++ language. These operators are intended to remove some of the ambiguity and dangers inherent in old-style C language casts.

`dynamic_cast` is used for casting polymorphic types. `static_cast` is used to cast nonpolymorphic types. `const_cast` can be used to remove the `const`, `volatile`, and `__unaligned` attributes. `reinterpret_cast` is used for simple reinterpretation of bits.

The `const_cast` and reinterpret_cast should be used as a last resort, since these operators present the same dangers as old style casts.

The `dynamic_cast` and `static_cast` operators move a pointer throughout a class hierarchy (derived class from base class). However, `static_cast` relies exclusively on the information provided in the cast statement and can therefore be unsafe.

In contrast to `dynamic_cast`, no runtime check is made on the `static_cast` conversion. The object pointed to by this cast may not be the expected object, in which case the use of the resulting pointer could be disastrous.

The value of a failed cast to pointer type is the null pointer. A failed cast to reference type throws a `bad_cast` exception.

The `static_cast` operator can explicitly convert an integral value to an enumeration type. If the value of the integral type does not fall within the range of enumeration values, the resulting enumeration value is undefined.

Any expression can be explicitly converted to type void by the `static_cast` operator. The destination void type can optionally include the const, volatile, or __unaligned attribute.

The `const_cast` operator can be used to remove the `const`, `volatile`, and __unaligned attributes from a class. This operator can explicitly convert a pointer to any object type or a pointer to a data member type that is identical except for the `const`, `volatile`, and __unaligned qualifiers. For pointers and references, the result will refer to the original object. However, a write operation through the resulting pointer, reference, or pointer to data member might produce undefined behavior.

The `reinterpret_cast` operator allows any pointer to be converted into any other pointer type. It also allows any integral type to be converted into any pointer type and vice versa. Misuse of the `reinterpret_cast` operator can easily be unsafe. Unless the desired conversion is inherently low-level, you should use one of the other cast operators.

Statements

Statements were covered in Chapter 3. The specifics that apply to classes in this topic will be covered in the next chapter. This section will discuss error handling.

Error Handling

Error handling in C++ is very different than in traditional Visual Basic. .NET adds exception handling to any language that runs on .NET, including Visual Basic and this is quite similar to C++ exception handling (exception handling is the way you handle errors in C++).

Microsoft C++ supports two kinds of exception handling: C++ exception handling (try, throw, catch) and structured exception handling (__try/__except, __try/__finally).

> **NOTE**
>
> The terms "structured exception handling" and "structured exception" or "C exception" refer to the structured exception handling mechanism provided by Win32 (try, except, finally). All other references to exception handling or "C++ exception" refer to the C++ exception handling mechanism (try, throw, catch).

Although structured exception handling works with C and C++ source files, it is not specifically designed for C++. Typically C++ programmers prefer to use C++ exception handling because it is integrated closely with the language.

.NET implements structured exception handling, choosing to implement the system provided exception handling instead of C++ exception handling.

C++ Exception Handling

The C++ language provides built-in support for handling anomalous situations, known as "exceptions," which may occur during the execution of your program. The try, throw, and catch statements have been added to the C++ language to implement exception handling. With C++ exception handling, your program can communicate unexpected events to a higher execution context that is better able to recover from such events. These exceptions are handled by code which is outside the normal flow of control. In other words exception handling code is never executed unless an exception occurs.

The statements enclosed within the `try` block are the guarded section of code. This is roughly equivalent to the `On Error Goto X` statement in Visual Basic. Throw raises an exception, like `Err.Raise` in Visual Basic. The catch clause handles the exception thrown by the throw expression, like the line label that `On Error` refers to in Visual Basic. The exception declaration statement indicates the type of exception the clause handles. The type can be any valid data type, including a C++ class. If the exception declaration statement uses ellipses (...), the catch will handle any type of exception, including a C exception. Such a handler must be the last handler for its corresponding `try` block.

The execution path for C++ exception handling works as follows. Control reaches the `try` statement by normal sequential execution. The guarded section (within the `try` block) is executed.

If no exception is thrown during execution of the guarded section, the catch clauses that follow the `try` block are not executed. Execution continues at the statement after the last catch clause following the try block.

If an exception is thrown during execution of the guarded section, or in any routine the guarded section calls that does not handle its own exceptions, an `exception` object is created from the object created by the `throw` operand. At this point, the compiler looks for a `catch` clause in a higher execution context that can handle an exception of the type thrown. The `catch` handlers are examined in order of their appearance following the `try` block. If no appropriate handler is found, the next dynamically enclosing `try` block is examined. This process continues until the outermost enclosing try block is examined.

If a matching handler is still not found, or if an exception occurs while unwinding but before the handler gets control, the predefined runtime function (`terminate`) is called.

If a matching `catch` handler is found the parameter is initialized to refer to the exception object. This might involve copying the `exception` object or simply getting the pointer. After the formal parameter is initialized, the process of "unwinding the stack" begins. First, all automatic objects that were constructed (but not yet destroyed) between the beginning of the `try` block associated with the catch handler and the exception's throw site are destroyed. Destruction occurs in reverse order of construction. The catch is executed and the program resumes execution following the last catch handler. Any other catch handlers are skipped; control can only enter a catch handler through a thrown exception, never through normal program flow.

The following code shows a simple example of a `try` block and its associated catch handler. This example detects failure of a memory allocation operation using the new operator.

```
#include <windows.h>
void main()
{
  int *iArr;
  try
  {
    iArr = new int[100];
    if (0 == iArr)
      throw "My array allocation failed";
  }
  catch (char *strErr)
  {
    cout<< "Exception: " << strErr << '/n';
  }
}
```

The operand of the throw specifies that an exception of type `char*` will be thrown. It is handled by a catch handler that has a parameter of type `char*`.

C++ exception handling brings a lot of power and flexibility to error handling. Not only can it deal with exceptions of varying types, but it also can automatically call destructor functions during stack unwinding, for all local objects constructed before the exception was thrown.

A throw with no operand rethrows the exception that is currently being handled. This type of throw should only appear in a catch handler or in a function called from a catch handler. The rethrown exception object is the original exception object, not a copy. The following code snippet demonstrates this.

```
try
{
  throw CmyException();
```

```
}
catch(...)
{
  //you can handle what you want
  throw;  //pass the exception on
}
```

If no matching catch handler can be found, the predefined function `terminate` is called. You are free to call the `terminate` handler in any of your `catch` handlers as well. The default action for the `terminate` function is to call abort. If you want some other function in your program to be called, call the `set_terminate` function with this function name. `set_terminate` can be called at any time. If `terminate` is called, it will be called with the last value passed to `set_terminate`.

Your custom function that you pass to `set_terminate` should terminate the program or current thread, ideally by calling exit. If it doesn't, and instead returns to its caller, `abort` will be called.

Structured Exception Handling

Structured exception handling is implemented in C and C++ through Microsoft extensions to the C language. The `__try`, `__except`, and `__try __finally` statements enable either C or C++ applications to handle events that would normally terminate the program.

The biggest difference in the way that structured exception handling works compared to C++ exception handling is the finally statement and the fact that all structured exceptions are of type unsigned `int`. C++ exception handlers can catch these exceptions with an ellipses type catch handler. So it is possible to mix code that uses both types of exception handlers.

A C exception can also be handled as a typed exception by using a C exception wrapper class. By deriving from this class, each C exception can be attributed a specific derived class.

Summary

This chapter examined additions to the C language provided by C++. This chapter gets many of the details of C++ out of the way in preparing for the discussion of classes, which follows in Chapter 5.

C++ Classes

IN THIS CHAPTER

Chapter 4, "C++ Basics," introduced the C++ language, talking mostly about its technicalities. Now we get to the fun stuff—classes, inheritance, and polymorphism. First, we'll get some basics of classes out of the way, and then we'll explore how to effectively use them.

In this chapter we will discuss the following items.

- *Classes*—The basics of classes, including Object-Oriented Programming (OOP) concepts and syntax of classes
- *Derived Classes*—Explores using derived classes—the syntax and the power of using derived classes

Classes

Classes make programming easier by encapsulating not only data, but the functions that operate on that data. This is the basic idea of any object-like class.

Visual Basic has classes, but the concept in Visual Basic is somewhat different than classes in C++. In Visual Basic, classes can have member variables, subs, functions, properties, and events. In C++, you have only member variables and functions. There are other differences that are addressed later in this chapter.

In this section, we will cover

- The popular object-oriented programming concepts
- The basic elements of a C++ `class`
- The naming conventions for classes
- The concept of class members
- The different types of member functions
- Member access in C++ classes
- The concept of friend functions

OOP Concepts

Traditional OOP concepts are universal, don't apply to any particular programming language, and are upheld by most programmers. Some languages allow better or "more pure" use of some of the concepts than other languages, but by and large they apply to most any language to some degree. In C++, classes provide implementation of these OOP concepts.

The following list summarizes these OOP concepts:

- *Abstraction*—An abstraction is the outside world's view of a class. It defines the functionality the class provides without regard to the technicalities of writing it. An abstraction is usually the same no matter what language you are using.

- *Encapsulation*—Containment of code within a defined unit, along with containment and hiding of data within that unit is a very basic OOP concept. In C++, you use classes to provide encapsulation.

- *Polymorphism*—Polymorphism is the ability to change. When talking about source code classes in C++, you usually mean that the functionality of the function can change in a derived class. Code that uses the base class or derived class does not usually need to know about these differences.

NOTE

There is an inherent danger when using polymorphism in derived classes. That is, the base class could be modified in such a way that the derived class would be broken. This obviously is not an ideal situation.

In Visual Basic, you obtain polymorphism in a very different way. Because Visual Basic objects are binary objects, they provide polymorphism by simply providing the same interfaces on different objects.

- *Inheritance*—Inheritance is the ability of a class to take on the characteristics of the class on which it is based. Visual Basic provides inheritance through the `Implements` keyword. `Implements` is a fairly weak inheritance tool, as anyone that has used it can attest.

NOTE

Inheritance in traditional Visual Basic involves inheriting an interface. There is no implementation that goes along with it.

In C++, when you inherit from a base class, you get the base class implementation. You can override functions and change the way they act, but the base class implementation is there by default.

Basics of Classes

There are several characteristics of classes that make them unique and useful to a programmer. This section will introduce some of those traits and cover the basics of different class types (`struct`, `union`, and `class`), class members, and classes compared to class instances.

In C++, class types actually encompass structs, unions, and classes. Our discussion of structs and unions from Chapter 3, "C Programming," is still valid in C++. We will refer to all of these declarations as class declarations, although classes will be the main focus. Remember that structs and unions do not provide all the features that classes do, so some of what we discuss is exclusive to classes.

Classes contain *members*—that is, the data items and functions within a class.

A class can contain the following items:

- *Class data members*—These typically hold the state of the object and define the attributes of the object. Unless they are static, the instance level variables and class data members are unique to the instance of the class. Visual Basic is very similar in this area except that it doesn't allow the static keyword on data items. Although Visual Basic classes have member variables to hold instance state like C++ classes, static variables would be implemented by using a public variable in a .bas module to achieve the same effect as a static C++ variable.

- *Constructor functions*—These initialize the object. (There can be zero, one, or several constructor functions.) Constructors are named the same as the class but can be overloaded to create several different constructors for one class. A constructor is roughly equivalent to a Visual Basic class Initialize event. In C++, there can be several constructors, whereas in VB there is only one Initialize event. The constructor in C++ and the Initialize event in VB are used for the same purpose—to initialize class members.

- *Destructor function*—This cleans up any memory or objects allocated in the class. (There is typically one destructor function.) The destructor is named the same as the class with a leading tilde (~). A destructor has no parameters and no return type. The Visual Basic class Terminate event is very similar to the C++ destructor function. It is not as effective as the C++ destructor because in Visual Basic it can be very tough to get to the Terminate event if objects are still allocated. For example, a loaded form in Visual Basic can keep a Terminate event from firing and can keep a class reference open. This doesn't happen in C++.

- *Classes also contain any number of member functions that define the behavior of the class*—C++ has only functions, whereas the Visual Basic classes have functions, subs, properties, and events. The Visual Basic class is fashioned very much after a COM object; the C++ class is not.

  Classes can be built to model real life objects, abstract objects, or (like many commercial class libraries) can model the operating system on which they run. Classes that model the operating system are actually useful and a functional use of implementation inheritance.

Class Instances

To understand the discussion in this chapter, you need to make a clear distinction between a class and a class instance. If you are used to working with Visual Basic classes, you are probably able to make this distinction already. If not, you need to grasp the concept before you proceed.

A class refers to the declaration and definition of a `class`. A class by itself can perform no operations. You must declare an instance of the class or instantiate a class object to use it. A class instance has its own set of member data (excluding static data that is shared between instances). The functions for a particular instance operate on that instance's data.

During the following discussions, you will read about both class definitions and class instances. Keep this distinction in mind while you are reading about classes.

Names

Classes are variable types, and the class declaration introduces a new type into a compilation unit. There is only one definition per compilation unit for each class. These class types can be used to declare objects. The C++ compiler type checks the use of these objects, just as it does primitive types. The following code demonstrates how the compiler will type check the class variable, and it will produce an error if you attempt to assign a class variable of one type to a class variable of another type.

```
class Line
{
public:
        int x1,y1,x2,y2;
};

class Square
{
public:
        int x1,y1,x2,y2;
};
Line l;
Square s;

s=l;  //error incompatible types
```

Class definitions can have global or class scope. Class definitions do not have block scope. Class variables (class instances) can have any scope just like a normal variable. If a class is defined within another class, it is called a *nested class*.

> **CAUTION**
>
> Nested classnames that have class scope can hide global classnames within their scope.
>
> Hiding a global scoped class with a class scoped class is not something that you should do. I simply mention it so that you don't accidentally do it.

The naming of classes in Visual Basic is very similar, except that nested classes are not supported. A class is global in nature in Visual Basic, and there is no way to change this.

Class Members

This section will cover class members, including member variables, member functions, member access control, and friend functions. The members that make up a class declaration and the way you access those members is a major portion of understanding classes.

Member Variables

A class is defined by its member functions and the data with which those functions operate. Member variables hold the "state" of the class instance. Each class instance gets its own copy of the member variables.

Initialization of class member variables cannot occur at the time of declaration. This produces an error. Because each instantiation of a class object has its own data instance, the correct way to initialize this data is through the class constructor. This is the same as Visual Basic. No executable code is allowed where data members are declared in Visual Basic.

Member Functions

As already mentioned, a class declaration can contain data and functions. The functions within a class are what distinguish a class from other structure (struct and union) type declarations. Any non-static function declared inside a class is a member function.

Member functions are accessed with the member selection operators (if they have the proper access) from outside the class, but require no member selection operators from inside the class. The code in Listing 5.1 demonstrates this. Notice the difference between the class variable and the pointer variable and the way the functions are accessed.

NOTE

In most of the samples in this chapter, you will use code that draws graphics. You can run the code by generating a C Windows "Hello World" application in the C++ environment.

To run the code, generate a new WIN32 Application and call it **chap5app**. Add a new include file to the project called **chap5.h**. The code in Listing 5.1 will be placed in those files (chap5app.cpp and chap5.h).

In some of the later samples, you will also have a chap5.cpp file that you will use for some of the function definitions.

LISTING 5.1   Accessing class members

```
//chap5.h
class Circle
{
public:
        int x,y,r;
        void SetCenter(int xr, int yr)
        {
                x = xr;   //no selection operators
                y = yr;
        }
        void SetRadius(int rr)
        {
                r = rr;
        }
};
//this code can be placed inside the WndProc of
//the chap5app.cpp file where indicated

//at the top of the function
Circle c;
Circle *pc = &c;

//in the WM_PAINT case selection
c.SetCenter(20,20);  //selection operator for object
pc->SetRadius(10);   //selection operator for pointer
```

There are a couple of choices when declaring and defining member functions. Remember that declaring a program element does not necessarily define that programming element (as covered in the previous chapter). You can either define the class with the declaration or separate the declaration and definition.

NOTE

In Visual Basic, there is no option to split the declaration and definition. You define the function. There is no declaration for Visual Basic functions outside of the definition, so the declaration and definition are together.

In C++, when you declare a class, you must at least declare all the functions that go in it. You can also define those functions at the time of declaration. The following code shows a class that declares and defines the function at the same time. When a member function is defined in the following manner, the function will be inline. You can use the `inline` keyword, but it will be redundant in this case.

```
//chap5.h
class Circle
{
public:
        int x,y,r;
        void SetCenter(int xr, int yr)
        {
                x = xr;   //no selection operators
                y = yr;
        }
        void SetRadius(int rr)
        {
                r = rr;
        }
};
```

By far, the most common way to define the member functions in a class is to declare the function at the same time as declaring the class (typically done in an `include` file) and then define the function later (typically done in a C++ source file). When you define the function this way, you must use the scope resolution operator (`::`) in your definition. In this case, the function will not be inline unless you explicitly define the function inline. The following code demonstrates a definition outside the class declaration.

```
//chap5.h
class Circle
{
public:
  int x,y,r;
  void SetCenter(int xr, int yr);
  void SetRadius(int rr);
};
//chap5.cpp
void Circle::SetCenter(int xr, int yr)
{
        x = xr;   //no selection operators
        y = yr;
}
void Circle::SetRadius(int rr)
{
        r = rr;
}
```

Static Functions

The static keyword can be applied to both data and functions. You typically use the static keyword for a function (or data) that will apply to all loaded instances of a class. A static function has no this pointer (which we will cover in a moment), and you will use the scope resolution operator to call it.

Visual Basic's static modifier doesn't work at all like C++'s static keyword. In VB, the static modifier isn't allowed on a member variable. You would have to use a Global variable to achieve what a static member variable does in C++. The static modifier on a VB function just means that the variables inside the function are static and hold their value between calls.

In the sample code in Listing 5.2, the CircleCount data member is static, as is the CircleCount function. Notice that the data member is defined at the file scope level in the .cpp file. This is necessary because in the class, the data member is not defined, just declared.

LISTING 5.2   Static Class Members

```
//chap5.h
class Circle
{
private:
  int x,y,r;
public:
  Circle(){count++;};

  void SetCenter(int xr, int yr);
  void SetRadius(int rr);
  static int CircleCount(){return count;};
  static int circlecount;
};

//chap5.cpp
#include "stdafx.h"
#include"chap5.h"

void Circle::SetCenter(int xr, int yr)
{
        x = xr;
        y = yr;
}
void Circle::SetRadius(int rr)
{
        r = rr;
}
```

LISTING 5.2   Continued

```
//chap5app.cpp
//place at file scope level
int Circle::count;

   //place in WndProc
   Circle::count=0;
   Circle c;
   Circle c1;
   Circle c2;

   //place in WM_PAINT in WndProc
   wsprintf(szHello,"%d",Circle::CircleCount());
   DrawText(hdc, szHello, strlen(szHello), &rt, DT_CENTER);
```

This code will result in the number 3 being printed in the window of the test application.

Non-static member functions have an implied `this` pointer that points to the object instance for which the function was invoked. Non-static member functions have direct access to other member functions and member data items. In Listing 5.2, the `SetCenter` and `SetRadius` functions are non-static and access data members in the class.

this

The `this` keyword is a `const` pointer to the instance for which the current function was called. Typically, you can access member functions and data from inside the class without explicitly using the `this` pointer.

Visual Basic has a similar reference called `Me`. The `Me` object in Visual Basic refers to the current object, whatever that object is (this includes class objects).

As the previous statement implies, by calling the `this` pointer a `const` type pointer, the value of `this` cannot be modified. It used to be possible to modify the `this` value in other versions of C++, but it is not possible in the current version of Microsoft C++.

At times, it might be handy or even necessary to use the `this` pointer. Typically, using the `this` pointer involves passing it to some procedure outside the scope of the class so that the outside procedure can call back into the correct instance of the class. I have done this in custom controls when subclassing window procedures. The subclass procedures must reside outside any class definition, but they need to call into the class instance to set properties and fire events.

Special Member Functions

Special member functions include constructors, destructors, conversion functions, the `new` operator, `delete` operator, and `assignment` operator. All of these special functions can be user defined for each class. The Visual Basic counterparts for the constructor and destructor have been before. The rest of these special functions do not have Visual Basic counterparts.

Constructors

I've already mentioned constructors; this section will cover them in more detail. A constructor has the same name as the `class` to which it belongs. It cannot return a value, nor can you access the address of the function. A constructor can be overloaded and can have any number of parameters or none at all.

A constructor is called whenever an instance of that class is created. This happens in several circumstances, some of them not so obvious. These circumstances include:

- When a variable of that class type is declared at a local level or at a global (file scope) level.
- When `new` is used to create a class object dynamically.
- When a temporary object is created and the constructor is called implicitly by the compiler or explicitly called by code.
- If the `class` is a data member of another `class` or the base class is a sub-object of a `class`.

In addition to executing the code that the class author places in the constructor, there are several things a constructor does when it is invoked for a class. It initializes the object's virtual base pointers (if derived from a virtual base class), calls the base class and member constructors, and initializes the object's virtual function pointers.

As said previously, a constructor has the same name as the `class`. A default constructor is one that can be called without parameters. This doesn't mean that a default constructor must have no parameters, but if it does, they must have default values so the constructor can be called without parameters.

A *copy constructor* is another special kind of function. It is a constructor with one parameter that takes a reference to an object that is of the same class. The copy can be accomplished with a member-wise copy or bit-wise copy. The semantics of the copy procedure are up to the programmer.

The example in Listing 5.3 shows a copy constructor.

LISTING 5.3   Copy Constructor

```
//chap5.h
class Circle
{
private:
```

LISTING 5.3   Continued

```cpp
  int x,y,r;
public:
  Circle(){count++;};
  Circle(Circle &cir);

  void SetCenter(int xr, int yr);
  void SetRadius(int rr);
  int GetCenterX();
  int GetCenterY();
  int GetRadius();
  Circle &operator=( Circle & );
};

//chap5.cpp
#include "stdafx.h"
#include"chap5.h"

Circle::Circle(Circle &cir)
{
  x=cir.GetCenterX();
  y=cir.GetCenterY();
  r=cir.GetRadius();
}

void Circle::SetCenter(int xr, int yr)
{
  x = xr;
  y = yr;
}
void Circle::SetRadius(int rr)
{
  r = rr;
}

int Circle::GetCenterX()
{
  return x;
}

int Circle::GetCenterY()
{
  return y;
}
```

LISTING 5.3   Continued

```
int Circle::GetRadius()
{
  return r;
}

Circle &Circle::operator=( Circle &cir )
{
  x = cir.GetCenterX();
  y = cir.GetCenterY();
  r = cir.GetRadius();
  return *this;
}

//chap5app.cpp
Circle c;
Circle c1;

c.SetCenter(20,20);
c.SetRadius(10);
Circle c2(c);
c1=c2;
```

There is a lot going on in this example. First, you have an overload of the constructor. This overload is a copy constructor and does a member-wise copy of the class. Notice that there are added functions to individually access the private members. You could have simply made the members public so you could copy the members directly, but using functions better follows OOP concepts by hiding the data from the outside world and just exposing the functionality.

Notice also that there is an assignment operator. This function does the same kind of copy that the copy constructor does.

In the chap5app code that uses these copy functions, notice that the copy constructor is used at the time that you declare the object. c2 is declared, defined, and initialized with the copy constructor.

c2 is copied to c1 using the assignment function in the Circle class. This is a good example of overloading an assignment operator to perform a copy.

Any other number of constructors can be supplied within the rules of overloading functions. The other constructors (besides the default constructors) must be called explicitly if they are to be used. If you supply no constructors, the compiler generates a default constructor and a default copy constructor.

Destructors

Destructors have been mentioned before, this section will explore more details of the destructor. Destructor functions are essentially the opposite of constructors; they are called when an object is destroyed. The destructors are named the same as the class they are contained in with a tilde (~) in front of the name. Destructors have no arguments, cannot specify a return type or return a value using the return statement, and cannot be declared as const, volatile, or static. However, they can be virtual.

Destructors are called when an automatic object goes out of scope, whether this is associated with a block scope variable that goes out of scope or when the program ends, causing global variables to go out of scope. The destructor is also called when the lifetime of a temporary object ends or when the delete operator is used to deallocate an object constructed with the new operator. The destructor can also be called explicitly. An explicit call of a destructor would be necessary for an object placed at an absolute address.

Conversions

Conversions are also a special type of member function. You can do a conversion by construction, where the constructor is the conversion function, or you can have special conversion functions that are not constructors.

Conversion constructors save time, allowing you to create a class based on a different variable type. For example, you might create a circle based on a rectangle representing the extents of the circle. Listing 5.4 demonstrates this concept. Conversion functions allow flexibility, permitting you to define the semantics of an assignment operation. A conversion function can allow several different overrides of the assignment operator—one for a copy assignment and others for a conversion.

Conversion can take place when you do an explicit type conversion or when an implicit type conversion takes place. A conversion function is applied only if it is unambiguous; otherwise, an error occurs.

> **NOTE**
>
> A constructor that can be called with a single parameter is a *conversion constructor*, unless that single parameter is a reference to the class type, in which case it is a *copy constructor*.

Listing 5.4 shows some conversion functions. Circle::Circle(RECT &rt) is the conversion constructor and Circle &Circle::operator=(RECT &rt) is a conversion routine. These functions have been added to the Circle class.

LISTING 5.4   Conversion Functions

```
//chap5.h
class Circle
{
private:
  int x,y,r;
public:
  Circle(){count++;};
  Circle(Circle &cir);
  Circle(RECT &rt);

  void SetCenter(int xr, int yr);
  void SetRadius(int rr);
  int GetCenterX();
  int GetCenterY();
  int GetRadius();
  Circle &operator=( Circle & );
  Circle &operator=( RECT & );};

//chap5.cpp
#include "stdafx.h"
#include"chap5.h"

Circle::Circle(Circle &cir)
{
  x=cir.GetCenterX();
  y=cir.GetCenterY();
  r=cir.GetRadius();
}

Circle::Circle(RECT &rt)
{
  x=rt.left + ((rt.right-rt.left)/2);
  y=rt.top + ((rt.bottom-rt.top)/2);
  r=((rt.bottom-rt.top)/2);
}

void Circle::SetCenter(int xr, int yr)
{
  x = xr;
  y = yr;
}
void Circle::SetRadius(int rr)
{
  r = rr;
```

LISTING 5.4   Continued

```
}

int Circle::GetCenterX()
{
  return x;
}

int Circle::GetCenterY()
{
  return y;
}

int Circle::GetRadius()
{
  return r;
}

Circle &Circle::operator=( Circle &cir )
{
  x = cir.GetCenterX();
  y = cir.GetCenterY();
  r = cir.GetRadius();
  return *this;
}

Circle &Circle::operator=( RECT &rt )
{
  x=rt.left + ((rt.right-rt.left)/2);
  y=rt.top + ((rt.bottom-rt.top)/2);
  r=((rt.bottom-rt.top)/2);
  return *this;
}

//chap5app.cpp
RECT rt={40,50,80,100};
Circle c(rt);
Circle c1;
c1=rt;  //yes this works, assign a RECT to a Circle
```

The overloaded constructor will convert from a rectangle (preferably a square) to a circle. It does that in the conversion constructor by centering the circle in the rectangle and drawing a circle with a radius of half the height of the rectangle.

Notice that you determine the semantics of this conversion. You could have made other choices, but this is the way that you have defined the conversion from a square to a circle.

Notice also that an overload of the assignment operator has been added. This is another way to do a conversion. Copies and conversions are very similar, except the conversion routine is converting from a different type.

Sometimes, the compiler will choose a conversion constructor based on the conversion needed. If you must maintain control over the conversion process, do not declare constructors with one parameter, use helper functions instead. Helper functions are just simple public functions to do the conversion, but because they are not overloading the assignment operator, they must be called explicitly.

Special Operators

If you provide custom implementations for the `new` and the `delete` operators, they will be used when the object is allocated with the `new` operator and deallocated with the `delete` operator. Either of these operators can have a global or a class scope, which means the class can provide functions global to your program that will perform the memory allocations. If they have class scope, both operator functions are static and cannot be overridden.

The `new` operator should allocate any required memory for the object and return a void * from that allocation. If the memory allocation fails, the `new` operator should return NULL or it is possible to throw an exception. Memory that is allocated with the `new` operator can be freed using the `delete` operator.

Member Access Control

It's already been mentioned that there are three levels of access that can be applied to member functions and data. These are public, protected, and private. This section will concentrate on those access controls.

In Visual Basic, only two levels of these member access controls exist—public and private. The `Friend` modifier in Visual Basic also acts like an access level modifier, which is covered in the section on `Friends`. Visual Basic does not have a protected access level. You cannot derive classes from base classes in VB. Because protected access allows derived classes to use class members from the base class, it isn't needed in VB.

Private access allows access to members only from within the class. Using this level of access control doesn't even allow access by derived classes. This might typically be used with data members that have "accessor" functions to manipulate and use the data.

Protected access allows derived classes access to member functions and data with this access specifier. Code outside the scope of the class or derived class cannot see these members.

Public access allows access to these member functions and data from anywhere that an instance of the class is declared. This level of access is typically applied to functions that are used to program the object. If you look at the circle used previously, it's easy to see that the

5

C++ CLASSES

member variables should be protected access, instead of private access, if you intend to derive other classes from it. The following code shows the protected and public access modifiers:

```
//chap5.h
class Circle
{
protected:
        int x,y,r;
public:
        Circle(){count++;};
        Circle(Circle &cir);
        Circle(RECT &rt);

        void SetCenter(int xr, int yr);
        void SetRadius(int rr);
        int GetCenterX();
        int GetCenterY();
        int GetRadius();
        static int CircleCount(){return count;};
        static int count;
    Circle &operator=( Circle & );
    Circle &operator=( RECT & );
};
```

Access to virtual functions is through protected or public member functions. A derived class cannot change the access type of the base class when overriding it.

friend Functions

friend functions are a rather odd OOP feature because they really are not OOP in nature. A friend function has global scope, but can access any access level of class members from the class in which they are declared. The actual definition can be in another class or at file scope level.

To state it as simply as possible, a friend function declaration within a class says, "This function can have access to anything within an instance of this class." Many times, you will see that one of the parameters of the friend function is a reference to the same class where the function is declared as a friend. This is because the friend function is really at file scope level, it has no knowledge of any object instance.

C++ friend functions are different from Visual Basic's friend keyword and can make the C++ friend functionality difficult to grasp at first for a VB programmer. In Visual Basic, the friend keyword modifies a method, property, or function so that it can be called from outside the class. The friend class routines can be accessed only from the project that the class is in, they are not part of the public interface. In VB, you access the `friend` function through normal object syntax, and the `friend` function has access to the member variables through the object instance from which they are called.

In C++, the `friend` function is scope level, so the object instance that the function accesses must come from a parameter or other declared object instance.

The `friend` keyword can also be used with an entire class, giving all of the functions in that class access to the private members of the class in which that the declaration appears.

Derived Classes

One of the most powerful features of C++ is the ability to write derived classes. This is a feature that was lacking in traditional Visual Basic, so in this section you won't find references to Visual Basic because they simply don't apply.

Classes are powerful in and of themselves. Visual Basic has proven this by providing classes that do not allow derived classes and yet are a useful and powerful programming model.

But when you add the ability to derive other classes from the classes, you create and override and change the functionality of the base classes, this programming model becomes even more powerful. Although Visual Basic has not been able to provide class implementation inheritance, this functionality will be part of the VB.NET platform. C++ has provided this programming model for many years.

Basics

Derived classes use inheritance. A derived class has one or more base classes from which it derives. The simplest form of inheritance is single inheritance, where you have one base class on which the derived class is based.

Some of the most difficult decisions that a programmer makes have to do with the design of classes and the hierarchy of those classes. This chapter has been using a `circle` object for the class example. A square or rectangle is another object that could have been used for an example. It seems that you could inherit from the rectangles to build a `chart` class. But this is more of a problem of composition than inheritance. Composition is a good way to use objects, but it is not inheritance in the traditional sense.

In this case, you're going to build from the `Circle` class a derived class that does pie shaped arcs. At first, this seems like you are going in reverse—can't a circle be *composed* of pie-shaped arcs? It can, but in reality, a circle is one of the simplest shapes to describe—a center point and a radius is all you need. With a pie shape arc, you also need to know where to start and end the arc.

First, look at the completed `circle` object, in Listing 5.6, including the drawing code. Notice in that code, the `Draw` procedure is virtual, which means it can be overridden to change its functionality.

> **NOTE**
>
> Overriding functions is one of the most important concepts for derived classes and although we've mentioned it already I want to review it again so that you are comfortable with the concept.
>
> To override a function, the function must be virtual in the base class. This means that the programmer of the base class must have an idea that the function should be overridden. Some functions are not appropriate for overriding and, if this is the case, the programmer of the base class can avoid that by not making the function virtual.
>
> After you have a base class and decide to use it to construct a derived class, the question then becomes how do you use the features of the base class. For example, which functions are you able to override and, from those, which ones do you have a need to override. This is one of things that point out how implementation inheritance is not "black box" programming. You have to know how the base class is constructed to use the base class effectively.
>
> Listing 5.6 is a class listing that you will use as a base class to demonstrate derived classes.

LISTING 5.6   Base Class

```
//chap5.h
class Circle
{
protected:
      int x,y,r;
public:
      Circle(){count++;};
      Circle(Circle &cir);
      Circle(RECT &rt);

      void SetCenter(int xr, int yr);
      void SetRadius(int rr);
      int GetCenterX();
      int GetCenterY();
      int GetRadius();
      static int CircleCount(){return count;};
      static int count;
   Circle &operator=( Circle & );
```

LISTING 5.6   Continued

```cpp
    Circle &operator=( RECT & );
        long lineColor;
        virtual void Draw(HDC);
};

//chap5.cpp
Circle::Circle(Circle &cir)
{
        x=cir.GetCenterX();
        y=cir.GetCenterY();
        r=cir.GetRadius();
}

Circle::Circle(RECT &rt)
{
        x=rt.left + ((rt.right-rt.left)/2);
        y=rt.top + ((rt.bottom-rt.top)/2);
        r=((rt.bottom-rt.top)/2);
}

void Circle::SetCenter(int xr, int yr)
{
        x = xr;
        y = yr;
}
void Circle::SetRadius(int rr)
{
        r = rr;
}

int Circle::GetCenterX()
{
        return x;
}

int Circle::GetCenterY()
{
        return y;
}

int Circle::GetRadius()
{
        return r;
}
```

5

LISTING 5.6   Continued

```
Circle &Circle::operator=( Circle &cir )
{
    x = cir.GetCenterX();
    y = cir.GetCenterY();
      r = cir.GetRadius();
    return *this;
}

Circle &Circle::operator=( RECT &rt )
{
      x=rt.left + ((rt.right-rt.left)/2);
      y=rt.top + ((rt.bottom-rt.top)/2);
      r=((rt.bottom-rt.top)/2);
    return *this;
}

void Circle::Draw(HDC hdc)
{
      HPEN linePen;
      HPEN oldPen;

      linePen = ::CreatePen(PS_SOLID,1,lineColor);
      oldPen = (HPEN) ::SelectObject(hdc, linePen);
      ::Ellipse(hdc, x-r,y-r,x+r,y+r);
      ::SelectObject(hdc, oldPen);
      ::DeleteObject(linePen);
}
```

The derived class, shown in Listing 5.7 is quite a bit simpler. However, note that there are some other things you could do in addition to what's already been done in this derived class. For one thing, you could do new copy and conversion functions.

LISTING 5.7   Derived Class

```
//chap5.h
class ArcPie : public Circle
{
private:
      float start, sweep;
public:
      long fillColor;
      void SetAngle(float st, float sw){start=st;sweep=sw;};
```

LISTING 5.7   Continued

```
        float Getstart(){return start;};
        float Getsweep(){return sweep;};
        virtual void Draw(HDC);
};

//chap5.cpp
//the draw function is an override of the base class
//implementation of the Draw function.
void ArcPie::Draw(HDC hdc)
{
        HPEN linePen;
        HPEN oldPen;
        HBRUSH fillBrush;
        HBRUSH oldBrush;

        fillBrush = ::CreateSolidBrush(fillColor);
        linePen = ::CreatePen(PS_SOLID,1,lineColor);
        oldPen = (HPEN) ::SelectObject(hdc, linePen);
        ::MoveToEx(hdc, x,y,NULL);
        ::BeginPath(hdc);
        oldBrush = (HBRUSH) ::SelectObject(hdc, fillBrush);

        ::AngleArc(hdc, x,y,(DWORD)r,start,sweep);
        ::LineTo(hdc, x, y);
        ::EndPath(hdc);
        ::StrokeAndFillPath(hdc);
        ::SelectObject(hdc, oldPen);
        ::DeleteObject(linePen);
        ::SelectObject(hdc, oldBrush);
        ::DeleteObject(fillBrush);
}
  //chap5app.cpp
  ArcPie a;  //declares an ArcPie instance
  a.SetRadius(30);  //sets the radius, base class function
  a.SetCenter(120,150);  //sets the center, base class function
  a.SetAngle(30,90);  //sets the angles, derived class function
  a.lineColor = 0xFF0000;  //line color, base class data member
  a.fillColor = 0x0000FF;  //fill color, derived class data member
  a.Draw(ps.hdc);  //derived class,  override of the base class function
```

5

The changes made in the derived class included adding the data members to hold the angle of the arc and the function to draw it. In addition, the Draw function was overridden and new code to do the drawing was supplied.

Notice, though, that the functions that handle setting the radius and center are only in the base class, and those functions provide that functionality for the derived class. Also, the data members that hold the radius and the center are in the base class but are used in the drawing function in the derived class.

As long as any class has only one base class, it is still a case of single inheritance. You can also have multiple levels of inheritance, wherein a class can be both a derived class and a base class.

In multiple levels of inheritance, a base class can be either a direct or an indirect base class. Derived classes can access base members (either public or protected) from code within the derived class. If the derived class has overridden or redefined the member, the scope resolution operator can be used to access those members.

Users of the derived class can access public members in the base class as though they are part of the derived class. In fact, class members and inherited class members are accessed exactly the same, just as though the inherited class members were part of the derived class which, through implementation inheritance, they are. You can see this in Listing 5.7 where you have base class members and derived class members both being used to program the object.

It is possible to cast a reference or pointer of a derived class to a base class type. Doing this would allow you to treat objects of different types as though they were all the same type (the base class). However, because the pointer is actually a pointer to an instance of a derived class, the functions in the derived class are called. The cast is for purposes of type checking only. You can only call the functions that are provided by the base class (type checking), but the function is actually called in the derived class (actual pointer).

Multiple Base Classes

A class can be derived from more than one base class. In a model of this type, the base classes are specified using a base list. The order of the base classes in the list is typically not important. It may affect the order in which constructors and destructors are called, but that typically isn't important.

In the multiple inheritance example in Listing 5.8, we've created a Squircle class. This is a combination of a circle and a square. They are drawn together using a simple override of the drawing function and then calling both base drawing implementations.

LISTING 5.8 Multiple Inheritance

```
//chap5.h
class Square
{
```

LISTING 5.8   Continued

```cpp
private:
  int x1,y1,x2,y2;
public:
  Square(){squarecount++;};
  Square(Square &sq);
  Square(RECT &rt);

  void SetSquareTL(int x, int y){x1=x;y1=y;};
  void SetSquareBR(int x, int y){x2=x;y2=y;};
  int GetTLX(){return x1;};
  int GetTLY(){return y1;};
  int GetBRX(){return x2;};
  int GetBRY(){return y2;};
  static int SquareCount(){return squarecount;};
  static int squarecount;
  Square &operator=( Square & );
  Square &operator=( RECT & );
  long fillColor;
  long lineColor;
  void Draw(HDC);
};

class Circle
{
protected:
  int x,y,r;
public:
  Circle(){count++;};
  Circle(Circle &cir);
  Circle(RECT &rt);
  void SetCenter(int xr, int yr);
  void SetRadius(int rr);
  int GetCenterX();
  int GetCenterY();
  int GetRadius();
  static int CircleCount(){return count;};
  static int count;
  Circle &operator=( Circle & );
  Circle &operator=( RECT & );
  long lineColor;
  virtual void Draw(HDC);
};

class Squircle : public Circle, public Square
{
```

LISTING 5.8   Continued

```cpp
public:
  virtual void Draw(HDC hdc)
  {
    Square::Draw(hdc);
    Circle::Draw(hdc);
  };
};
//chap5.cpp
Square::Square(Square &sq)
{
  x1=sq.GetTLX();
  y1=sq.GetTLY();
  x2=sq.GetBRX();
  y2=sq.GetBRY();
}

Square::Square(RECT &rt)
{
  x1=rt.left;
  y1=rt.top;
  x2=rt.right;
  y2=rt.bottom;
}

Square &Square::operator=( Square &sq )
{
  x1=sq.GetTLX();
  y1=sq.GetTLY();
  x2=sq.GetBRX();
  y2=sq.GetBRY();
  return *this;
}

Square &Square::operator=( RECT &rt )
{
  x1=rt.left;
  y1=rt.top;
  x2=rt.right;
  y2=rt.bottom;
  return *this;
}


void Square::Draw(HDC hdc)
{
```

LISTING 5.8 Continued

```cpp
    HBRUSH lineBrush;
    HBRUSH fillBrush;
    RECT rt;
    rt.top=y1;
    rt.left=x1;
    rt.right=x2;
    rt.bottom=y2;

    fillBrush = ::CreateSolidBrush(fillColor);
    lineBrush = ::CreateSolidBrush(lineColor);
    ::FillRect(hdc, &rt, fillBrush);
    ::FrameRect(hdc, &rt,lineBrush );
    ::DeleteObject(fillBrush);
    ::DeleteObject(lineBrush);
}



//circle class definitions
Circle::Circle(Circle &cir)
{
    x=cir.GetCenterX();
    y=cir.GetCenterY();
    r=cir.GetRadius();
}
Circle::Circle(RECT &rt)
{
    x=rt.left + ((rt.right-rt.left)/2);
    y=rt.top + ((rt.bottom-rt.top)/2);
    r=((rt.bottom-rt.top)/2);
}

void Circle::SetCenter(int xr, int yr)
{
    x = xr;
    y = yr;
}
void Circle::SetRadius(int rr)
{
    r = rr;
}

int Circle::GetCenterX()
{
```

LISTING 5.8   Continued

```
  return x;
}

int Circle::GetCenterY()
{
  return y;
}

int Circle::GetRadius()
{
  return r;
}

Circle &Circle::operator=( Circle &cir )
{
  x = cir.GetCenterX();
  y = cir.GetCenterY();
  r = cir.GetRadius();
  return *this;
}

Circle &Circle::operator=( RECT &rt )
{
  x=rt.left + ((rt.right-rt.left)/2);
  y=rt.top + ((rt.bottom-rt.top)/2);
  r=((rt.bottom-rt.top)/2);
  return *this;
}

void Circle::Draw(HDC hdc)
{
  HPEN linePen;
  HPEN oldPen;

  linePen = ::CreatePen(PS_SOLID,1,lineColor);
  oldPen = (HPEN) ::SelectObject(hdc, linePen);
  ::Ellipse(hdc, x-r,y-r,x+r,y+r);
  ::SelectObject(hdc, oldPen);
  ::DeleteObject(linePen);
}

//chap5app.cpp
//WndProc
  Squircle s;
```

LISTING 5.8   Continued

```
//WM_PAINT case
  s.SetSquareTL(40,40);
  s.SetSquareBR(100,100);
  s.SetCenter(70,70);
  s.SetRadius(20);
  s.Circle::lineColor = 0xFF0000;
  s.Square::lineColor = 0xFF0000;
  s.fillColor = 0x0000FF;
  s.Draw(ps.hdc);
```

Multiple inheritance can introduce name ambiguities. In other words, it may be possible to get to a function or data members along more than one path, and these functions might be totally different and in different base classes. When this happens, qualifying the name is the only way to resolve the issue. You can see this in Listing 5.8 in the class implementation, where you call the base draw implementations, and in the chap5app.cpp, where you set the line colors.

Using Declaration

Another way to qualify ambiguous names is through the using declaration introduced in Chapter 4. The using declaration is used mainly with classes.

The using declaration introduces a name into the declarative region in which the using declaration appears. The name becomes a synonym for an entity declared elsewhere. It allows a name from a specific namespace to be used without explicit qualification. This is in contrast to the using directive, which allows all the names in a namespace to be used without qualification. The following code shows a simple using declaration.

```
class X
{
  void y(char);
  void z(char);
};
class H:X
{
  using X::y;
  void y(int) {y('x')}
}
```

When used to declare a member, a using declaration must refer to a member of a base class. For example

```
class G
{
```

```
  int y(char);
};
class H:X
{
  using X::y;
  using G::y;   //illegal G is not a base of H
}
```

A name defined by a using declaration is an alias for its original name. It does not affect the type, linkage, or other attributes of the original declaration. A using declaration for a single name can only refer to a name if it is unique within the declarative region. The following code demonstrates a using declaration:

```
class X
{
  int i;
  void y(char);
  void z(char);
};
class H:X
{
  int i;
  void y(int);
  void z(char);
  using X::i;   //error - i declared twice
  using X::y;   //ok - function, overloaded with different types
  using X::z;   //error function, same types
}
```

When a using declaration introduces a name from a base class into a derived class scope, member functions in the derived class override virtual member functions with the same name and argument types in the base class.

So you can take the previous example and change the order of the using (using X::z;) and the declaration of the function z in class H (void z(char);), and the using statement would then override the z function from the base class. This is demonstrated in the following code.

```
class X
{
  int i;
  void y(char);
  void z(char);
};
class H:X
{
  int i;
```

```
    void y(int);
    using X::z;
    void z(char);  //now ok, z overrides base implementation
    using X::i;  //error - i declared twice
    using X::y;  //ok - function, overloaded with different types
}
```

The using declaration can make accessing members in a different namespace much simpler than having to qualify the name every time it is used.

Abstract Classes

Abstract classes exist solely for the purpose of acting as a base class for derived classes and cannot be instantiated as objects. However, you can use pointers and references to an abstract class. Abstract classes equate loosely to the implements keyword in Visual Basic.

In VB, the Implements keyword simply forces a programmer to use and expose an interface. All of the elements of the interface must be implemented in the VB class. The abstract class does force the derived class to implement functions. However, while the Implements key word can provide no functionality, an abstract class can have functions that do provide functionality for the derived classes.

An abstract class contains at least one pure virtual function. A class with a pure virtual function cannot be instantiated and is termed an *abstract* class. A class will be abstract if it inherits a pure virtual function and does not provide an implementation for it, so your derived classes can be pure "by accident" if you don't provide an implementation for a pure function.

Summary

This chapter has focused on C++ classes. You will use these concepts in later chapters to build components in C++ code. It's imperative to understand classes and how they are used in C++. Reading this chapter alone will not mean you have mastered classes. You have to put them into practice, which you'll do in the following chapters.

C++ and Windows

IN THIS CHAPTER

Visual Basic has traditionally hidden much of the operation of the platform from the programmer and of course there is always a lot of talk about platform independence, which by definition would not require a lot of understanding of any particular platform.

Hidden functionality and platform independence are nice things when you can manage them; your ability to do so depends mostly on the application. Some applications need very few system services beyond basic things like file access. Other programs, however, rely on certain system services, and consequently you end up programming to the underlying system.

Many people argue that platform independence is a good thing; cross-platform code would certainly benefit from not having to know anything about the systems it is running on. But in practice you seldom are insulated at that level from the underlying platform. Visual Basic and .NET do a good job of hiding the details of the system, but C/C++ does not. But even the .NET classes are very much fashioned after the Windows operating system.

Ultimately, a basic understanding of the platform that you program on is helpful. This chapter will expose you to much of the underlying system and functionality of Windows, and how this can be accessed from C++. My intent is to help you write better software by understanding what is happening underneath the system. You may be able to write code that ports more easily to other platforms by avoiding programming practices that are platform dependant. Most of the code that you will look at in this chapter is written in bare C.

How the Windows System Works

I'll begin by talking about processes and threads, and then move on to messages and yielding. These are some very basic system-level issues that as a Visual Basic programmer you have probably heard about, but might not have grasped at the level that you need to use them effectively.

Processes and Threads

Although threading is traditionally considered an advanced subject, it makes sense to start with this and with the message subsystem because these ideas are basic to the way that WIN32 systems work.

In the good old 16-bit days, you didn't have to worry much about this stuff. Windows 16-bit was a multitasking system, but it was *non-preemptive*. (This means that one program must stop executing and give up processor time in order for another process to run.)

A WIN32 program that runs on a single thread, but has multiple windows, can suffer the same fate the 16-bit system does when a process does not yield.

32-bit Windows has preemptive multitasking and this means that each process or thread will get its own time slice. While this appears to solve the yielding crisis that existed in 16-bit, it doesn't do anything for a single threaded program that doesn't yield to allow its own UI to update.

For example, suppose you have a very tight set of code that processes and updates some status window to tell you where you might be within this code. If the code and the window are running on the same thread, the window will never get a paint message unless the code yields and allows the window to update. I will explain the yielding process in detail in the later section, "Message Pumps."

Message Subsystem

The message subsystem is what ties Windows together. Windows has been message-based since 16-bit versions. There are arguments for and against message-based operating systems, but combining true preemptive processing with a message-based system has proved to be quite successful.

Message Queues

Message queues are the means by which Windows programs receive their input and communicate with the system. There is one "master" message queue per system, and a "window" message queue for each thread that handles user input. All threads are created without message queues—the message queue gets attached to the thread when the thread makes a GDI (Graphics Device Interface) call. In other words if the thread interacts with the user, through the screen or the keyboard, it needs a message queue.

User input in the form of keyboard or mouse input is posted to the system queue, which in turn finds the window to which to direct the messages. The system queue then "posts" the message to the message queue attached to the thread that created the window. Posting the message preserves the order in which the messages on the queue will be handled.

In Visual Basic you typically had little control over the message queue. However timing within message queues will be important to you as you learn how to write Windows code in C and C++. In C you find that you have a lot of control, and this comes in handy quite often.

For example, with the heightened level of control in C/C++ you can write code that can look at the messages in the message queue without removing them. This would allow you to watch for a certain message and exit that code block when it arrives.

You can also preserve message processing order by using PostMessage. You have limited use of PostMessage in Visual Basic, but in C and C++ you have complete control including being able to create custom messages for a window.

Message Pumps

Message pumps (also called message loops) are the "animal" that both allows code to service message queues and permits message-based windows to receive their messages. Message pump code extracts messages from the message queue for a particular thread, and dispatches them to the proper window to be handled. A message pump is usually running on a UI thread when no other code on the thread is running. Typically a message pump contains three base functions in a continuous loop. I'll explore those functions in Listing 6.1 shortly.

In Visual Basic you will be familiar with servicing a message queue by using DoEvents. There are other ways in Visual Basic to service the message queue (not having any VB code running puts the VB program in a message loop) and there are ways to force window updates without the message pump (.Refresh).

Typically entering a message loop is termed "yielding." However that term really grew out of 16-bit technologies. There you only had one thread and the whole system would stop if a program didn't yield by entering a message loop. In 32-bit, other processes will continue to run, even if your process doesn't enter a message loop. However, as I pointed out before, the window messages in your program will not get serviced when you stop the message pump.

C programs, unlike DoEvents in Visual Basic, do not have a simple way of giving up processing to the message queue. If you write a piece of code in C that is going to take a while to execute you need to start a thread for that code, write the code so that it can be interrupted and resumed, or write a message loop with it.

Except for the thread option above, the other methods all rely on a "message pump."

Message Pump—Main Requirements

Listing 6.1 is a code snippet that demonstrates a message pump. Note that I'm simply detailing the main requirements of the message pump. This message pump does not have all the code that your message pump may require. In addition to the code shown, your message pump may require TranslateAccelerator (to handle accelerator keys) or IsDialogMessage (to handle keyboard messages in a dialog).

LISTING 6.1   Message Pump

```
MSG msg;
while (GetMessage(&msg,NULL,0,0))
{
    TranslateMessage(&msg);
    DispatchMessage(&msg);
}
```

A loop similar to this one is started on any thread that has UI associated with it. (I'll be more detailed about how this loop gets started in the following section on how a Windows program works.)

Now let's take a closer look at the code. `GetMessage` retrieves a message from the thread's queue. `TranslateMessage` is important for keyboard messages, but isn't for purposes of the discussion here.

`DispatchMessage` is the one that is interesting to us. This routine calls the procedure associated with the window specified in the `msg` structure.

The message structure holds all the information about a message, such as the window that the message goes to, the message number, the parameters that go with the message, the mouse position, and the time stamps for certain types of messages.

It is during `DispatchMessage` that most of the code actually executes. In other words, it typically takes a Windows message to make something happen in a Windows program.

The message pump is stopped while the code executes because `DispatchMessage` is simply a function call. Execution in this loop will not resume until the call to `DispatchMessage` returns. If you do something that takes an hour, then the message loop is "hung" for an hour. If you do this in a 16-bit program, the whole system hangs. In a 32-bit environment, the program's windows will become unresponsive because you've hung the UI thread for the program.

Avoid Hanging Message Loops

So how do you get around these problems? In 16-bit you really only had two options. Write code that could be resumed (code that remembers its state so it can stop processing and resume where it left off) or provide another message pump within the code. In 32-bit, you have one more option: Start a "worker thread" to handle the process that consumes so much time. Multithreaded programs have a whole new set of issues associated with them, but they do solve this problem.

You can write code that can be resumed. Code that requires a long time to execute commonly runs within a loop that has either a counter or a condition for exiting the loop. Because of the message queue and the fact that the message pump is a loop, you can use that to your advantage to write code that can be resumed to handle a long process. Consider the code snippet in Listing 6.2.

LISTING 6.2   Resuming Code

```
HandleOurCustomMessage(dword wp, long lp)
{
    //to start the process, we send our custom message
```

LISTING 6.2   Continued

```
//with wp set to 1 and lp set to the iterations
if (wp < lp)
{
    //do work here
    wp++;      //increment wp
    //seed the process
    PostMessage(ourhwnd,WM_OURCUSTOMMESSAGE,wp,lp);
}
}
```

If this procedure is written to respond to a custom Windows message, Listing 6.2 is one way you could write a procedure that wouldn't stop the message loop. Some other part of the program would start the process by sending or posting this custom message. Let's follow the process:

When the message is dispatched and this function executes, it posts a message that will end up in the message queue, and that will get dispatched and ultimately cause the function to be executed again. This whole time the message pump continues running and dispatching other messages.

The only thing you have to do to stop this process is to not post the custom message. In this routine, you will stop posting the custom message when wp is incremented to equal lp. So when you start this routine, you have to send values in wp and lp where lp is greater than wp in order for the function to be resumed.

This type of code is not used a lot in 32-bit. You'd see this technique pretty often in 16-bit code. However, I have used it in a control, not for lengthy processing but to handle the mouse in a control.

Using Message Pumps While Processing

The other way you can handle long processing is by writing message pumps right in the loop that runs for a long period of time. Look at the code snippet in Listing 6.3.

LISTING 6.3   Using a Message Loop During Processing

```
MSG msg;
for(x=1;x<y;x++)
{
    //do processing
    if (PeekMessage(&msg,NULL,0,0, PM_REMOVE))
    {
```

LISTING 6.3   Continued

```
        TranslateMessage(&msg);
        DispatchMessage(&msg);
    }
}
```

Notice that in this code you use `PeekMessage`. `PeekMessage` must be used while you are trying to run code. `GetMessage` will not return until it has a message. `PeekMessage` will return immediately whether it has a message or not. This lets this loop continuously execute, but handle messages on this thread.

PostMessage Versus SendMessage

SendMessage and PostMessage are pertinent to the discussion of the message queue because of their interaction with it—or, in the case of SendMessage, its lack of interaction with the message queue.

I've mentioned PostMessage a couple of times. External events like keyboard and mouse messages place messages in the message queue. `PostMessage` also places messages in the message queue. `PostMessage` returns after placing the message in the queue and the program continues to execute. The message is placed at the end of the queue. Because messages are processed FIFO (first in first out), the messages that are already in the queue will be processed before one placed in the queue by PostMessage. This means that the processing of the message sent with PostMessage may be delayed.

With `SendMessage` the message queue is bypassed and the message is sent directly to the window. Essentially the window procedure is called directly without going through the message pump. This means that messages may sit in the message queue while a message sent by `SendMessage` is processed. The program flow could encounter a message pump, so it would be possible to process messages from the message queue while in the `SendMessage` call.

The way these API calls handle messages may be quite important when it comes time to choose which API to use to process a message that you need to send to another window.

How a Windows Program Works

Message queues and pumps are integral to how a "normal" Windows program works. By normal, I mean a program with at least one window—it doesn't matter whether the program is written in C, C++, C++ with MFC, C#, or Visual Basic. They may be hidden from you, buried under Visual Basic Forms or .NET classes, but the basics of a Windows program are always there.

Window Class

A Window class is at the base of any window in the system. A Window class contains several things that a window uses—of utmost importance it holds the address of the Window procedure. Every Windows program that has at least a single window must create a Window class; typically this is done in the InitApplication routine.

Creating a Main Window

A window can be created almost anywhere in a program. The main program window is typically created in an InitInstance procedure and is based on an existing Window class. It uses the Window procedure specified in the Window class.

- The Window Procedure—The procedure is where most user code is written. Whether you are writing a Windows program or a control, the class procedure is where the action is.

  The Window procedure ultimately is called when the window receives a message. Through various mechanisms, depending upon the type of program, the message will eventually make it to code that will handle the message.

- The Message Loop—I've already had a lot to say about the message loop. This is the mechanism that gets the message from the thread's queue to the window procedure.

- The Windows API—This is an important aspect of the Windows system. I will talk about the Windows API when it fits the context of the discussion, but it is not the focus of this book. Working with C++ and C you can't write code without using the Windows API, so I will certainly cover some of the APIs.

Base Services

Windows services can best be broken down into non-UI (User Interface) and UI features. Non-UI features include things like the clipboard, IO, and timers.

Clipboard

The clipboard can be thought of as a temporary storage area in the computer's memory. It can hold data in a variety of formats, including formats that you haven't even thought of yet.

Typically the clipboard is used for the cut, copy, and paste commands in editors and other programs that work with data in this manner.

Visual Basic (and .NET) has some fairly easy-to-use objects that access this functionality. In C and C++, this functionality is somewhat more tedious to program.

Device Input and Output

You haven't had to do the dirty programming of going out and getting device input since the days of programming in DOS. Someone has to do it though and the code to do this resides in the Windows system. As I stated before, the system queue gathers the messages from input devices like the keyboard and determines where they will be sent.

Handling standard devices is an integral part of Windows now and if you want to program to an input device (like a keyboard) you usually add that code within the Window procedure. In Visual Basic you are provided Keyboard and mouse events. In C you have the same type of events available but in the form of a Windows message.

Handles and Objects

Several types of handles are used to refer to objects within Windows. (I am not using the word *object* as it refers to a programming unit, like a class in C++. Nor am I using it to refer to a binary object, like a COM object.)

In this section *object* refers to a basic Windows element, like a window or a drawing surface or a font. These objects are used to provide the basic functionality in Windows. For example, you can't draw on something without a device context.

In order to refer to such objects you must use a handle. These handles may in most cases be thought of as identifiers (although in 32-bit they can sometimes be locations in memory). Usually you use the handle along with an API function to perform some function with an object.

Most often in Visual Basic you don't have to worry about these handles, although they are provided within many programming objects. Most controls have an hwnd property, which is a window handle. Some have an hdc property, which is a device context handle. However many programming objects—for example, font and picture objects—do not expose these handles in VB.

Let's look at some of the basic objects that require handles and some of the things that you might use those handles for. They fall into two general groups: handles defined in User and handles defined in GDI. Windows, menus, timers, and memory are user objects. Device contexts, brushes, pens, fonts, and bitmaps are GDI objects.

User Objects

Obviously, the most familiar handle is the hwnd (handle to a window). Most programmers are familiar with window handles and the fact that they identify a specific window within the system. Window handles are fickle though. They come and go. You should not depend on a window handle being valid over a long period of time. You should validate a window handle before using it. IsWindow is the API call to use to validate a window handle. Listing 6.4 shows how you might use this API before trying to paint to the window. Typically you use window handles right within the window procedure. In this case the window handle will be passed in with the message. Don't store the window handle for later use, it can change. In Visual Basic, you use the handle without checking the validity, but typically you get that handle from a form or a control and you can be pretty sure that it is valid, unless you try to store it and use it later.

In C you need to check it, especially inside control code. Controls are not always guaranteed a valid window handle. If it isn't valid it is usually NULL, but using IsWindow is the best procedure for checking the handle.

For example, one of the problems that you can generate with a NULL window handle is screen flash. An InvalidateRect with a NULL window handle will invalidate the entire screen, causing the whole screen to redraw.

GDI Objects

The hdc (handle to a device context) is the next most familiar handle. Many programmers are aware of this handle, but unless you've done some GDI code, you might not be aware of some of the finer points of hdcs. This is a very limited resource. It is critical in its use and handling. If you mishandle an hdc, it wont be long before the whole system comes crashing down about your ears.

> **NOTE**
>
> I should qualify these statements somewhat. They apply when using common device contexts, which are global to the system and limited in number. You can use a private device context that is private to the window that it belongs to, but for simple work, you usually don't do that. Private device contexts use about 800 bytes of memory for each context. That doesn't sound like much, but if it's the type of window that might have many instances, like a control, then using private device contexts is not appropriate.

GDI Objects include brushes, pens, bitmaps, fonts, palettes, and regions. In a general discussion of GDI objects you would usually separate out palettes and regions because they behave and are used somewhat differently.

With brushes, pens, bitmaps, and fonts you generally have a create, select, delete cycle that must be used to ensure that you do not have resource leakage. This means that you will create the object, select it into a device context, draw with it, select it out of the device context, and then delete it. Listings 6.4 and 6.5 demonstrate the complete cycle. Listing 6.4 shows the Visual Basic code. Listing 6.5 shows the C code that accomplishes the same thing. The VB code is a complete listing; all that has to be added to a normal VB EXE is a button and this code will run. The C code on the other hand must be placed in C program and that listing is just too long to show here.

LISTING 6.4   GDI Object Cycle

```vb
'Visual Basic example GDI object cycle
Private Declare Function IsWindow Lib "user32" (ByVal hwnd As Long) As Long
Private Declare Function GetDC Lib "user32" (ByVal hwnd As Long) As Long
Private Declare Function CreatePen Lib "gdi32" (ByVal nPenStyle As Long, _
                                     ByVal nWidth As Long, _
                                     ByVal crColor As Long) As Long
Private Declare Function SelectObject Lib "gdi32" (ByVal hdc As Long, _
                                        ByVal hObject As Long) As
Long
Private Declare Function DeleteObject Lib "gdi32" (ByVal hObject As Long) As
Long
Private Declare Function ReleaseDC Lib "user32" (ByVal hwnd As Long, _
                                     ByVal hdc As Long) As Long
Private Declare Function Ellipse Lib "gdi32" (ByVal hdc As Long, _
                                     ByVal X1 As Long, _
                                     ByVal Y1 As Long, _
                                     ByVal X2 As Long, _
                                     ByVal Y2 As Long) As Long


Private Sub Command1_Click()
  Dim hwnd As Long
  hwnd = Me.hwnd
  If IsWindow(hwnd) Then
    Dim hdc As Long
    Dim holdpen As Long
    Dim pen As Long

    hdc = GetDC(hwnd)                 'get's a device context
    pen = CreatePen(PS_SOLID, 1, &HFF)   'creates a pen
    holdpen = SelectObject(hdc, pen)     'selects the pen into the context
    'any gdi routine that uses the pen
    'can be used here, like DrawTo or Rectangle
    Ellipse hdc, 10, 10, 40, 40
    SelectObject hdc, holdpen         'selects the pen out of the context
    DeleteObject pen                  'gets rid of the pen
    ReleaseDC hwnd, hdc               'releases the device context
  End If

End Sub
```

LISTING 6.5   GDI Object Cycle

```
if (IsWindow(hwnd))
{
    HDC  hdc;
    HPEN holdpen;
    HPEN pen;

    hdc = GetDC(hwnd);                   //get's a device context
    pen = CreatePen(PS_SOLID,1, 0xff);   //creates a pen
    holdpen = SelectObject(hdc,pen);     //selects the pen into the context
    //any gdi routine that uses the pen
    //can be used here, like DrawTo or Rectangle
    SelectObject(hdc, holdPen);          //selects the pen out of the context
    DeleteObject(pen);                   //gets rid of the pen
    ReleasdeDC(hwnd, hdc);               //releases the device context
}
```

This is a normal GDI "sandwich." The outer wrapper is made up of the HDC functions—GetDC and ReleaseDC, in this case. Inside that are the GDI drawing objects, in this case CreatePen and DeleteObject. Inside that are the functions that select GDI drawing objects in and out. SelectObject is always used for that. Using C++ objects can make your code simpler because you can use constructors and destructors to handle much of the initialization and cleanup.

When you select an object into a device context, you should always save the old object. You select the object out by using SelectObject with the old handle. This works because device contexts are always created with GDI drawing objects created and selected into the context. Only one drawing object of each type can be selected into a device context at a time.

Menus use handles and probably are not as familiar to Visual Basic programmers as some other handles. Visual Basic takes care of menus for you and it isn't necessary to deal with menu handles within Visual Basic.

In C, menu handles enable you to respond to choices from the menus. Of course, the same thing happens in Visual Basic, but VB fires an event to allow you to respond to the choices so a VB programmer doesn't have to deal with the handles.

Memory Handles

Memory allocation can also use handles. This was very common in 16-bit. Memory with handles is possible in 32-bit but is only there for compatibility reasons. You shouldn't use handles when allocating memory in 32-bit. It simply slows the memory access down. I'll try to clarify this a little.

In 16-bit, you used moveable memory to allow the memory manager to swap that memory to disk. If you allocated fixed memory in 16-bit, it defeated the memory manager and memory wouldn't swap to disk. In 32-bit, the memory manager can swap fixed memory. So there is no real reason to allocate moveable memory in 32-bit. Moveable memory uses a handle and you have to lock the memory to get an actual pointer to the memory. With fixed memory, the memory allocation returns the actual pointer. There is no need to lock and unlock the memory. This is why using fixed memory is faster than moveable memory. It also uses fewer resources (no handles). Listing 6.6 shows examples of both types of memory allocation.

LISTING 6.6   Memory

```
{
    HANDLE     hmem;
    LPVOID pmem;
    LPVOID fpmem;

    //this works in 32 bit, but is the
    //16 bit way of doing things
    hmem = GlobalAlloc(GHND, 1024);
    pmem = GlobalLock(hmem);
    //pmem may be used in here
    GlobalUnlock(hmem);
    GlobalFree(hmem);

    //32 bit way
    fpmem = (LPVOID) GlobalAlloc(GPTR, 1024);
    //fpmem is a memory pointer and may
    //be used here
    GlobalFree(fpmem);
}
```

NOTE

More controlled ways of allocating memory exist now. For example, in .NET-managed code you would never allocate memory in this manner. You would use New to allocate the objects and the CLR would handle creating these objects and managing the memory. This is a much more civilized way of doing things.

Hooks

Several system hooks can be used in very specific situations. These hooks typically use call back procedures and involve some rather difficult programming techniques.

Some of the things that are possible with hooks are

- Process or modify messages meant for the dialog boxes, message boxes, scroll bars, or menus for an application (WH_MSGFILTER).

- Process or modify messages meant for all the dialog boxes, message boxes, scroll bars, or menus for the system (WH_SYSMSGFILTER).

- Process or modify messages for the system whenever a GetMessage or a PeekMessage function is called (WH_GETMESSAGE).

- Process or modify messages whenever a SendMessage function is called (WH_CALL-WNDPROC).

- Record or play back keyboard and mouse events (WH_JOURNALRECORD, WH_JOURNALPLAYBACK).

- Process, modify, or remove keyboard events (WH_KEYBOARD).

- Process, modify, or discard mouse events (WH_MOUSE).

- Respond to certain system actions, making it possible to develop computer-based training (CBT) for applications (WH_CBT).

These hooks may be useful from time to time, but as a rule they should be avoided. The reason to avoid these hooks is that they can degrade system performance.

All hooks place a hook function in order to get between some functionality of Windows. How hard the hook is on performance depends on where the hooks are placed and what they hook. System-level hooks impact performance of every program running. Thread-level hooks only impact the thread that they are installed on.

Obviously you need to avoid system hooks when you can. System hooks that send a lot of messages through to the filter function are especially bad. WH_CALLWNDPROC, WH_CBT, WH_DEBUG, and WH_GETMESSAGE are especially severe when set at a system level.

In addition to a decreased impact on system performance, thread hooks have other advantages as well. Using a thread hook doesn't require packaging the hook function in a separate DLL. This is required in a system hook. You just discovered another use for a C DLL like you'll study in the next chapter.

NOTE

There are a couple more hooks worth mentioning that aren't common hooks: a low-level keyboard hook and a low-level mouse hook. These hooks were introduced in NT4, service pack 3 and can be used in NT4-SP3 and above and Windows 2000.

These hooks get every keystroke in the system and can stop any keystroke (except the Ctrl+Alt+Del). You can even get at and remove the Alt+Esc and the Alt+Tab. Ctrl+Alt+Del must be handled in a "GINA" DLL. A GINA DLL can intercept and block Ctrl+Alt+Del and it (of course) must be written in C.

You can find documentation on these two hooks under WH_KEYBOARD_LL and WH_MOUSE_LL.

Thread hooks do not need to share data from a DLL with other processes. Thread hooks do not cause events to be serialized.

System hooks must be able to share data between processes or the system will crash. System hooks will be called by every thread in the system causing those messages to go through that one hook function (that is, it creates a bottleneck).

SetWindowsHookEx, UnHookWindowsHookEx, and CallNextHookEx are used to manage hook functionality in Windows. Table 6.1 lists the possible hooks that can be managed with these functions.

TABLE 6.1 Hooks

Hook	Possible Scope
WH_CALLWNDPROC	Thread or System
WH_CBT	Thread or System
WH_DEBUG	Thread or System
WH_GETMESSAGE	Thread or System
WH_JOURNALRECORD	System Only
WH_JOURNALPLAYBACK	System Only
WH_FOREGROUNDIDLE	Thread or System
WH_SHELL	Thread or System
WH_KEYBOARD	Thread or System
WH_MOUSE	Thread or System
WH_MSGFILTER	Thread or System
WH_SYSMSGFILTER	System Only

WH_CALLWNDPROC is documented with the CallWndProc function. Windows calls this function whenever the SendMessage function is called. Filters can process the message, but cannot modify it, although this was possible in 16-bit. This hook drains system performance significantly.

WH_CBT is documented with the CBTProc function. The CBT hook is specialized and intended for computer-based training. This hook receives very specialized information from the system during certain messages that allow the programmer to coordinate the hooked application and the CBT application.

WH_DEBUG is documented with the DebugProc function. This hook is called when another hook function is about to be called. Filters cannot modify the values of this hook, but can stop the next hook from being called by returning a non-zero value.

WH_GETMESSAGE is documented with the GetMsgProc function. This hook is called when the GetMessage or PeekMessage is about to return a message. The message can be modified by the filter function.

WH_JOURNALRECORD is documented with the JournalRecordProc function. WH_JOUR-NALPLAYBACK is documented with the JournalPlaybackProc function. Journal hooks are used to record and play back events. These hooks are system only and so affect all Windows-based applications.

WH_FOREGROUNDIDLE is documented with the ForeGroundIdleProc function. Windows calls this hook when there is no user input to process. If the hook is thread level, it is only called when that thread is the current thread. It is for information only, both wParam and lParam are 0.

WH_SHELL is documented with the ShellProc function. This hook is called when actions happen to top-level windows. This hook is for notification only.

WH_KEYBOARD is documented with the KeyboardProc function. This filter is called when the GetMessage or PeekMessage function is about to return a WM_KEYUP, WM_KEY-DOWN, WM_SYSKEYUP, WM_SYSKEYDOWN, or WM_CHAR message. Windows will notify the function if the message is being removed from the queue or not. The filter function can tell Windows to discard the message.

WH_MOUSE is documented with the MouseProc function. This filter is called when the GetMessage or PeekMessage function is about to return a mouse message. Windows will notify the function whether the message is being removed from the queue. The filter function can tell Windows to discard the message.

WH_MSGFILTER is documented with the MessageProc function. Windows calls this message when a dialog box, a message box, a scroll bar, or a menu receives a message. It is also called when the Alt+Tab or Alt+Esc keys are pressed while the application that set the hook is active.

WH_SYSMSGFILTER is documented with the SysMsgProc function. This hook is identical to the WH_MSGFILTER except that it is system wide. This filter is called before the WH_MSG-

FILTER. If this filter returns TRUE, then the WH_MSGFILTER for the same message will not be called.

How about a small sample app that can either take in a ThreadID or ProcessID and "preview" all mouse and keyboard messages? The premise could be a macro script recorder that might feed a "test" program or log keystrokes to a text file as an audit tool.

Registry

I could write a whole book about the registry. I'll try to keep my comments in check here. With the introduction of the registry, Microsoft decided that it was a good idea to place all configuration information in the registry.

Lately Microsoft has decided that perhaps putting everything in the registry wasn't that good of an idea after all. It makes programs more difficult to install and uninstall. It makes it impossible to just copy a program from one computer to another, like you did in the DOS days, and expect it to run.

The registry is still where program configuration information is written and Windows does not have a set of easy routines to get at registry information for you. On the plus side, you can decide where to place your program configuration information if you use the API routines. If you use Visual Basic's routines to place registry information, you know that you were limited to a particular section in the registry. Certainly you need to be sensible about where you place information in the registry, but you may want it someplace besides "Microsoft/VB and VBA Program Settings."

Timers

Visual Basic programmers are familiar with the timer that is supplied in the intrinsic control. That custom control, like most controls, uses an event to fire the timer. The VB control does this internally, whereas in C you must use the timers provided in the system.

If you have the VB control, why might you want to use the timers in C? Because there are times when you might write code that requires a timer.

After timers are created they send WM_TIMER messages to the Window that they are associated with. Timers do not have to be associated with a window. They can specify a function to call when the timer expires. However, a timer must run on a thread that is serviced by a message pump, even if the timer specifies a function instead of a window handle.

TIP

Don't try to start a timer on a worker thread, because the callback function will never be called.

Timer messages are low priority, so even if the WM_TIMER message gets sent right when the timer expires, it still could take the window a while to process it. Also, like WM_PAINT messages, no matter how many WM_TIMER messages are in the queue they will be combined into one WM_TIMER message.

The timer sample shown in Listing 6.7 shows how to set and release the timer, and use the timer messages when they are sent. Notice in the SetTimer that you use an ID of 1 and 1000 as the interval. The ID is unique to the window that the timer is set for and ignored if you use a function. The interval is one second and the function pointer is null, which means that this timer posts WM_TIMER messages to the message queue.

LISTING 6.7   Timers

```
//some function, usually a property, method or init
{
    //a timer must be set with setimer
    //in a control you would probably
    //check for run mode
    SetTimer(m_hwnd, 1, 1000, NULL);
}

//some function, usually a property, method or destructor
{
    KillTimer(m_hwnd, 1);
}

//window procedure for m_hwnd
{
    case WM_TIMER:
        //here we do the work involved
        //with the timer
}
```

GDI

All programmers have to deal with the GDI (graphics device interface). The hottest thing today are Internet applications and people are sacrificing the user interface experience to write the code that handles distributed programs.

Users will sacrifice some usability in the program in order to be able to use it though any browser from anywhere in the world. These things are certainly important to today's computing environment. Still, in most distributed environments, companies decide on the specific browser and other software that must be in place both on servers and end users machines. Only the most generic code can exist cross platform.

In many instances there are still WIN32 components in the software. Programs have to deal with local devices, like scanners and printers.

So I still think it is important to know how to deal with system-specific code, like GDI. Windows systems continue to add features to the GDI code, features that users want, so this type of programming is far from dead and in fact could make a comeback when the Internet pipe gets big enough.

The strict definition of GDI is the part of Windows that communicates between the program and the device drivers that actually run the devices. This code will always be there; the only question is, will programmers be coding to it?

Direct use of GDI happens whenever you control the display characteristics of something right down to the pixels that go on the display or printer. You do this quite often in custom control programming, which is a big part of writing support code in C and C++. If you use a Windows API to draw text or a line, you are using GDI.

Back in Listing 6.5, I introduced the GDI cycle or "sandwich," as some people call it. Drawing with GDI objects require a little thought and the following of some very strict rules to guard against system failures and resource leakage.

In an earlier section, "Handles and Objects," I introduced most of the GDI objects that a programmer typically sees. Being successful with GDI means you have to use those objects consistently within a set of constraints. C++ or .NET objects can make this process easier to manage, because a C++ object has a destructor that can delete the objects when done. However, it just can't relieve the programmer of all the responsibility of GDI drawing without being too cumbersome.

GDI code has no real alliance with any language and I can write it in Visual Basic as well as C. Some things are easier to do in C, but it can be accomplished in either language.

Simple drawing code is fairly simple to understand. Some of the more difficult concepts have to do with logical (page) and device coordinates and translating between them. Mapping modes are also difficult to understand and deal with.

Table 6.2 shows the different mapping modes available and where you are likely to see them.

TABLE 6.2   Mapping Modes

Mapping Mode	Description	Typically Used
MM_ANISOTROPIC	Each unit in page space is mapped to an application-specified unit in device space. The axis may or may not be equally scaled (for example, a circle drawn in world space may appear to be an ellipse when depicted on a given device). The orientation of the axis is also specified by the application.	Where HIMETRIC units are used, this mapping mode allows placing the origin at the top—left, which is easier to handle in code. It is used a lot in metafile play-back also.
MM_HIENGLISH	Each unit in page space is mapped to 0.001 inch in device space. The value of x increases from left to right. The value of y increases from bottom to top.	Typically you might find this in word processing or desktop publishing.
MM_HIMETRIC	Each unit in page space is mapped to 0.01 millimeter in device space. The value of x increases from left to right. The value of y increases from bottom to top.	Typically you might find this in word processing or desktop publishing. These units are also used in COM objects.
MM_ISOTROPIC	Each unit in page space is mapped to an application-defined unit in device space. The axes are always equally scaled. The orientation of the axes may be specified by the application.	
MM_LOENGLISH	Each unit in page space is mapped to 0.01 inch in device space. The value of x increases from left to right. The value of y increases from bottom to top.	Typically you might find this in word processing or desktop publishing.

TABLE 6.2   Continued

Mapping Mode	Description	Typically Used
MM_LOMETRIC	Each unit in page space is mapped to 0.1 millimeter in device space. The value of x increases from left to right. The value of y increases from bottom to top.	Typically you might find this in word processing or desktop publishing.
MM_TEXT	Each unit in page space is mapped to one pixel; that is, no scaling is performed at all. When no translation is in effect (this is the default), page space in the MM_TEXT mapping mode is equivalent to physical device space. The value of x increases from left to right. The value of y increases from top to bottom.	This is the default mapping mode and is the most common in C/C++ programming.
MM_TWIPS	Each unit in page space is mapped to one twentieth of a printer's point (1/1440th inch). The value of x increases from left to right. The value of y increases from bottom to top.	Typically found in Visual ..... Basic

Usually you'll find pictures and drawings that show you the relationships between logical and device coordinates. That doesn't really relate to what has to happen in the code. First your GDI code can work with pixels (MM_TEXT mapping mode, device coordinates) unless you need features like zoom. In that case you'll have to work in some other coordinate system (usually MM_ANISOTROPIC) that allows you to switch from a 1:1 relationship.

When you set up a window that allows zooming, your coordinate system becomes some multiplier of the device coordinates. All mouse coordinates and drawing code are converted by this multiplier.

DPtoLP and LPtoDP are the way to make many of the conversions that you'll need. The only problem with these routines is that they need an HDC with the mapping mode set up properly.

Knowing what these units are and how to translate between them is important. Most often what you see as C/C++ programmers supporting Visual Basic are pixels (MM_TEXT), HIMETRIC, and TWIPS. Sometimes these are not the mapping modes, but are the units that the mapping modes are expressed in. For example it is common to use HIMETRIC units, but MM_ANISOTROPIC mapping mode to get the origin at the top left of the coordinate system.

Listing 6.8 shows conversion functions for converting between twips and pixels. These do not use DptoLP or LPtoDP because you aren't really interested in the mapping mode; you're interested in converting between twips and pixels whatever the mapping mode. You might use these conversions when firing mouse events in a custom control. Visual Basic always expects the mouse coordinates in the scale of the container, which is most often twips.

LISTING 6.8   Functions for Converting Between Twips and Pixels

```
#define TWIPS_PER_INCH 1440
int RoundDiv(long x, short y);
#define RoundDiv(x,y) (int)((x+y/2)/y)

int XPixelsToTwips(int xPixels, HDC pdc)
{
    int     iTwipsPerPixel;
    int     iLogPixels;
    HDC     dc;

    if (pdc == NULL)
    {
        dc = CreateIC(_T("Display"), NULL, NULL, NULL);
        iLogPixels = GetDeviceCaps(dc, LOGPIXELSX);
        DeleteDC(dc);
    }
    else
    {
        iLogPixels = GetDeviceCaps(pdc, LOGPIXELSX);
    }
    if (0==iLogPixels)
        iLogPixels=1;
    iTwipsPerPixel = TWIPS_PER_INCH / iLogPixels;
    return(xPixels * iTwipsPerPixel);
}

int YPixelsToTwips(int yPixels, HDC pdc)
{
    int     iTwipsPerPixel;
    int     iLogPixels;
    HDC     dc;
```

LISTING 6.8   Continued

```
    if (yPixels < 0)
        yPixels=yPixels;
    if (pdc == NULL)
    {
        dc = CreateIC(_T("Display"), NULL, NULL, NULL);
        iLogPixels = GetDeviceCaps(dc, LOGPIXELSY);
        DeleteDC(dc);
    }
    else
    {
        iLogPixels = GetDeviceCaps(pdc, LOGPIXELSY);
    }

    if (0==iLogPixels)
        iLogPixels=1;
    iTwipsPerPixel = TWIPS_PER_INCH / iLogPixels;
    return(yPixels * iTwipsPerPixel);
}

int XTwipsToPixels(int xTwips, HDC pdc)
{
    int     iTwipsPerPixel;
    int     iLogPixels;
    HDC     dc;

    if (pdc == NULL)
    {
        dc = CreateIC(_T("Display"), NULL, NULL, NULL);
        iLogPixels = GetDeviceCaps(dc, LOGPIXELSX);
        DeleteDC(dc);
    }
    else
    {
        iLogPixels = GetDeviceCaps(pdc, LOGPIXELSX);
    }

    if (0==iLogPixels)
        iLogPixels=1;
    iTwipsPerPixel = TWIPS_PER_INCH / iLogPixels;
    return(RoundDiv(xTwips, iTwipsPerPixel));
}

int YTwipsToPixels(int xTwips, HDC pdc)
{
```

LISTING 6.8   Continued

```
int     iTwipsPerPixel;
int     iLogPixels;
HDC     dc;

if (pdc == NULL)
{
    dc = CreateIC(_T("Display"), NULL, NULL, NULL);
    iLogPixels = GetDeviceCaps(dc, LOGPIXELSY);
    DeleteDC(dc);
}
else
{
    iLogPixels = GetDeviceCaps(pdc, LOGPIXELSY);
}

if (0==iLogPixels)
    iLogPixels=1;
iTwipsPerPixel = TWIPS_PER_INCH / iLogPixels;
return(RoundDiv(xTwips, iTwipsPerPixel));
}
```

Summary

In this chapter you explored some of the basics of the Windows operating system as it affects application programming.

C DLL Basics

IN THIS CHAPTER

This chapter looks at the mechanics of writing function-based DLLs. In today's computing environment, you might raise some eyebrows by writing a C/C++ DLL to support a Visual Basic program. After all, now that OLE, COM, COM+, ActiveX, and .NET have come along, there's no need to write support code in DLLs anymore. But as with standard modules in Visual Basic, standard C DLLs have their place.

Sometimes using DLLs can just be the best and possibly only way to achieve an end—it also can be very fast. If you understand how COM and COM+ work, then you can appreciate a DLL for its speed. Furthermore, a DLL is typically somewhat easier to write than a comparable control or COM object. You can combine it with a type library to make it easy to use. For example, in Visual Basic you can browse the functions in a DLL that has type information.

Tutorial for Creating a Simple C DLL

This first section steps though the process of creating a simple project in Visual C++ and covers the basic steps required to write the DLL and the routines that are part of the DLL. I will explicitly walk you through the steps required to build a DLL that is compatible with Visual Basic.

This section covers the following items:

- Using the wizard to create the base project and files
- Exporting the function
- Prototyping the function
- Writing the function contents
- Calling the function and debugging from Visual Basic

Using Visual C++ to Create the DLL

You'll use Visual C++ 6.0 to create a new DLL project. Visual Studio includes a wizard to lead you though the creation of a new DLL, as shown in Figure 7.1. I chose to create a simple DLL. This generates the CPP file and the include file, and places the DllMain function for you. Name this DLL sampDLL.dll.

DLLMain Function

All DLLs have a DLLMain function, sort of like WinMain for Windows executable files written in C or simply the Main function for console-based programs. This is the function where execution begins.

> Visual Basic programmers have a `Main` function that can be used in EXEs or DLLs. Its functionality is slightly different depending on whether it is a "regular" EXE, an ActiveX EXE, or an ActiveX DLL (the only kind of DLL you can make).
>
> You can opt to have the `DllMain` function in your source code. If you see DLLs without this code, this simply means that Visual C is linking in its standard version of this routine. The standard version of the routine does what the routine in your sample does: It simply returns `TRUE`.
>
> So why put this code in? To be sure that you understand what is happening. Sometimes you will need to place code in this routine, and without first seeing this routine, you wouldn't even know where to start. With this in mind, you can choose to leave this routine out of your DLL source code in the future.

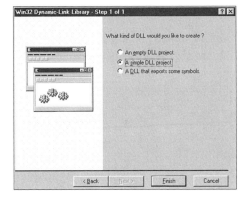

FIGURE 7.1
Visual C++ DLL Wizard.

Exporting the Function from C

To successfully use an exported function from a C DLL in a Visual Basic program, certain requirements must be met. Visual Basic expects this exported DLL function to work like a Windows API call. The following list specifies these requirements:

- Arguments are passed from right to left. This is a Pascal convention, not the default in C.

- Arguments are to be passed by value unless you specify a pointer or a reference type. By default, Visual Basic passes all arguments by reference; arguments passed by reference contain the 32-bit address of the argument rather than the value of the argument. However, most functions in an exported DLL expect the value of the argument rather than the 32-bit address. To pass an argument by value, use the `ByVal` keyword in Visual Basic when declaring the function.

- Stack maintenance is handled by the called function. Again, this is a Pascal convention, not the norm in Visual C++; however, it *is* normal in Visual Basic.

- The function name is case-sensitive. Under Win16, function names are not case-sensitive, but under Win32, function names *are* case-sensitive.

- Name decoration cannot be handled by Visual Basic without using an alias in the declaration.

After this, you're ready to add some code. To meet the requirements for a Visual Basic function, you will do several things in your C code. You should declare the function in such a way that the stack maintenance is correct and then export the function in a way to remove name decoration.

The Visual C++ keyword that can perform the correct stack maintenance and parameter order is _stdcall. WINAPI is also defined as _stdcall in Windows.h and is a convenient way to do this.

The _stdcall keyword decorates the function name with a preceding underscore and appends @*n*, where *n* is the number of bytes required to contain the function's arguments and the return value. For example, if you create a function called Foo and use the _stdcall keyword to provide stack maintenance, the function is defined as follows:

```
int WINAPI Foo (int nIndex);
```

The following is the exported name result:

```
_Foo@8
```

Note the preceding underscore that is added by the _stdcall keyword.

To export the call, you can use either the _declspec(dllexport) keyword or a DEF file EXPORT section. The _declspec(dllexport) keyword exports the function but maintains the name decoration. The following example shows how to implement both the _stdcall and _declspec(dllexport) keywords on a function called Foo:

```
_declspec(dllexport) int _stdcall Foo (int nIndex);
```

You'll probably see a lot of sample code written this way, however to make the routine compatible with Visual Basic you need to go a little farther. A DEF file will export the function name and remove the name decoration. The example in Listing 7.1 shows how the EXPORT section of a DEF file is implemented for a function called Foo:

LISTING 7.1   Example of C prototype using *extern* *"C"*

```
EXPORTS
  Foo
```

To export the function properly, you'll make some additions to the DLL projects you started. You can follow along and write the code as you go, or you can cheat just a bit and use the supplied code that is already written for you. In any case, you will add a definition file and place the previous export in it.

To do this, create a new file within the C++ environment and place the export in it. Save it as sampdll.def.

Now you must add this definition file to your project. Refer to Figure 7.2.

FIGURE 7.2

Visual C++ project workspace.

Right-click Source Files, and add the sampdll.def file to the project. Your workspace window should now look like Figure 7.3.

FIGURE 7.3

Visual C++ project workspace with DEF file added.

Prototyping the Function

Now you can prototype the function. A prototype is known in Visual Basic as a declaration. You don't call it that in C, however, because a declare is something different in C. You can refer to the section "Functions" in Chapter 2 for a basic discussion of prototypes.

One thing to remember and avoid: If you are working with a CPP file (C++), you must also guard against some more name decoration produced by C++. I recommend that you always work with C++ files so that you have the power of C++ at your command. To protect against the C++ name mangling, you can use the extern "C" definition. This is shown in Listing 7.2.

The DLL project that you have created does not have an include file beyond the stdafx.h. Add an include file now and place the following prototype in it. The name doesn't really matter beyond making the rest of this sample work. Name this file sampleDLL.h and use that name in the CPP file.

LISTING 7.2   Example of C prototype using extern "C"

```
#ifdef __cplusplus
extern "C"
{
#endif     //__cplusplus
     int WINAPI Foo ( int nIndex );
     //follow with other prototypes that you want protected from name mangling
#ifdef __cplusplus
}
#endif     //__cplusplus
```

Be sure to add this include in the CPP file just below the stdafx.h include.

```
#include "stdafx.h"
#include "sampleDLL.h"
```

This method demonstrates a way to write the prototype within an .h file. This include file can be included within either a C or a C++ module. As you can see from the ifdef, the extern "C" statement is not used if the code is in a C file, but it is used if the file being compiled is a C++ file. The extern "C" is required only on the prototype. I have gotten in the habit of doing this just so that the name decoration doesn't sneak up on me—the extern "C" will never hurt you unless you actually want the name decoration. Because you're using Visual Basic here, you won't need that decoration.

Writing the Function

The function is now prototyped, so you should write the actual function. I'll keep the first one fairly simple: It will just return the parameter passed as a result of the function. This is certainly not the most challenging function that you will undertake, but it will demonstrate several points. Listing 7.3 shows the entire CPP file. Name this one sampDLL.cpp.

LISTING 7.3   Example of C Procedure

```
#include "stdafx.h"
#include "sampdll.h"

BOOL APIENTRY DllMain( HANDLE hModule,
                       DWORD  ul_reason_for_call,
                       LPVOID lpReserved
                     )
{
    return TRUE;
}
int WINAPI Foo ( int nIndex )
{
    return nIndex;
}
```

You can now compile the DLL project. Be sure that you are set for debug mode—this is done from the Build menu.

Before building the project make sure you have the following files and code included in the project.

Sampdll.def   Listing 7.1

Sampdll.h   Listing 7.2

Sampldll.cpp   Listing 7.3

You should be able to build the sample now.

Starting Visual Basic from the C++ Environment

Now you'll set up Visual C to use Visual Basic as a debugging environment, compile the project, start Visual Basic, and then debug the DLL.

Precompiled Headers

C++ has a feature called precompiled headers to speed compiling. This feature compiles the headers included in the stdafx.h file into a PCH file, which in this case is windows.h. For the small DLL, these files are a couple of megabytes. For controls, which also contain the OLE header files, this precompiled header can be 8MB or 9MB. I know that drive space is cheap, but there are limits.

If you don't want these large precompiled header files hanging around, you can turn off this feature in the Project Settings dialog box, shown in Figure 7.4. Be sure to turn

7

C DLL BASICS

this off for each CPP file in the project, and be sure to do it for both debug and release modes. You can also remove the `stdafx.cpp` file from the project. Its only purpose is to provide the precompiled header. You'll still have to turn off precompiled headers in the other source files.

If you don't mind using the disk space, you don't have to change this. I got into this habit when I was working on OLETools at BeCubed. With 64 controls at 6–8MB each, total disk space was about 500MB, or .5GB. This was when drives of 1GB and 2GB were common, so it was a big deal to me.

If you set your project like this, it will take longer to compile, but not all that much longer. If you compile the project with the precompiled headers turned on even one time, you'll have to delete the PCH file manually to get rid of it, even after you turn off this feature.

You will use the Project Settings dialog box for several things—it's instructive to look through it to see what is available. You can access this dialog box from the Project, Settings menu selection; it is a little tricky to use until you become accustomed to how it works.

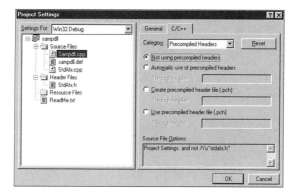

FIGURE 7.4

Project Settings—turning off precompiled headers.

You first need to make a configuration change in the Project Settings dialog box—you should do this for any C/VB project that will use user-defined structures (UDTs). Change your Project Settings dialog box to match the screen in Figure 7.5. Notice that in the left pane, I have chosen the setting for all configurations and have selected Code Generation on the right from the C/C++ tab. Now, from the Struct Member Alignment drop-down menu, change this value to 4 bytes. (I'll explain this change in more detail in "How to pass and use Structures (UDTs)" later in this chapter).

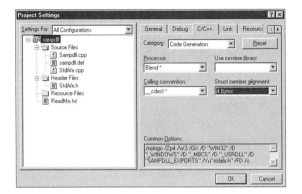

FIGURE 7.5

Project Settings—struct alignment.

This setting matches the struct alignment for Visual Basic 32-bit, and this matters when you start using structures between the two languages.

One more change is necessary for the Project Settings dialog box, and then you'll be ready to compile and test the DLL. When debugging a DLL, you must set the debug target in C++ to something that will load the DLL. In this case, you'll simply use the Visual Basic development environment. Set your Project Settings dialog box as shown in Figure 7.6. Use the button to the right to bring up a Browse dialog box so you can browse for the Visual Basic exe; it will typically be in the directory shown in this figure.

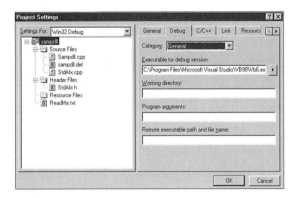

FIGURE 7.6

Project Settings—debug target.

Now that you have the debug target for C++ you can compile the DLL and get started testing it. To compile the DLL, choose the Build sampdll option from the Build menu. If everything completes with no errors, press F5 to start the debug process. This launches Visual Basic, where you'll actually use the DLL you've written.

Declaring and Using a Function from Visual Basic

Here you are, back in Visual Basic—what now? Well, if you've ever declared and called an API function, then you'll be right at home. If not, roll up your sleeves, and let's get to work. Before you actually get to the code and call the routine, let's discuss some aspects of declaring functions in Visual Basic. I'll discuss some particulars of declaring the routine and passing the parameters to the C routine.

Let's say we have a routine that meets the requirements I listed earlier. Our routine must be declared in Visual Basic before you can use it.

When you write a declaration for a C routine in Visual Basic, you must first determine the type of parameters, how they are passed, and the return value (if any).

In this case, you have a routine that has one `int` parameter and that returns an `int` as a result of the routine. Unlike Visual Basic, where the default way to pass a parameter is by reference, in C the default is to pass a parameter by value. Let's take a moment to clarify the difference.

If a parameter is passed by value, the actual variable value is placed on the stack during the call to the function. The called function gets this value from the stack, but this function cannot access the original variable—it can access only the value that is on the stack. In contrast, when a parameter is passed by reference, this means that the address of the original variable is placed on the stack; the function retrieves this address and actually works with the value at the variable location in memory. Thus, the function is free to change the parameter's value when the parameter is passed by reference.

Notice that the default in Visual Basic (previous to .NET) is to pass parameters by reference. In this first case, you are using `ByVal` to force this routine to pass the parameter by value.

This line is an example of declaring a parameter by value:

```
Declare Function Foo Lib "libname.dll" (ByVal nIndex As Long) As Long
```

In contrast, this line is an example of declaring a value by reference:

```
Declare Function Foo Lib "libname.dll" (ByRef nIndex As Long) As Long
```

Some functions can vary in the way they pass values from the DLL. The `LPARAM` parameter in the `SendMessage` API is an example of this type of behavior. It can contain various types of variables depending on the message being processed. A common way to handle this is by using an alias to declare different functions.

This line is an example of using an alias to provide two routines that call the same routine, one by value and the other by reference:

```
Declare Function Foobyval Lib "libname.dll" Alias "Foo" (ByVal nIndex As Long)
As Long
Declare Function Fooref Lib "libname.dll" Alias "Foo" (ByRef nIndex As Long) As
Long
```

Another way to do the same thing is by using As Any to declare the parameter and then calling the function in any manner that you prefer.

```
Declare Function Foo Lib "libname.dll" (nIndex As Any) As Long
```

Then use the ByVal keyword to pass the parameter by value, or place the variable in the call with the ByRef keyword to pass the parameter by reference.

7

C DLL BASICS

ByRef **Keyword**

I am using the ByRef keyword in the samples in this chapter. In reality, in Visual Basic 6 the default is by value as I mentioned before. This means the routine will work the same way from VB6 whether you use the ByRef keyword or not.

I use it here for clarity. .NET changes this default convention, so it's a good idea to get used to specifying explicitly what you want.

This line shows an example of using the function by value:

```
x = Foo (ByVal nIndex)
```

Here's an example of using the function by reference:

```
x = Foo (ByRef nIndex)
```

Now that you understand a little about declaring functions and passing parameters, let's add a declaration to the sample Visual Basic program and call the function.

I'll use the As Any declaration and explore what goes on the stack for the routine. Notice that all the routines that you previously declared used a Long variable in the Visual Basic declares. A C int and a C long are the same type of variable in 32-bit—they are 4-byte integers, or longs. A Visual Basic integer, a 2-byte integer, is the same as a C short.

Start Visual Basic and begin a new EXE. You will need to add a standard module to place the declares. Although this is not absolutely necessary, it is the cleanest or most effective way to this. If you place the declares in a form, you must make them private, and then the declared function can be used only within that form.

```
Declare Function Foo Lib "libname.dll" (nIndex As Any) As Long
```

NOTE

If you are using the supplied code, the parameter to this function is declared ByVal. If you want to follow along in code, you'll need to change the declaration temporarily.

Notice that the libname.dll will have to be changed to the name of the DLL that you are working with. If that DLL is not on the path, you'll also need to include the full path to the DLL. This typically will be the case when you are working in the environment. If you distribute a program that uses function calls like this, only the DLL filename will appear in the declare. You will depend upon the DLL being on the computer's path or in the program's directory during execution of the program.

Once you have the function declared, let's call it and look at the results. Put a button on the form, and place a couple lines of code in it.

```
Private Sub Command1_Click
    Dim lvar as Long
    lvar = 5
    Debug.Print Foo(ByRef lvar)
    Debug.Print Foo(ByVal lvar)
End Sub
```

Now run the project and click the button. You will see two values in the debug window. I can't tell in advance what the first one will be—this is the address of the lvar variable. The second value printed will be the value of the lvar variable—in this case, 5. Let's take a moment to understand what happened.

Because you declared a function that takes a long value, you can actually pass a long variable to it or the address of most any variable. This is because addresses are four bytes long. You declared the parameter in the routine As Any, so you were free to pass the variable by reference even though the routine was actually designed to take a long by value. In practice, you will usually declare and pass variables of the type that the routine is expecting.

In calling the routine, you first passed the address of the variable, which is what you see printed first in the debug window. Then you passed the value of the variable, which you see printed second in the debug window.

Debugging the C++ Code

Debugging C++ code can be very frustrating for a Visual Basic programmer. In Visual Basic, you have an IDE that allows debugging at a level that is not experienced in many languages, including C++.

C++ has recently added some things that try to make the experience better, but I find the traditional way of debugging in C++ to work best. This is a code, compile, and test sequence that is repeated until the program behaves as you want it to.

The technique that is often used in Visual Basic is one to let it crash, fix it (because it dumped you on the code that crashed), and then go on. My name for that approach is the "run until it doesn't crash" approach. This doesn't work in the C++ environment. C++ isn't going to crash and dump on the line of code and then allow you to fix it and go on. This is just the nature of what you are doing, which is debugging an executable file. A sample will demonstrate what I am talking about.

First, if you are still in Visual Basic, exit now and get back to this project in C++—you might want to save your work first. Don't use the menu choice in C++ to stop debugging because it shuts down VB rather ungracefully, causing you to lose your work.

Place the following code in the C routine you've been working with, and then compile it in C++. This routine will give you a warning about the runtime error that will occur. The whole point of the example is to generate the error, so ignore the warning. Then run Visual Basic from the C++ environment so you are debugging in VB.

```
int WINAPI Foo ( int nIndex )
{
    int x=2;
    x = x / 0;
    return nIndex;
}
```

Load the sample that calls this routine, run the program, and invoke the routine. Your VB program will generate the divide-by-zero error and dump on the line that generated the error, which is the call to the Foo function. Notice that C++ didn't help you out here at all—this is typical of a runtime error in C.

You can debug the routine by placing a breakpoint in the Foo routine and commanding Visual Basic to continue running. This will drop you on the breakpoint in Visual C and enable you to step trace the function and find the line generating the error. (Remember, C++ step into is F11, not F8; step over is F10, not Shift+F8).

Stepping through it still generates the same results. You end up back in Visual Basic with an error message, but at least you've found the line.

C++ Runtime Errors

I have found that many times when the C code generates a runtime error in this way, the Visual Basic message box is displayed behind C++.

7

C DLL BASICS

> This can make it difficult to tell what happened. You might still be trying to step trace, and the machine is just sitting there beeping at you.
>
> If this is happening to you, switching back to the VB form using the Taskbar will bring up the error message that you can't see.

Tutorial Summary

In review, so far you've learned how to write and export a C/C++ function from a DLL so that it can be called from Visual Basic. You've also learned how to declare that routine in Visual Basic and call it.

What you have done so far in this chapter demonstrates a very simple DLL that supports Visual Basic. Now I will delve into the intricacies of writing DLLs that support Visual Basic. I will no longer provide every single step required: Instead, the code will be presented, and you will place the code in the project and then compile and run the projects based on the examples provided earlier.

Passing Numeric Variables

Passing numeric variables to C routines is the simplest form of calling functions from Visual Basic. This is what you have done in the first example. You need to know only whether the variable should be passed by value or by reference. The defaults for the two languages are opposite, so the probability of messing this up is high.

Four-Byte Integers (Longs)

In Listing 7.4, you'll find a few simple C prototypes, followed by the Visual Basic declarations. These routines demonstrate how you might handle a four-byte integer parameter. Most Visual Basic programmers know this as a `long`, but in 32-bit C, this is an `int` or a `long`. I am showing the C code using `int`, but I could just as well have used `long` within the C code.

LISTING 7.4   A Listing for Visual Basic Long Calls

```
//C prototype, parameter is by value
int WINAPI Foo ( int nIndex );

'VB Declaration, parameter is by value
Declare Function Foo Lib "libname.dll" (ByVal nIndex As Long) As Long

//C prototype, parameter is by reference
int WINAPI Foo ( int *nIndex );
```

LISTING 7.4   Continued

```
'VB Declaration, parameter is by reference
Declare Function Foo Lib "libname.dll" (ByRef nIndex As Long) As Long
```

Now let's add a by reference routine to the C code, recompile it, and call it. If you're still in Visual Basic, exit back to Visual C++. When you're there, add the prototype and code to the C sample DLL.

The prototype is added to the sampdll.h file. Keep it within the extern "C" declaration.

```
int WINAPI FooRef ( int *nIndex );
```

The implementation is in the CPP file:

```
int WINAPI FooRef ( int *nIndex )
{
    //since nIndex holds a pointer you
    //use the * to reference the value.
      *nIndex += 10;
    return *nIndex + 5;
}
```

Don't forget to remove the code in the function Foo that generates the error the function Foo should look like the following code.

```
int WINAPI Foo ( int nIndex )
{
    return nIndex;
}
```

Notice that in the by reference function, you refer to the value of the referenced variable with the * operator. This is the indirection operator and may be used either on the left or the right side of the expression.

Also, don't forget to add the function to the DEF file.

```
EXPORTS
    Foo
    FooRef
```

You can start Visual Basic and now change the declarations as follows:

```
Declare Function Foo Lib "libname.dll" (ByVal nIndex As Long) As Long
Declare Function FooRef Lib "libname.dll" (ByRef nIndex As Long) As Long
```

Let's add the following code to the Click event now, and see the results:

7

C DLL BASICS

```
Private Sub Command1_Click
    Dim lvar as Long
    lvar = 5
    Debug.Print Foo(lvar)
    Debug.Print FooRef(lvar)
    Debug.Print lvar
End Sub
```

The results in the debug window will be as follows:

```
5
20
15
```

This is because the function Foo simply returns lvar. Function FooRef returns lvar + 15. FooRef also modifies the variable lvar by adding 10 to it, which is shown in the last Debug.Print statement.

You can generate and call similar functions that use a Visual Basic integer, single, double, or Boolean data type.

Two-Byte Integers (Integer)

The main thing to remember about Visual Basic integers is that they translate to C shorts. Other than that, they are handled in the same manner as longs. The following lines show how to prototype in C and declare in VB, a function that uses a C short, both by reference and by value:

```
//C prototype, parameter is by value
short WINAPI Foo ( short nIndex );

'VB Declaration, parameter is by value
Declare Function Foo Lib "libname.dll" (ByVal nIndex As Integer) As Integer

//C prototype, parameter is by reference
short WINAPI Foo ( short *nIndex );

'VB Declaration, parameter is by reference
Declare Function Foo Lib "libname.dll" (ByRef nIndex As Short) As Short
```

Four-byte Real (Single)

A Visual Basic single translates to a C float. The following code demonstrates the float/single data type in a function:

```
//C prototype, parameter is by value
float WINAPI Foo ( float nIndex );
```

```
'VB Declaration, parameter is by value
Declare Function Foo Lib "libname.dll"  (ByVal nIndex As Single) As Single

//C prototype, parameter is by reference
float WINAPI Foo ( float *nIndex );

'VB Declaration, parameter is by reference
Declare Function Foo Lib "libname.dll" (ByRef nIndex As Single) As Single
```

Eight-Byte Real (Double)

Finally, this is a data type that is the same in Visual Basic and C, with no ambiguities. This is the only numeric type that has a one-to-one name relationship with C. The following code shows the C prototypes and the VB declares for the double type:

```
//C prototype, parameter is by value
double WINAPI Foo ( double nIndex );

'VB Declaration, parameter is by value
Declare Function Foo Lib "libname.dll" (ByVal nIndex As Double) As Double

//C prototype, parameter is by reference
double WINAPI Foo ( double *nIndex );

'VB Declaration, parameter is by reference
Declare Function Foo Lib "libname.dll"  (ByRef nIndex As Double) As Double
```

Boolean

The Boolean data type turns out to be a rather interesting little animal. In Visual Basic, the Boolean data type is two bytes and is allowed to have one of two values: 0 or -1 (ffff hex). This translates to a short or, in more recent terms, a VARIANT_BOOL (which is defined as a short). The following code shows how to handle a Visual Basic Boolean:

```
//C prototype, parameter is by value
short WINAPI Foo ( short nIndex );

'VB Declaration, parameter is by value
Declare Function Foo Lib "libname.dll" (ByVal nIndex As Boolean) As Boolean

//C prototype, parameter is by reference
short WINAPI Foo ( short *nIndex );

'VB Declaration, parameter is by reference
Declare Function Foo Lib "libname.dll" (ByRef nIndex As Boolean) As Boolean
```

C programmers are familiar with a BOOL type with possible values of 1 and 0. The C BOOL type in 32-bit is four bytes (a true study in inefficiency). There is no real reason to use this type in Visual Basic unless you are forced to call a routine with this type parameter. Declare it as a long if you have to deal with it.

Currency

The Visual Basic currency type has no actual counterpart in C/C++. In reality, its bit structure is like that of an eight-byte integer. Of course, the currency type is a decimal number with four decimal places. It is stored as an eight-byte integer divided by 10,000.

It is possible to pass the currency data type to DLLs, but I'm not sure why you would. The Windows 64-bit integer math routines are very crude, and these routines are the way you would have to manipulate the LARGE_INTEGER type in C. It has more use in some Windows APIs where the LARGE_INTEGER type is used. You can replace the call with the currency type and then multiply the result by 10,000.

Using Strings

If you haven't read the section "Strings and Things," in Chapter 4, you may want to do so before going through this discussion. That section discusses string types, Unicode, and other string issues related to the Windows system and programming languages.

Here I will talk about passing and using three types of strings from Visual Basic to C. These are the C strings formed by passing a basic string by value, the BSTR, and the byte array passed as a C string.

Passing C Strings (ByVal)

This is the most common way to pass strings to a DLL routine. Almost all WinAPI functions receive their strings this way. It might be confusing at first to try to understand why this works, and you may think that Visual Basic is doing some black magic underneath all of this. That is not the case, though, and the reason it works is quite simple.

To understand, you first must know something about the string type that Visual Basic uses—what they are and how they are constructed. Internally, Visual Basic uses a BSTR, which is an OLE string type that consists of a header and a zero-delimited string (asciiz). The header contains a pointer to this string and the length; you are not really concerned about the format of the header, except that the first part of it is a pointer to the C type string.

Visual Basic normally passes variables by reference, passing a string with no ByVal qualifier would pass a pointer to the start of this header or, by definition, a pointer to a BSTR. However, passing this variable ByVal would place the address of the C string on the stack, which is exactly what most C DLLs are looking for (a pointer to a C string). So, there you have it—no more mystery.

Function return values of this type are not allowed because there is no corresponding data type in Visual Basic. The C procedure can modify a string passed to it as a parameter in this manner because it does have the address. However, it cannot modify the length, so you must make sure that the string is long enough to handle whatever the C routine will do to it.

Listing 7.5 shows a sample with a C string as a parameter.

LISTING 7.5   VB and C Implementation of a String

```
//C prototype
int WINAPI Foo ( LPTSTR lpStr );
'VB Declaration, parameter is by value
Declare Function Foo Lib "libname.dll" (ByVal str As String) As Long
```

Within the C function, work with the string in a normal manner—it is an array of characters, like any other C string. One thing of interest to note is that 32-bit Visual Basic will convert this string from Unicode to ANSI when passing control from Visual Basic to C, and from ANSI back to Unicode on the way back in. This can affect performance dramatically.

Handling a BSTR

With BSTR type as passed by reference to a DLL routine, you discover a little bit of madness. This variable, which by definition contains a Unicode string, is converted to ANSI by Visual Basic, just like any string in a call to a DLL routine.

> **NOTE**
>
> This truly does not make a lot of sense. Let me say now that this Unicode-to-ANSI conversion and back is an animal of declared functions in Visual Basic. This does not happen (unexpectedly) in COM objects or any routines defined with a type library. This is demonstrated in the section "Type Libraries and DLLs" in Chapter 8.

The BSTR is the string type used internally by Visual Basic; Visual Basic also uses a Unicode representation of strings internally. The fact that it is converted to an ANSI string by Visual Basic when passed to a DLL routine—and, of course, back to Unicode when passed back—is troublesome. This conversion includes function return values. You should take that into consideration when working with the string in the DLL. Most of the functions that deal with OLE strings assume that the string part is Unicode, but when using a BSTR passed into a DLL from Visual Basic, the string will be ANSI.

If you pass a BSTR to a DLL function, you should be sure that the DLL function is expecting one. If the function is a declared function, it should also be expecting the string to be in ASCII format.

A piece of good news is that you can use a BSTR as the result of a function. There are OLE functions to manipulate this string type. The routines that manipulate a BSTR are shown here. Note that the OLE routines shown are the routines that offer byte operations because Visual Basic converts the strings to ASCII before your DLL function sees the BSTR.

```
SysAllocStringByteLen

SysAllocStringByteLen

SysFreeString

SysStringByteLen
```

Let's take a look at a C prototype and a Visual Basic declaration that would use a string in this manner.

In working with the string in the C routine, you'll use the appropriate OLE functions and, in this case, return an uppercase representation of the string.

Listing 7.6 shows how to handle the BSTR type. You can add the C code to the sampdll project you have been working with and it will compile. If you receive a number of errors, check the stdafx.h file and be sure that the following line is not present or is commented out. This definition will leave out many things in the windows.h header, including the BSTR type.

```
#define WIN32_LEAN_AND_MEAN
```

LISTING 7.6   VB and C Implementation of BSTR

```
'VB Declaration, parameter is by reference
Declare Function UpperCaseByRef Lib "libname.dll" (ByRef str As String) As
➥String

//C prototype, parameter is by reference
BSTR WINAPI UpperCaseByRef ( BSTR *lpStr );

BSTR WINAPI UpperCaseByRef (BSTR *pbstrOriginal)
{
    BSTR bstrUpperCase;
    int i;
```

LISTING 7.6 Continued

```
        int cbOriginalLen;
        LPSTR strSrcByRef, strDst;

        cbOriginalLen = SysStringByteLen(*pbstrOriginal);
        bstrUpperCase = SysAllocStringByteLen(NULL, cbOriginalLen);
        strSrcByRef = (LPSTR)*pbstrOriginal;
        strDst = (LPSTR)bstrUpperCase;
        for(i=0; i<=cbOriginalLen; i++)
            *strDst++ = toupper(*strSrcByRef++);
        return bstrUpperCase;
}
```

Notice that within this routine, you are using only the byte functions when working with the BSTR. Notice also that you are using only LPSTR (not LPTSTR) because the string will *always* be ASCII, never Unicode, even if you compile the DLL as Unicode.

In Chapter 8, the section called "Type Libraries and DLLs" looks at how to write a DLL function that can receive strings in Unicode format.

Passing Byte Arrays

The byte data type was added to Visual Basic to have an in-memory way of representing data with an unknown or binary format. Programmers traditionally had done this with the string data type. This methodology carried with it a certain lack of efficiency and a general lack of elegance to the code. The byte data type was born to handle data of this type.

The byte data type can be used as a simple variable. In this context, it is really a numeric data type and corresponds to the char data type in C. The most common way to use a byte data type is as an array. When used in this manner, a byte array is same as character arrays in C, except that they don't necessarily end with a terminating ASCII 0.

A byte array can be substituted at any time for a C string (Visual Basic string passed ByVal), as long as you terminate the array with a character 0. The prototype and usage in C is exactly the same as a C char string. In Visual Basic, the Declare can be done in such a way that either a string or a byte array can be passed to a particular routine.

Here is a sample DLL function that will enable you to pass either a Visual Basic string or a byte array:

```
//C prototype
int WINAPI Foo ( LPSTR lpStr );
'VB Declaration, parameter is as any
Declare Function FooStr Lib "libname.dll" ( str As Any ) As Long
```

7

C DLL BASICS

To use this with a string, enter this line:

```
a& = FooStr ( ByVal somestring$)
```

To use this with a byte array, enter this line:

```
a& = FooStr ( ByRef abytearray(0) )
```

The default way for Visual Basic to pass variables is by reference. Placing the first element of an array in a call to a function places the address for that element on the stack. This is also the address for the start of the array—in this case, the start of the C string.

Note that this technique passes the address for the start of the data in the array, not the array itself. There is a difference in passing the data of the array and passing the array itself. I will discuss this when I talk about passing arrays to functions.

One thing of note about byte arrays is that they can be much faster than intrinsic Visual Basic strings. This is due to several issues. First, in terms of calling declared functions, the string represented by byte arrays do not undergo the Unicode-to-ANSI and ANSI-to-Unicode conversions on the way in and out of the call. If a call is happening repeatedly, this can be very important.

If the ultimate representation of the string is to be ANSI, there is no real advantage to carrying the string in Unicode. Byte arrays can be ANSI internally and can be converted to Unicode when this is required.

Second, the overhead associated with Visual Basic strings is not imposed on byte arrays. This is easy to see in a large repeated concatenation of strings. The speed difference when using a byte array compared to a Visual Basic string can be hundreds of times. A concatenation can be much more difficult to write for a byte array, but it can be worth it.

Passing and Using Structures (UDTs)

You can pass a user-defined type (UDT) by reference to a function. Visual Basic also allows functions to return a user-defined type. You cannot pass a UDT by value to a DLL function. A user-defined type is returned in the same way it would be with any other function, as demonstrated in the code example that follows.

It is important to make sure that the UDT as defined in Visual Basic is of the same size as the C structure defined in the DLL by enforcing a strict one-to-one alignment of corresponding members in both UDTs. This can be a problem because Visual Basic packs user-defined types on a dword (four-byte) boundary. So, compile your C code with a four-byte struct member alignment compiler setting. The default setting is eight bytes, so you must change this in your C DLL. I typically do this in any DLL I write to support Visual Basic, although this is the only real reason for doing this.

An integer in VB is always two bytes, whereas an int in C is four bytes. If the C type is int, the VB type will have to be long. Otherwise, if short and long are used in C, the corresponding integer and long types can be used in VB.

It is also important to note that again strings will be converted to ANSI. So, a declaration of String * 10 will be 10 bytes when the structure is passed to C, even though the representation of the string within Visual Basic requires 20 bytes.

The function in Listing 7.7 shows how to pass and return a user-defined type (UDT) from a DLL function. This UDT contains all possible data types that you are concerned with. The DLL function, called from Visual Basic takes a UDT by reference, and returns a copy of the UDT to Visual Basic. The DLL function modifies the members of the passed UDT, which is reflected back in VB. You can add this code to the same sampdll project, again make sure the LEAN_AND_MEAN definition is removed.

The size of the UDT passed to the DLL will be 76 bytes (after padding), if you check the sizeof(udtRet) in the following example that is what you get. However, the size of the UDT actually stored by VB is 88 bytes. The extra 12 bytes account for the fact that the fixed-length string member, strg, is stored as a Unicode string (and padded to a four-byte alignment), and the Unicode string in the string is converted to ANSI when the DLL routine is called. Visual Basic will report the length of the structure at 72. This is what you actually get if you add the lengths of the variables. However the number reported by VB does not include the padding required by the byte alignment and it counts the UNICODE string as 11 characters.

If this all seems pretty confusing, it is. The good news is as long as you set your byte alignment to 4 in the C++ compiler and match the variables properly, it will work.

LISTING 7.7 C Implementation of a UDT

```c
#include <windows.h>
#include <ole2.h>
#define MAXSIZE 11

#define CCONV _stdcall
#define NOMANGLE

typedef struct
{
    short intgr;        //integer
    long lng;           //long
    float sng;          //single
    double dbl;         //double
    LARGE_INTEGER cur;          //currency
    double dtm;         //date
```

LISTING 7.7   Continued

```
    short bln;          //boolean
    BYTE byt;           //byte
    VARIANT vnt;         //variant
    BSTR vstrg;          //variable length string
    char strg[MAXSIZE];    //fixed length string
    short array[1][1][2];     //array of integers (2 Bytes in VB)
} UDT;

UDT WINAPI CopyUDT(UDT *pUdt)
{
    UDT udtRet;
    int i, cbLen;
    LPSTR strSrc;
    int cbOriginalLen;

    // Copy Passed-in UDT into the UDT that has to be returned
    udtRet.intgr = pUdt->intgr;
    udtRet.cur = pUdt->cur;
    udtRet.lng = pUdt->lng;
    udtRet.sng = pUdt->sng;
    udtRet.dbl = pUdt->dbl;
    udtRet.dtm = pUdt->dtm;
    udtRet.bln = pUdt->bln;
    udtRet.byt = pUdt->byt;
    udtRet.array[0][0][0] = pUdt->array[0][0][0];
    cbOriginalLen = SysStringByteLen(pUdt->vstrg);
    udtRet.vstrg = SysAllocStringByteLen((const char *)pUdt->vstrg,
➡cbOriginalLen);

    // must initialize all Variants
    VariantInit(&udtRet.vnt);
    VariantCopy(&udtRet.vnt, &pUdt->vnt);

    strncpy(udtRet.strg, pUdt->strg, MAXSIZE-1);

    // Modify members of passed-in UDT
    cbLen = SysStringByteLen(pUdt->vstrg);
    strSrc = (LPSTR)pUdt->vstrg;
    for(i=0; i<cbLen; i++)
        *strSrc++ = toupper(*strSrc);

    pUdt->array[0][0][0]++;
    VariantChangeType(&pUdt->vnt, &pUdt->vnt, NULL, VT_BSTR);
```

LISTING 7.7 C ontinued

```c
    pUdt->intgr++;
    pUdt->lng++;
    pUdt->sng += (float)1.99;
    pUdt->dbl += 1.99;
    pUdt->cur.LowPart += 1999;
    pUdt->dtm++;
    pUdt->bln = ~pUdt->bln;
    pUdt->byt = toupper(pUdt->byt);
    strncpy(pUdt->strg, "Bill", MAXSIZE-1);
    return udtRet;
}
```

Notice that once again, you should be careful to use the byte functions when working with the BSTR. This is critical because the string will be expressed as ANSI.

Listing 7.8 shows some sample code in Visual Basic that might call this function

LISTING 7.18 C Implementation of a UDT

```vb
'these first lines should so in a VB module
Declare Function CopyUDT Lib "sampdll.dll" (u As UDT) As UDT
Type UDT
    intgr As Integer
    lng As Long
    sng As Single
    dbl As Double
    cur As Currency
    dtm As Date
    bln As Boolean
    byt As Byte
    vnt As Variant
    vstrg As String
    strg As String * 11
    arr(0, 0, 1) As Integer
End Type
'the following lines go in a button click
Private Sub Command1_Click()
    Dim u As UDT
    Dim uResult As UDT
    u.arr(0, 0, 0) = 1
    u.arr(0, 0, 1) = 1
    u.bln = True
    u.byt = 1
    u.cur = 500
```

7

C DLL BASICS

LISTING 7.18   Continued

```
    u.dbl = 456.76
    u.dtm = Now
    u.intgr = 6
    u.lng = 12
    u.sng = 234.56
    u.strg = "a test"
    u.vnt = "A variant"
    u.vstrg = "Another test"
'here's the function call
    uResult = CopyUDT(u)
    Debug.Print uResult.arr(0, 0, 0)
    Debug.Print uResult.arr(0, 0, 1)
    Debug.Print uResult.bln
    Debug.Print uResult.byt
    Debug.Print uResult.cur
    Debug.Print uResult.dbl
    Debug.Print uResult.dtm
    Debug.Print uResult.intgr
    Debug.Print uResult.lng
    Debug.Print uResult.sng
    Debug.Print uResult.strg
    Debug.Print uResult.vnt
    Debug.Print uResult.vstrg
End Sub
```

Passing and Using Variants

A Visual Basic variant and a C variant have the same format, so it becomes quite easy to analyze the content of a variant in a C DLL and even return a variant as a result of a function. A variant can be passed by value or by reference.

Note that a variant can contain a string—specifically, a BSTR—and by now you are accustomed to Visual Basic converting all strings to ANSI. This is the one exception. A BSTR inside a variant is *not* converted to ANSI and back. Consequently, you are working with a Unicode string in the DLL.

Following is a simple C prototype, followed by the Visual Basic declaration.

```
//C prototype, parameter is by value
short WINAPI VariantArg(VARIANT vt)
'VB Declaration, parameter is by value
Declare Function VariantArg Lib "libname.dll" (ByVal vt As Variant) As Integer
//C prototype, parameter is by reference
```

```
short WINAPI VariantArg(VARIANT *vt)
'VB Declaration, parameter is by reference
Declare Function VariantArg Lib "libname.dll" (ByRef vt As Variant) As Integer
```

This is a short sample that demonstrates how to use a variant in a C DLL. This code can be added to the same sampdll project. This function also requires the removal of the LEAN_AND_MEAN definition in the stdafx.h file.

```
short WINAPI VariantArg(VARIANT vt)
{
    int i;
    char *pcBuf;
    if (vt.vt == VT_DISPATCH)     // variant is an object
        return -1;
    else if (vt.vt == VT_BSTR)
    {      // variant is a string
        i = SysStringLen(vt.bstrVal);
        pcBuf = (char *)malloc(i + 1);
        WideCharToMultiByte(CP_ACP, 0, vt.bstrVal, i, pcBuf, i, NULL, NULL);
        i = atoi(pcBuf);
        free(pcBuf);
        return (short)i;
    }
    else if (vt.vt == VT_I2)      // variant is an integer
        return vt.iVal;
    else     // variant is something else
        return -3;
}
```

Notice that a variant that contains a BSTR is an exception to Visual Basic's habit of converting Unicode string data to ANSI. The string contained in the BSTR passed as a variant will be left as a Unicode string. In this particular function, you are converting the string to ANSI yourself. This is not necessarily required, but it is shown here for demonstration purposes. It is perfectly fine to use the BSTR in Unicode format.

The following code can be used in Visual Basic to call this function.

```
'put this in a module
Declare Function VariantArg Lib "sampdll.dll" (ByVal vt As Variant) As Integer
'this goes in a button click
Private Sub Command1_Click()
    Dim v As Variant
    V = 4
    Debug.Print VariantArg(v)
End Sub
```

7

C DLL BASICS

Passing and Using Arrays

Two ways exist by which to pass arrays to DLL functions; more to the point there is one way to pass the array and one way to pass only the data.

When an array is passed to a DLL function, Visual Basic actually passes a pointer to a pointer to a SAFEARRAY structure, or LPSAFEARRAY FAR *. Safe Arrays contain information about the number of dimensions and their bounds. The data referred to by an array descriptor is stored in column-major order (the leftmost dimension changes first), which is the same scheme used by Visual Basic, but different than that used by Pascal conventions or C. The subscripts for SafeArrays are zero-based.

When you pass only the data, the information about the subscripts is not passed, so you would have to determine size in some other manner. Also, because multidimension Visual Basic arrays are stored somewhat differently than C arrays, this would have to be taken into consideration.

The OLE 2.0 APIs can be used to access and manipulate the array. Table 7.1 lists the OLE 2.0 functions that access arrays.

TABLE 7.1   Safe Array Functions

Visual Basic Command	OLE API
Lbound	SafeArrayGetLBound
Ubound	SafeArrayGetUBound
	SafeArrayGetElement
	SafeArrayGetElemsize
	SafeArrayGetDim

The OLE API function SafeArrayGetDim returns the number of dimensions in the array, and the functions SafeArrayGetLBound and SafeArrayGetUBound return the lower and upper bounds for a given array dimension. All these functions require a parameter of type LPSAFEAR-RAY to describe the target array.

When working with string arrays, if you decide to create a string array within a DLL, be sure to create the new elements in the string array as Unicode strings. This is required because VB uses Unicode to store strings internally, but it converts them to ANSI on the way into a DLL. VB normally converts them back to Unicode on the way out of the DLL, but because I am talking about an array that has been *newly created inside the DLL* and passed back as a variant, VB will not know enough to do the conversion.

The example demonstrates passing and returning arrays of strings, but it can easily be modified to work for arrays of any permitted data type. The sample copies an entire array but changes only one element of that new array to a Unicode string. If the entire array were to be copied properly, all the elements would have to be modified to Unicode. You can avoid this by simply passing an array of variants instead of an array of strings.

The main point of the sample is to introduce you to safe arrays and to be sure that you understand what happens to strings when passed through an array.

LISTING 7.9   C Implementation of Arrays

```
VARIANT WINAPI CopyArray(LPSAFEARRAY FAR *ppsa)
{
    VARIANT vnt;
    SAFEARRAY     sa2;
    LPSAFEARRAY   lpsa2=&sa2;      BSTR element = NULL;
    long rgIndices[] = {0,1,2};
    // Must initialize variant first
    VariantInit(&vnt);

    // copy the passed-in array to the array to be returned in
    // variant
    SafeArrayCopy (*ppsa, &lpsa2);
    // Get the value of the string element at (0,1,2). This will
    // be an ANSI string.
    SafeArrayGetElement (lpsa2, rgIndices, &element);

    // Convert this to Unicode, as VB4 (32-bit) will not do
    // so for you, as the string is inside an array *NEWLY
    // CREATED* inside the DLL!
    unsigned int length = SysStringByteLen(element);
    BSTR wcElement = NULL;

    wcElement = SysAllocStringLen(NULL, length*2);
    MultiByteToWideChar(CP_ACP,MB_PRECOMPOSED,(LPCSTR)element,__
        -1, (LPWSTR)wcElement, length*2);

    // Put this Unicode string back into the corresponding
    // location in the array to be returned
    SafeArrayPutElement (lpsa2, rgIndices, wcElement);
    SysFreeString (wcElement);
    SysFreeString (element);
    element = SysAllocString((BSTR)"Hello Again!");

    // Modify the same element (0,1,2) of the passed-in array
    SafeArrayPutElement (*ppsa, rgIndices, element);
    SysFreeString (element);
```

LISTING 7.9   Continued

```
// store the array to be returned in a variant
vnt.vt = VT_ARRAY|VT_BYREF|VT_BSTR;
vnt.pparray = &lpsa2;

return vnt;
}
```

Unicode and ANSI

I've given a lot of attention to the Unicode/ANSI issue in Visual Basic because it is an important consideration when working with C DLLs. I'm sure that the developers of Visual Basic struggled with this issue some bit before coming to the decision to make Visual Basic Unicode internally.

The first question might be, was it wise to make Visual Basic Unicode internally? This was done with the very first version that was 32-bit-compatible (version 4). The fact that the developers based Visual Basic on OLE technology at the time really left them no choice. Internally, Visual Basic had to be compatible with OLE internals, and OLE knows nothing about ANSI—it speaks Unicode.

Then, of course, there was the issue of what to do with API calls—most would expect the strings to come to them in ANSI form, particularly because the predominant system at the time was Windows 95. This was the only way to allow Visual Basic to be compatible with all operating systems in one executable.

If you write C routines to be called from Visual Basic that involve strings, or even if you call Windows APIs, it is advisable to be aware of what is happening to the strings. That is why I will recap all the issues and circumstances under which Visual Basic does or does not make these conversions.

This list defines the behavior of strings as they are passed to and from library functions. This list assumes that the function is called based on a declaration within Visual Basic. The type library method of calling functions, although I haven't talked about it yet, is listed here:

- **ByVal string parameter** —Converted to ANSI on the way to the routine, and converted back to Unicode on the way back.
- **ByRef string parameter (BSTR)** —Converted to ANSI on the way to the routine, and converted back to Unicode on the way back.

- **Function result as string**—Converted to Unicode on the way back. Don't build the result of a declared function in Unicode, or it will be converted again and become "double Unicode."

- **Byte array parameter**—Not converted. Byte arrays remain in the form in which they are passed.

- **UDT containing fixed-length string**—Converted to ANSI on the way to the routine, and converted back to Unicode on the way back.

- **UDT containing BSTR**—Converted to ANSI on the way to the routine, and converted back to Unicode on the way back.

- **String arrays**—Converted to ANSI on the way to the routine, and converted back to Unicode on the way back (yes, the *entire* array).

- **Function result as string arrays**—Because these are passed back within variants, no conversions are made. You should ensure that string arrays that you create as a result of a function are Unicode.

- **Variant parameter containing BSTR**—Not converted. The variant is the exception to this Visual Basic rule of converting strings.

- **Function result as a variant containing a BSTR**—Not converted.

- **Function defined in a type library containing a string**—Conversions made to strings based on their type. Consequently, Unicode strings (BSTR and LPWSTR) will come through as Unicode strings. ANSI strings (LPSTR) will be translated to ANSI and back.

When you first observe the list, it appears that not a lot of logic is applied here. In reality, a lot of thought went into this to give programmers flexibility and to keep from breaking any more 16-bit code than was absolutely necessary.

The fact is that Visual Basic is Unicode internally—you have to deal with that. Because many of the systems running today still run on ANSI-based operating systems (Windows 95/98), then it stands to reason that a lot of your DLL code might want these strings in ANSI form. Microsoft has saved you the trouble of coding that into every routine, but C and C++ programmers are not afforded that luxury. If they have Unicode strings, they must always be aware of that format and deal with it themselves, either by writing code or by setting compiler options.

You have the capability to get the strings to the DLL functions in either ANSI or Unicode format. All you have to do is decide which you need and then set up the function properly within Visual Basic.

So which format should the strings follow? That really depends upon the function. If you are simply modifying the string in some manner and handing it back to Visual Basic, then you really don't need the overhead of the conversion. For example, the uppercase function that I demonstrated earlier to show how BSTRs are passed is *not* the way to write that function; all the conversions just slow it down.

However, consider what would happen if you wanted to call a Windows API from the DLL. Unless you were coding for NT or Windows 2000 *exclusively*, you might as well let Visual Basic do the conversion. To be compatible with both ANSI and Unicode operating systems, you must call the ANSI versions of the Windows API.

Summary

In this chapter, I explained how to write C DLLs. I also looked closer at handling variable types between Visual Basic and C. This information can serve you well in other areas besides writing function-based DLLs.

While function-based DLLs are not the most modern means of supplying code to Visual Basic programs, they are the most enduring of any of the add-on technologies. VBXes are gone, ActiveX controls will probably follow in their path, but DLLs still endure. This is because they are a basic technology in the operating system.

C DLL Practical Examples

IN THIS CHAPTER

This chapter looks at some more advanced issues of DLLs. Because this technology is no longer mainstream, I'll also provide some concrete examples of why you might use a DLL, along with the actual sample code to do this, in order to demonstrate the value of understanding this technology.

In addition, this chapter explores using type libraries with a DLL. It also explores subclassing, teaches you to write a DLL that supports InstallShield, and looks at extended stored procedures and callbacks.

Type Libraries and DLLs

So far, this book has established one advantage of using type libraries with a DLL: avoiding the unnecessary translation of Unicode strings to ANSI. Another advantage is that the functions look more "native" to the Visual Basic programmer. No `Declare` statements are necessary to define these functions. You simply add a reference to the type library to your Visual Basic program, just like any other object you might use.

You also pick up a little performance, and not just because of the string issue. `Declare` statements are actually "late-bound" at runtime, whereas type library information is "early-bound" at compile time.

Using type libraries moves DLLs into an object like structure. You should remember, though, that a DLL has no concept of instances: You don't create variables that hold references to the DLL; you simply call the functions within the DLL.

How can type libraries help you? What would you use them for? I use them to provide functionality that I think should be intrinsic to Visual Basic but isn't. A good example of this might be a routine that trims all types of whitespace, not just spaces.

Can you write these routines in Visual Basic code? Absolutely, but if you do, you have one of two options for implementation: You can use the Visual Basic source code directly from a standard module, or you can build it into a Visual Basic object. Both methods have pitfalls—in particular, building it into a VB object makes the use of the routines rather clunky.

The following section demonstrates building a DLL that includes type library information through a simple tutorial.

Tutorial for Creating a DLL Including Type Library Information

First, look back to the start of Chapter 7, "C DLLs," at the section titled "Tutorial for Creating a Simple C DLL," where you used Visual C++ to create a DLL. Instead of repeating that discussion here, refer back to it and follow it to create your base files for a new DLL. (The project example delivered with the book is called TypeDLL. You might load this project if you do not want to step through each instruction here.)

> **NOTE**
>
> ### Backward `instr`
>
> I am using a backward `instr` function that exists in Visual Basic 6 (InstrRev). I wrote this for earlier versions of Visual Basic and am using it here as an example.

Writing the Implementation

After you have built your base files, add a new window to the project. Add the code for the .h file. Remember, this is where you use the extern "C" constants, and all of the function prototypes go in this file. Save it as TypeDLL.h. Listing 8.1 shows the include file.

LISTING 8.1   C Prototypes for TypeDLL.dll

```
//TypeDLL.h has function prototypes
#ifdef __cplusplus
extern "C"
{
#endif    //__cplusplus
    long WINAPI TypeDLL_BkInstr(LPWSTR sBase, LPWSTR sSearch);
    long WINAPI TypeDLL_strLen(LPSTR sTest);
#ifdef __cplusplus
}
#endif    //__cplusplus
```

Remember that, while you are writing the implementation for these routines in the CPP file, you should include this header file at the top of the CPP file. Listing 8.2 shows the implementation for the two routines that I am demonstrating.

LISTING 8.2   C Implementation for TypeDLL.dll

```
#include "windows.h"
#include "typeDLL.h"
long WINAPI TypeDLL_BkInstr(LPWSTR sBase, LPWSTR sSearch)
{
    LPWSTR    sTemp=NULL;
    BOOL      bComp=FALSE;
    long      i;
    //this is forwarn instr right now
```

LISTING 8.2   Continued

```
    if (lstrlenW(sBase) > lstrlenW(sSearch))
    {
        for (sTemp = sBase + lstrlenW(sBase) -
lstrlenW(sSearch);sTemp>=sBase;sTemp--  )
        {
            bComp=TRUE;
            for (i=0;i<lstrlenW(sSearch);i++)
            {
                if (*(sTemp + i) != sSearch[i])
                    bComp = FALSE;
            }
            if (bComp)
                break;
        }
    }
    if (bComp)
        return (long) (sTemp - sBase + 1);
    else
        return 0;
}

long WINAPI TypeDLL_strLen(LPSTR sTest)
{
    return lstrlen(sTest);
}
```

One thing to notice about this code is that the BkInstr function uses wide strings, and you are calling the wide character APIs in this routine. In the strLen routine, you are using the ANSI versions of the APIs because the string is an ANSI string. The strings will come through in the correct formats because of the type library you'll add later. Visual Basic converts strings to ANSI or leaves them in Unicode based on the type of parameter in the type information.

Now add another new window to the project, and place the DEF file code. The code that follows is again similar to the code at the beginning of the chapter. Save this file as TypeDLL.DEF.

```
LIBRARY TypeDLL.DLL
DESCRIPTION 'Type Lib Sample DLL'
EXPORTS
    TypeDLL_BkInstr
    TypeDLL_strLen
```

Adding the DLL as a Reference

Next, add a third new window to the project. This file will hold the type library source code.
Save this file as TypeDLL.IDL. Listing 8.3 shows the code that will allow you to add this DLL
to Visual Basic as a reference.

LISTING 8.3   IDL File for TypeDLL.dll

```
// TypeDLL.idl
[
// Use GUIDGEN.EXE to create the UUID
uuid(638B5760-3F8A-11d4-8D97-00A0CC21CD54),
helpstring("TypeDLL - sample dll with Type information"),
// Assume standard English locale.
lcid(0),
// Version number to keep track of changes.
version(1.0)
]
    library TypeDLLLib
    {
    // Define any Enumerations or structures here
    // Now define the module that will "declare" your C functions.
    [
    uuid(638B5761-3F8A-11d4-8D97-00A0CC21CD54),
    helpstring("Sample functions exported by TypeDLL.dll"),
    dllname("TYPEDLL.DLL")
    ]
    module DLLFunctions
    {
    [
        entry("TypeDLL_BkInstr"),
        helpstring("Backward Instr.")
    ]
    long __stdcall BkInstr([in] LPWSTR sBase, [in] LPWSTR sSearch);
    [
        entry("TypeDLL_strLen"),
        helpstring("Test routine.")
    ]
    long __stdcall strLen([in] LPSTR sTest);
    }
    };
```

Let's take a look at this file before we move on. This is an IDL source file. You will use it to
define the routines that are exported from the DLL. The first section of the file between the

8

C DLL PRACTICAL
EXAMPLES

square brackets ([and]) defines the type library; it contains the UUID that will be placed in the registry, and a few other items. The UUID is the most important item in this section. Create it using the GUIDGen tool that comes with Visual C++. (Just search the Program Files directory; it will be there. When you find it, add it to your Tools menu in Visual C++.)

You then have the library section itself. This section is bracketed by curly braces ({ and }) and extends to the end of the source code. The next section within square brackets contains the definition of the module section. It can contain a UUID, although it doesn't really require one. The main thing in this section is the DLL name.

After that, the contents of the module section are contained within another set of curly braces. This extends to the end of the library section that contains it. Within the module section lie the function prototypes.

These prototypes have a section within square brackets that contains an entry line. This entry line defines the routine name as it is exported from the DLL. The entry attribute is equivalent to the Alias statement within Visual Basic declarations. Other attributes may be placed within this section. The help string and the uses get last error attributes are a couple of examples.

After each section that contains the entry attribute is the function prototype. You define it with the name that you want the Visual Basic programmer to see. The parameter names are what you want the VB programmer to see as well. The parameter types are C-based, however, not Visual Basic types. The VB programmer will see basic types within the VB environment.

NOTE

I have seen include files that contain definitions that basically define the VB types as the correct C types so that the VB types may be used within the functions. I don't see this as an advantage for you, though. You are trying to learn C here, not hide it from the VB programmer. However if you feel that you need to do this, here is an example of how to use a typedef to achieve this:

```
typedef BSTR     String;
```

This statement (which is placed just inside the curly braces for the library section) defines String as the same type as BSTR. With this statement in place, you can now use the String statement and the BSTR statement interchangeably within the IDL file.

You can also place definitions for UDTs and enumerated types (Enums) at the start of the library section in the IDL source file. Enums can be a great way to get constants defined within your program. I'll explore both of these things in the section "Some Finer Points of the IDL File." Right now, let's finish building the DLL.

Combining the Type Library into the DLL

You need to create one more file. In this demonstration, you will combine the type library into the DLL as a resource. This keeps you from having two files around and is just a little cleaner. You might not want to do this, however, because it also makes it easy for anyone to see how your DLL functions when it is distributed with a program. In other words, the type library information is required for the development environment but is not needed when you distribute your compiled program.

To combine the type library information into the DLL, you need to create a .RC file. This file has one line in it, as follows. Save this file as TypeDLL.rc.

```
1 TYPELIB "TypeDLL.tlb"
```

Configuring the Project

You've created all the source files that you need, so now you must configure the project so that it will build everything. Add the DEF file, the .RC file, and the .IDL file to the project.

Because the .RC file loads the type library information from the main project directory, you'll have to make sure that it is created there. Use the Project Settings dialog box to change the output file on the Link tab so that the .TLB file is created in the project directory. Then the line in the .RC file will work.

You should be able to build and work with the .DLL now. If you have trouble with Visual Basic finding the file, you can change the Output File Name option on the Project Settings dialog box so that it places the .DLL in the path for Visual Basic to find it. You can also find the DLL through the Browse functionality built into the References dialog box in Visual Basic.

Some Finer Points of the IDL File

You have worked with the basic format of the IDL file in the previous section. Now let's take a look at doing some more interesting things with the IDL file as it relates to constants and structures.

Constants are somewhat simpler than structures, so I'll talk about them first. There are actually two ways to define a constant in an ODL/IDL file. One is through the actual const statement. The other is with the typedef enum statement. Listing 8.4 show samples of each.

LISTING 8.4 IDL Examples of Constants

```
 [ helpstring("Setting a high bit in a long with a hex number") ]
const long HI_BIT = 0x80000000;
[ helpstring("Setting a high bit in a short with a decimal number") ]
const short HI_BIT_2 = -32768;
```

LISTING 8.4   Continued

```
[ helpstring("Setting double const") ]
const double pi = 3.14159265;
[ helpstring("Defining a const string") ]
const LPSTR "Some String";
[ helpstring("Enum constants Example") ]
typedef enum {
    [ helpstring("Left") ]
    enLeft = 0,
    [ helpstring("Right") ]
    enRight = 1,
    [ helpstring("Center") ]
    enCenter = 2
} myAlignment;
```

The enumerated type is useful only for numeric constants and is a convenient way to group related constants together. The values are optional; if left off, the constant values would increment by 1 for each element. If you assign values, they do not have to increment by 1 or even be in sequence.

The const statements allow the definition of various types of constants, as shown in Listing 8.4. So, if you want a string or a double constant value, you would need to use a const statement.

User-defined types or structs in the C world are a little more interesting than the constants. First, not all data types will work. If you look at the structure you used in this chapter in the section titled "How to pass and use structures" to demonstrate structures in a DLL, you find that the fixed-length string and currency data types are not accessible though the UDT in automation. This is because Visual Basic must do the variable translations for you. This means that you can't match unlike variable types, such as currency and LARGE_INTEGER, or date and double, just because you know it will work. In addition, Visual Basic just doesn't understand some data types, such as char arrays. The following code is an example of a structure:

```
typedef struct
{
    short intgr;      //integer
    long lng;         //long
    float sng;        //single
    double dbl;       //double
    VARIANT_BOOL bln;       //boolean
    BYTE byt;         //byte
    VARIANT vnt;         //variant
    BSTR vstrg;         //variable length string
```

```
    short array[1][1][2];      //array of integers (2 Bytes in VB)
} UDT;
```

Now that you've placed this code in the IDL file, you need to be able to use it. You could make up the include files yourself, but there is no reason to do this. You can specify that the MIDL compiler output an include file based on the IDL file. This is done in the Project Settings dialog box. The generated include file can even replace the function prototypes that you've been putting in your own include file, but only if the prototype name and the entry name are the same, as in the following code, which exports a Good.h file:

```
[
        entry("BkInstr"),
        helpstring("Backward Instr.")
]
        long __stdcall BkInstr([in] LPWSTR sBase, [in] LPWSTR sSearch);
```

Either way, you can use the include file for the structure definitions.

I'll have plenty more to say about IDL when I explain COM objects and ActiveX controls. Here I have touched the surface, and using a type library certainly makes a DLL more usable.

Adding Resources to a DLL

You previously used a .RC file to hold the line for the type library information that was included into the DLL as a resource. Other types of resources can be included in your DLL as well. These include accelerators, bitmaps, cursors, dialog boxes, HTML, icons, menus, strings, toolbars, and version information, as well as the type library information.

You can edit resource files (.RC files) and manually enter the resource information. However, Visual C++ manages the content of a resource file within the UI, and this is a very good way to attach resource information to an executable file, including DLLs.

Visual Basic can use resource files directly within the environment. VB uses `LoadResString`, `LoadResPicture`, and `LoadResData` to load information from the resource file.

However, I'm talking about DLLs here and the resource information that can go along with them. Resources added to DLLs can have several advantages aside from the resources inside Visual Basic. First, you can replace the DLL without recompiling the Visual Basic executable, so you could decide at installation time which DLL to use. This could help with issues such as internationalization.

Samples of C DLLs

Now, let's take a look at a few practical examples. These samples address some real-world problems using routines from a standard function based DLL.

Subclassing

By whatever name you want to call it, subclassing is the process of replacing a window's function address with one of your own. This way, the messages for that window are directed to this new function. You may want to refer to the section "The Window Procedure," in Chapter 6, "C ++ and Windows," if you haven't looked at it yet.

The process that I will talk about here will work equally well in a COM object or an ActiveX control. The only difference is that you might want to get a reference to the object that you are dealing with. As with the sample presented here, you may want a reference to some object in Visual Basic. I'll demonstrate how to get that information to your Window procedure so that those objects can be referenced from that procedure.

Any Windows procedure must reside outside any class object that you have and must be exported in the same manner as the routines that you have already been writing. The only difference is that the Window procedure has a strict format to which it must adhere.

In the subclass DLL, you will write a procedure to subclass a Window, a procedure to remove the subclass from the Window, and a procedure that is the actual subclass procedure itself. In the subclass procedure, you will also pass a reference to a window so that you can set the text of that window from the subclass procedure.

Because you do not have events in a DLL that you can fire, you need some other mechanism to use the results of the subclass procedure. In this sample, you will do this by passing a reference to a window handle and using SendMessage to notify the window.

Refer to Listing 8.5. This is the source code to a DLL that demonstrates how to subclass a window. The routine in this DLL will subclass a window and set the text in a second window based on the highlighted menu item. Listing 8.6 shows a Visual Basic listing that uses this DLL to place the menu captions into a text box as they are highlighted.

In this DLL you allow subclassing of only one window to a single level. It is possible to subclass multiple windows and to any number of levels. By *levels*, I mean it is possible to set multiple subclasses on the same window. The only rule to follow there is you must remove them in the same order that you set them.

You use the SetProp routine to store the window handle where you will display the menu item. This allows you to retrieve this window handle and set the text from the subclass procedure.

Look at the SubClassWindow procedure. This is the procedure that sets up the subclass. First you check to make sure you have a valid window to subclass and to communicate with. Next you make sure you're not already subclassing something. After that you can use SetWindowLong to set the subclass. Notice that you pass the address of the subclass procedure (SubClassWinProc) within this function call. If you were successful, you set the other window handle into the custom properties within the window.

The UnSubClassWindow procedure is even simpler. You check to make sure you are subclassing a window. Then you remove the custom props and use SetWindowLong to put back the original procedure.

The SubClassWinProc is where you do the dirty work. This is the procedure that after subclassing will be getting the messages that were bound to the subclassed window. You must be a good citizen in this procedure. What happens to the window messages now is completely up to you. Typically they are forwarded on with the CallWindowProc routine. You can see this in the latter part of the procedure.

You can also find a call to the UnSubClassWindow procedure in this routine. Part of being a good citizen is ensuring that the subclass procedure gets cleaned up after the window is destroyed. You do that by calling the UnSubClassWindow procedure in the WM_DESTROY. If you remove the subclass before the WM_DESTROY, this procedure will never see that message; this is just insurance.

Now to the reason that you wrote the subclass procedure to start with. That is intercepting messages and doing interesting things with them. Here you are grabbing the WM_MENUSELECT message, getting the menu caption and setting this text into the window handle stored in the custom props.

LISTING 8.5 SUBClass Example

```cpp
// SUBPROC.cpp : Defines the entry point for the DLL application.
//


#include "stdafx.h"
#include <atlbase.h>
#include <atlconv.h>

FARPROC         m_lpfnOrigProc=NULL;
VOID WINAPI UnSubClassWindow(HWND hwnd);

BOOL APIENTRY DllMain( HANDLE hModule,
                       DWORD  ul_reason_for_call,
                       LPVOID lpReserved
                     )
{
    return TRUE;
}


//-------------------------------------------------------------------
// Sub class routine for target control window proc.
```

LISTING 8.5   Continued

```c
//---------------------------------------- ----------------------------------
LRESULT __declspec( dllexport) CALLBACK SubClassWinProc(HWND hwnd, UINT msg,
WPARAM wp, LPARAM lp)
{
        LONG rc;
    WORD    whi;
    WORD    wlo;
    HWND    hwndMain=NULL;
      UINT     tmsg=msg;
    HWND ctl=NULL;
    static HWND    s_hwndlast;
    char cStr[1024];

        //get the window handle
    whi = (WORD) GetProp(hwnd, "MyCallBackHi");
    wlo = (WORD) GetProp(hwnd, "MyCallBackLo");
    ctl = (HWND) MAKELONG(wlo, whi);

    //if we get a good handle
    if (ctl)
    {
        switch(msg)
        {

            //our test simply tracks the menu
            //text and set's it into the window
            //whose handle is stored in our custom props
            case WM_MENUSELECT:
            {
                if (MF_POPUP & HIWORD(wp))
                    GetMenuString((HMENU)lp,LOWORD(wp),cStr,1024,MF_BYPOSITION);
                else
                    GetMenuString((HMENU)lp,LOWORD(wp),cStr,1024,MF_BYCOMMAND);
                SetWindowText( ctl, cStr) ;
                return 0;
            }
            break;
            case WM_DESTROY:
            {

            }
        }
    }
```

LISTING 8.5   Continued

```
    //handle getting the message to the original proc
    if (m_lpfnOrigProc)
    {
        rc = CallWindowProc((WNDPROC) m_lpfnOrigProc, hwnd, msg, wp, lp);
    }
    if (ctl)
    {
        switch(msg)
        {
            //safety valve, in case we forget
            //this is done after forwarding the
            //message to the original proc
            case WM_DESTROY:
            {
                UnSubClassWindow(hwnd);
            }
        }
    }
    return rc;
}


BOOL WINAPI SubClassWindow(HWND hwnd, HWND ctl)
{
    if (!::IsWindow(hwnd))
        return(FALSE);  // Invalid hwnd parameter

    if (!::IsWindow(ctl))
        return(FALSE);  // Invalid ctl parameter

    if (m_lpfnOrigProc)
        return FALSE;   // Already are subclassing

    //set in our window proc
    //this subclasses the window
    m_lpfnOrigProc = (FARPROC)::SetWindowLong(hwnd, GWL_WNDPROC,
➥(DWORD)SubClassWinProc);

    //if this was successful
    if (m_lpfnOrigProc)
    {
        //set up our custom props that hold the
        //window handle to communicate with
```

LISTING 8.5   Continued

```
        SetProp(hwnd, "MyCallBackHi", (HANDLE) (HIWORD (ctl)));
        SetProp(hwnd, "MyCallBackLo", (HANDLE) (LOWORD (ctl)));
    }
    return TRUE;
}


VOID WINAPI UnSubClassWindow(HWND hwnd)
{
    // Make sure we're actually subclassing before we undo it.
    if (m_lpfnOrigProc)
    {
        //take out our custom properties
        RemoveProp(hwnd, "MyCallBackHi");
        RemoveProp(hwnd, "MyCallBackLo");
        //set the window proc back
        ::SetWindowLong(hwnd, GWL_WNDPROC, (LONG)m_lpfnOrigProc);
        m_lpfnOrigProc = 0L;
    }
}
```

The Visual Basic 6 program in Listing 8.6 shows how to use the subclass example. Here you are subclassing the form, which has some menu items on it. You have a text box (txtResult) where you will display the highlighted menus. You will have to build a VB project and add the text box and the following code. In addition you will need to change the Lib statements which reference the sample DLL. Your paths will be different.

LISTING 8.6   Using the SUBClass Example from Visual Basic

```
Private Declare Function SubClassWindow Lib "C:\Books\C++ for VB\Chap 7 -
DLLs\SUBPROC\Debug\subproc.dll" (ByVal hwnd As Long, ByVal ctl As Long) As Long
Private Declare Sub UnSubClassWindow Lib "C:\Books\C++ for VB\Chap 7 -
DLLs\SUBPROC\Debug\subproc.dll" (ByVal hwnd As Long)


Private Sub Form_Load()
    SubClassWindow Me.hwnd, txtResult.hwnd
End Sub

Private Sub Form_Unload(Cancel As Integer)
    UnSubClassWindow Me.hwnd
End Sub
```

The only thing you need to do for Listing 8.5 in addition to what has been presented here is place the code in a project and add an appropriate .DEF file to export the required functions. The following code presents a definition file that will work:

```
;subproc.def

LIBRARY        "subproc.dll"

EXPORTS
    SubClassWinProc
    SubClassWindow
    UnSubClassWindow
```

You can do the preceding method of subclassing in conjunction with a control. For example, if you wanted to write a control that would display menu captions as they were highlighted, this subclass procedure could be placed in a control and instead of communicating with a window, a reference to the control could be passed and the results of the subclass used by calling into the control's class. You do this in Chapter 10, "C# Basics," in the subclassing section there.

Support of InstallShield

InstallShield supports the use of DLLs to extend the installation environment. Although it also supports the use of executables to do the same thing, it is not really safe to try to write a Visual Basic executable and use it in this circumstance. This is because that executable has dependencies that the target machine may not have in place.

When you are writing utilities to use in an installation program, you want as few dependencies as possible. A C DLL works pretty well for this. You'll take a look at a simple DLL that will read a registry entry made by the setup program and tell you whether a program is installed. If the program is installed, this DLL will then launch the program, based on that registry setting.

InstallShield calls these types of DLLs extensions. That is pretty much what they are, an unrestricted extension to the InstallShield process.

Most of this process is exactly what you have gone through already. You'll write an exported function in a DLL and make it available for use in InstallShield. (I will not get into the specifics of using the DLL in InstallShield.)

To be used in InstallShield, the DLL function requires a specific prototype. You can prototype and export the function in the same manner as Visual Basic–compatible functions. As such it can be tested from Visual Basic.

```
CHAR WINAPI Foo(HWND hwnd, LPSTR szSrcDir, LPSTR szSupport, LPSTR szInst,
➡LPSTR szRes)
```

Here, hwnd is the InstallShield main window handle. SzSrcDir is the source directory <SRCDIR>. SzSupport is the support directory <SUPPORTDIR>. SzInst is the Installation directory <INSTALLDIR>. SzRes is not used.

Listing 8.7 is a simple routine that checks the registry for a program path and name and runs that program if found.

LISTING 8.7   InstallShield Extension

```c
#include "windows.h"
CHAR WINAPI RunEXE(HWND hwnd, LPSTR szSrcDir, LPSTR szSupport,
➥LPSTR szInst, LPSTR szRes)
{
    HKEY hKey=0;
    DWORD    type;
    DWORD    cbData=1024;
    char     data[1024];

    //get the reg setting
    RegOpenKeyEx(HKEY_CURRENT_USER,"Software\\mysoftware",0,0,&hKey);
    if (hKey)
    {
        RegQueryValueEx(hKey,"EXE ",0,&type,(LPBYTE)data,&cbData);
        data[cbData]=0;
        RegCloseKey(hKey);
        //exec it
        if (32 < WinExec(data,SW_SHOW))
            return 1;
    }
    return 0;
}
```

The routine exits with a return value of 1 if the program is found or 0 if it is not. A value of 1 would cause the InstallShield script to stop executing. This routine would allow a setup script to check for the installation of a program and, if there, run it, or if not, install it.

Extended Stored Procedures

Extended stored procedures (ESPs) are a way to write stored procedures for SQL Server in C++, and are another place where you can take advantage of DLLs. (Although it is possible to write ESPs for other versions of SQL Server, you'll address SQL Server 7 and later.) In this section you'll present a sample of a stored procedure written in C. You will need SQL Server 7 or later to compile and use the sample.

> **CAUTION**
>
> Understand that these procedures run in SQL Server's address space. You should use every precaution to make sure the routines are well debugged and sufficiently error-trapped. If they crash, they will likely take SQL Server with them. There's a fairly complex way to remote these procedures on another SQL Server machine so that you won't crash your main server; however, that server would go down if they crash. Using another server is viewed as only an interim solution for troubleshooting purposes. Ultimately, the routines simply must be very stable.

There are several reasons why you might want to write stored procedures in C, but the one that is most compelling to me is the increased power obtained in the C language, as compared to the internally generated stored procedures. You can simply do things in C that are not possible otherwise.

For example, SQL Mail is written in extended stored procedures, a very powerful email/database solution. Also in a stored procedure in C it would be possible to gather data from other sources. One example of this might be doing a credit card authorization in an extended stored procedure and storing the authorization number in the database.

First, you'll take a look at how to access SQL server using the Open Data Services API.

> **NOTE**
>
> Open Data Services is the API that you use from an Extended Stored Procedure to access SQL Server. You should know a little about this API to write these procedures— and if the procedures are fairly complex, you might need to know a *lot* about this API. This is not a book about Open Data Services, so I'll leave it up to you to explore the topic if necessary.

You start again by generating a Win 32 DLL. This time, however, you'll use a wizard specifically for extended stored procedures. (The sample included with the book is called SPPROC.DLL, and it can be found at www.samspublishing.com.)

When your project has been generated, you then need to point Visual C++ to the library and include files for the "Open Data Services" include and library files directories. These library and include files reside within the SQL Server installation. The svr.h and the opends60.lib files are used from these directories.

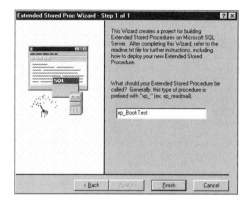

FIGURE 8.1
Extended Stored Procedure Wizard.

Figures 8.2 and 8.3 show how to add these directories. This dialog box is accessed from the Tools, Options menu selection. These settings are global to all projects.

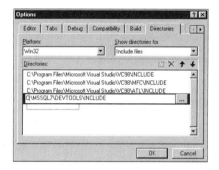

FIGURE 8.2
Add directory to include files path.

When you've done that, verify that the link statement contains the library file opends60.lib; this library file contains the ODS APIs that you will use in the project. The wizard will place this library file here for you—I just want to be sure that you know it's there and why.

If you look at the source code, shown in Listing 8.8, you find that the wizard has placed a good bit of code for you. This procedure put in here by the wizard demonstrates some calls to the ODS APIs and is a pretty good starting point for learning about extended stored procedures.

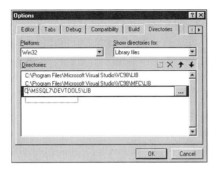

FIGURE 8.3
Add directory to library files path.

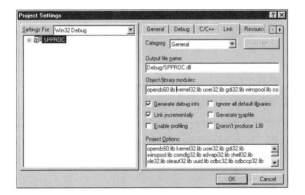

FIGURE 8.4
Add library to link statement.

LISTING 8.8   C Listing of Extended Stored Procedure

```
#include <windows.h>

//Include ODS headers
#ifdef __cplusplus
extern "C" {
#endif

#include <Srv.h>

#ifdef __cplusplus
}
#endif
```

LISTING 8.8   Continued

```
#define XP_NOERROR    0
#define XP_ERROR      1
#define MAXCOLNAME    25
#define MAXNAME       25
#define MAXTEXT       255

#ifdef __cplusplus
extern "C" {
#endif

RETCODE __declspec(dllexport) xp_BookTest(SRV_PROC *srvproc);

#ifdef __cplusplus
}
#endif

RETCODE __declspec(dllexport) xp_BookTest(SRV_PROC *srvproc)
{

    DBSMALLINT i = 0;
    DBCHAR colname[MAXCOLNAME];
    DBCHAR spName[MAXNAME];
    DBCHAR spText[MAXTEXT];

    // Name of this procedure
    wsprintf(spName, "xp_BookTest");


    //Send a text message
    wsprintf(spText, "%s Sample Extended Stored Procedure", spName);
    srv_sendmsg(
            srvproc,
            SRV_MSG_INFO,
            0,
            (DBTINYINT)0,
            (DBTINYINT)0,
            NULL,
            0,
            0,
            spText,
            SRV_NULLTERM);

    //Set up the column names
    wsprintf(colname, "ID");
```

LISTING 8.8   Continued

```
    srv_describe(srvproc, 1, colname, SRV_NULLTERM, SRVINT2,
            sizeof(DBSMALLINT), SRVINT2, sizeof(DBSMALLINT), 0);
    wsprintf(colname, "spName");
    srv_describe(srvproc, 2, colname, SRV_NULLTERM, SRVCHAR, MAXNAME, SRVCHAR,
➡0, NULL);

    wsprintf(colname, "Text");
    srv_describe(srvproc, 3, colname, SRV_NULLTERM, SRVCHAR, MAXTEXT, SRVCHAR,
➡0, NULL);


    // Update field 2 "spName", same value for all rows
    srv_setcoldata(srvproc, 2, spName);
    srv_setcollen(srvproc, 2, strlen(spName));

    // Send multiple rows of data
    for (i = 0; i < 3; i++)
    {
        // Update field 1 "ID"
        srv_setcoldata(srvproc, 1, &i);
        // Update field 3 "Text"
        wsprintf(spText, "%d) Sample rowset generated by the %s extended
➡stored procedure",
                i, spName);
        srv_setcoldata(srvproc, 3, spText);
        srv_setcollen(srvproc, 3, strlen(spText));
        // Send the entire row
        srv_sendrow(srvproc);
    }

    // Now return the number of rows processed
    srv_senddone(srvproc, SRV_DONE_MORE | SRV_DONE_COUNT, (DBUSMALLINT)0,
➡(DBINT)i);
    return XP_NOERROR ;
}
```

8

This procedure demonstrates building and returning a three-row set of data.

One item that the wizard doesn't take care of involves a routine that essentially returns a version number for SQL Server. Microsoft highly recommends writing and exporting this function, but its Extended Stored Procedure Wizard does not place this code within the DLL. At any rate, the prototype and the procedure is shown in Listing 8.9. As always the prototype goes within the extern "C" declarator.

LISTING 8.9   Required Export for Extended Stored Procedures

```
#include <windows.h>

//Include ODS headers
#ifdef __cplusplus
extern "C" {
#endif

#include <Srv.h>        // Main header file that includes all other header
files

#ifdef __cplusplus
}
#endif
__declspec(dllexport) ULONG __GetXpVersion();

__declspec(dllexport) ULONG __GetXpVersion()
{
    return ODS_VERSION;
}
```

After you've done this, you can compile and place your Extended Stored Procedure into SQL Server. When it's compiled, place the DLL in the MSSQL7\BINN directory—better yet, change the link output of your project to point to that directory. You can do this through the SQL Server Enterprise Manager or with Transact SQL statements. You can then call the Extended Stored Procedure(s) in the DLL.

One major issue remains: how to debug your stored procedures. Everyone would like to write flawless code the first time and not have to debug the code, but that rarely works. The fact of the matter is, you have to be able to run the code within a debugger.

The way you do this is similar in nature to the way you debugged DLLs using Visual C++ and Visual Basic. This time, however, you're using SQL Server.

NOTE

I think it goes without saying that you would not want to use your production server for debugging. You also need to have Visual C++ and SQL Server on the same machine to debug.

Here is the procedure you will follow to debug an extended stored procedure DLL:

1. Load the project into Visual C++.
2. Compile for debug, and be sure that the DLL is placed where it can be used. MSSQL7\BINN is a good spot.
3. Register the stored procedure.
4. Stop SQL Server.
5. Set the debug target to use SQL Server. In the Settings dialog box on the Debug tab, set the target to C:\MSSQL\BINN\SQLSERVR.EXE. Set the program arguments entry to -c, and set the working directory to C:\MSSQL\BINN.

This will run the SQL Server executable out of the debugging environment of C++. You can then set a break point in your extended procedure and use a program that calls the extended procedure. The breakpoint will cause C++ to break on that line, and you can debug the DLL.

Callbacks, Hooks, and Other Nasty Things

Some system services are rather difficult to program and might not even be possible in Visual Basic. Callbacks are one service of this type. Although Visual Basic can now provide a callback procedure address, it is troublesome to code this procedure.

The VB AddressOf operator is troublesome because normal debugging techniques may not work within the procedure and because VB is so strongly typed. An example will demonstrate what I mean.

Listing 8.10 is an example of using a Visual Basic callback to evaluate the fonts in a system. The main points to notice here are the amount of code and the way in which the string must be handled.

If you want to run the Visual Basic code in Listing 8.10, simply place the code in a standard module and call the routines from any place that is convenient. Some of the routines use a list box as a parameter. To call those routines, just place a list box on a form and pass a reference to that list box in the call to the procedure.

LISTING 8.10   VB Listing of Callback

```
'Font enumeration types
Public Const LF_FACESIZE = 32
Public Const LF_FULLFACESIZE = 64
```

LISTING 8.10   Continued

```
Type LOGFONT
      lfHeight As Long
      lfWidth As Long
      lfEscapement As Long
      lfOrientation As Long
      lfWeight As Long
      lfItalic As Byte
      lfUnderline As Byte
      lfStrikeOut As Byte
      lfCharSet As Byte
      lfOutPrecision As Byte
      lfClipPrecision As Byte
      lfQuality As Byte
      lfPitchAndFamily As Byte
      lfFaceName(LF_FACESIZE) As Byte
End Type

Type NEWTEXTMETRIC
      tmHeight As Long
      tmAscent As Long
      tmDescent As Long
      tmInternalLeading As Long
      tmExternalLeading As Long
      tmAveCharWidth As Long
      tmMaxCharWidth As Long
      tmWeight As Long
      tmOverhang As Long
      tmDigitizedAspectX As Long
      tmDigitizedAspectY As Long
      tmFirstChar As Byte
      tmLastChar As Byte
      tmDefaultChar As Byte
      tmBreakChar As Byte
      tmItalic As Byte
      tmUnderlined As Byte
      tmStruckOut As Byte
      tmPitchAndFamily As Byte
      tmCharSet As Byte
      ntmFlags As Long
      ntmSizeEM As Long
      ntmCellHeight As Long
      ntmAveWidth As Long
End Type
```

LISTING 8.10 Continued

```vb
' ntmFlags field flags
Public Const NTM_REGULAR = &H40&
Public Const NTM_BOLD = &H20&
Public Const NTM_ITALIC = &H1&

'   tmPitchAndFamily flags
Public Const TMPF_FIXED_PITCH = &H1
Public Const TMPF_VECTOR = &H2
Public Const TMPF_DEVICE = &H8
Public Const TMPF_TRUETYPE = &H4

Public Const ELF_VERSION = 0
Public Const ELF_CULTURE_LATIN = 0

'   EnumFonts Masks
Public Const RASTER_FONTTYPE = &H1
Public Const DEVICE_FONTTYPE = &H2
Public Const TRUETYPE_FONTTYPE = &H4

Declare Function EnumFontFamilies Lib "gdi32" Alias _
    "EnumFontFamiliesA" _
    (ByVal hDC As Long, ByVal lpszFamily As String, _
    ByVal lpEnumFontFamProc As Long, LParam As Any) As Long
Declare Function GetDC Lib "user32" (ByVal hWnd As Long) As Long
Declare Function ReleaseDC Lib "user32" (ByVal hWnd As Long, _
    ByVal hDC As Long) As Long

Function EnumFontFamProc(lpNLF As LOGFONT, lpNTM As NEWTEXTMETRIC, _
    ByVal FontType As Long, LParam As ListBox) As Long

    Dim FaceName As String
    Dim FullName As String
    FaceName = StrConv(lpNLF.lfFaceName, vbUnicode)
    LParam.AddItem Left$(FaceName, InStr(FaceName, vbNullChar) - 1)
    EnumFontFamProc = 1
End Function

Sub FillListWithFonts(LB As ListBox)
    Dim hDC As Long
    LB.Clear
    hDC = GetDC(LB.hWnd)
    EnumFontFamilies hDC, vbNullString, AddressOf EnumFontFamProc, LB
    ReleaseDC LB.hWnd, hDC
End Sub
```

Things are much simpler looking in C. With C, all the declarations are done and the Unicode conversion is not necessary. Notice in Listing 8.11 how easy it is to handle the string in the SendMessage call by using a cast. It's also easier to handle the procedure address.

LISTING 8.11   C Listing of Callback

```
int WINAPI EnumFontFamProc(LOGFONT *lpNLF, NEWTEXTMETRIC *lpNTM, DWORD
FontType, LPARAM LParam)
{
    SendMessage((HWND) LParam,LB_ADDSTRING,-1,(LONG) lpNLF->lfFaceName);
    return 1;
}

void WINAPI FillListWithFonts(HWND LB)
{
    HDC hDC = GetDC(LB);

    SendMessage(LB,LB_RESETCONTENT,0,0L);
    EnumFontFamilies (hDC, NULL, (FONTENUMPROC) EnumFontFamProc, (LONG) LB);
    ReleaseDC (LB, hDC);
}
```

There are some other uses for C DLLs that you haven't written examples for here. This includes system hooks. A system-wide hook can't be placed in an EXE file, they must reside in a DLL. In fact, a system-wide hook is a "trick" that you can use to "inject" your DLL into every process that runs in the system. That particular subject is beyond the scope of this book. Chapter 6 discusses hooks in more detail.

A GINA (Graphics Identification and Authentication) DLL is another application for a DLL. This is an NT (or WIN2000) DLL (the default GINA DLL is msgina.dll) and it handles the login at startup. It handles automatic login if that is configured. It also handles the CTRL+ALT+DEL event.

Replacing the GINA DLL with your own DLL is the only reliable and documented way of disabling the CTRL+ALT+DEL in these operating systems. A custom GINA DLL is also used for special authentication equipment, like card readers.

Summary

In this chapter you were presented with some useful examples of C DLLs. These techniques can take you beyond your everyday VB programming and allow you to accomplish things that are difficult or impossible to do in Visual Basic.

Components and Controls

IN THIS CHAPTER

The objective in this chapter will be to talk about components and, in particular, ActiveX controls that can be used in Visual Basic. One of the major uses I've made of C++ is in writing controls that support other technologies, such as Visual Basic and Internet Explorer. For a complete discussion, the chapter starts with components in general and then moves into controls specifically.

This chapter will cover the following topics:

- What constitutes a component.
- The basics of inheritance and some of the terms involved with inheritance.
- The basics of COM.
- The different types of ActiveX controls that we can build.
- Different technologies available for constructing controls.
- Writing an ATL control in detail.
- How to create a control based on a Windows base class—we use an EDIT control as an example.
- Composite controls and the different challenges they present.

Basics of Components

Component programming has been around a while. It hasn't always been called that, but since programming began, programmers have been breaking their code up into reusable units to make things easier.

One of the first ways of breaking code up was through library functions, which were covered in Chapter 7, "C DLL Basics," and Chapter 8, "C DLL Practical Examples." Function-based programming encapsulated code, but did nothing for data. You could put code into linkable object modules and later runtime linkable DLLs, but all the data had to be passed into the routines. Programmers even used global data in these libraries to store certain static data, but it was a long way from encapsulating the data.

When programmers began encapsulating data with the code, they started calling their programming units objects. Object-Oriented Programming (OOP) languages gave programmers their first opportunity to use components. Although implementation inheritance is somewhat different from a COM object, for example, it is a component. Data could be encapsulated by the object, and the user of the object didn't even have to know it was there or what form it was in.

Components and Inheritance

In this section, you'll go over the following definitions and what they mean:

- Inheritance
- Abstraction
- Encapsulation
- Polymorphism
- Interface inheritance
- Implementation inheritance
- Containment
- Delegation
- Aggregation

Inheritance Defined

The term *inheritance* has been applied to several different technologies, some of which bear little resemblance to inheritance, so finding a universal definition is difficult.

Visual Basic programmers have held to a definition of inheritance that includes the way they use binary components and the fact that Visual Basic has the `Implements` keyword.

Inheritance is the ability of a derived class to take on the characteristics of the class on which it is based. This is easy to see in implementation inheritance, but it is harder to see with binary objects. Inheritance with binary objects might more properly be called composition.

There are other concepts that are important to inheritance, many of which exist in binary objects. Inheritance can't be fully understood without addressing these concepts.

Abstraction

An *abstraction* is the outside world's view of an object. It defines the functionality the that object provides without regard to the technicalities of writing it.

Abstraction can include concepts that go beyond the software element. For example, the abstraction may have a method that turns on a machine. This obviously cannot be done without some physical device to make the connection.

Encapsulation

Encapsulation of code within a defined unit, along with encapsulation of data within that unit, is a very basic concept of inheritance. Encapsulation is the ability of an object to contain and hide information about the object.

After all, how can you inherit something unless it is in a structured unit. Source code classes and binary objects both support encapsulation.

Polymorphism

Polymorphism is essentially the ability to change. This means that the methods or properties can exist in several interfaces and have the same name. In programming, you go even further and say that your code that manipulates these objects should be able to call a method that exists in many objects without even knowing the type of object with which it is working.

There are two basic ways to achieve polymorphism. Inheritance-based polymorphism references objects through some base class. The actual objects could be a derived class of this base class. This works because the derived class inherits all the properties and methods of the base class. It can override those procedures and change the way they work or allow the base class to handle them.

CAUTION

There is an inherent danger when using this type of polymorphism. The base class could be modified in such a way that the derived classes would be broken. Obviously, this is not an ideal situation.

The other way to achieve polymorphism is through interface inheritance. This is typically a much "safer" way to use polymorphism.

Inheritance

While you can provide a strict definition of inheritance, in practice, it can actually take several forms. In this section you'll learn about the different types of inheritance.

Interface Inheritance

If you base an interface on another interface, you obtain the interface definition, not an implementation. All interfaces in COM are based on IUnknown and, as a result, have QueryInterface, AddRef, and Release definitions. You can actually implement these functions yourself within your interface; the definition is what is inherited.

You do not typically inherit complex interfaces beyond a single level. This has to do with the complications that would result from a change in a base interface. Of course interfaces are immutable; when an interface is created with a unique ID, it can't be changed. So instead, you create a new interface—ISomething and ISomething2. Now, if there are a lot of interfaces based on ISomething, there's a lot of work to be done to update them when ISomething2 is created. Consequently, you avoid establishing multiple levels of interface inheritance that would result in this problem.

Instead, you will typically add multiple interfaces to an object rather than trying to create a deep object hierarchy. You might view this as a form of inheritance, an object inherits this interface from the abstract class that defines it.

Interfaces specify the properties, methods, and events that a component exposes. You inherit an interface—in VB6 through the `Implements` keyword, in C# through the class statement, and in VB.NET through the `Inherits` keyword. When you inherit an interface, no functionality comes with it. You must provide the functionality within your component.

Because interfaces are contracts, their sole purpose is to make sure that a client knows how to access the properties, methods, and events of the component.

Implementation Inheritance

Implementation inheritance is typically restricted to source code. A compiled program would not have the information required for this type of inheritance. .NET and languages like it are somewhat different. .NET has a lot of metadata associated with a component, and the component isn't delivered compiled.

A .NET component uses a Just in Time (JIT) compiler to build actual executable code. The intermediate language (IL) has enough information to actually process it back to compiled code. So there is certainly enough information to handle implementation inheritance.

You accomplish implementation inheritance by creating classes based on other classes. When you do this, your class inherits all of the functionality of the base class. If the class has public properties, methods and events, those are inherited as well. Events have to programmed in a particular way to override them—this is discussed in Chapter 11, "C# Application," when you write a .NET control.

Of course, C++ uses implementation inheritance in its source code classes. This is the way that most OOP constructs work, through source code. When you use C++ classes, the complete source code is there, and the derived class can inherit all the functionality of the base class.

Delegation

Binary objects use containment and delegation; this process is a form of inheritance. This might also be called composition, but whatever you call it, this is a great way to reuse code.

With delegation, you write a component that exposes its own properties and methods just like any component. You also create an instance of some object that has some of the functionality that you need in your component. Your component's properties and methods simply call the applicable properties and methods in the contained object. In other words, your component delegates the work to the object that contains the required functionality.

A good example of delegation would be a Visual Basic custom control that uses constituent controls. The capabilities of these constituent controls are exposed to the user of the custom control through properties in the custom control.

You would typically use delegation if you need to modify some of the properties or methods in the contained object. If you don't, aggregation may be a better way to accomplish your task.

Aggregation

Aggregation is a way to use a contained object without having to implement a ton of methods and properties. With aggregation, the interfaces in the contained object are simply exposed as though they belong to the containing object.

The only drawback to using aggregation is that both the inner object and the outer object must be written with this in mind. The outer object is the one that you have development control of, so there's no problem providing the functionality there. The inner object must be "aggregatable."

Visual Basic programmers will find this concept somewhat foreign. This is because Visual Basic, prior to .NET, didn't support aggregation. You had to write this code in C or C++.

In .NET, all objects are aggregatable, but you typically wouldn't want to write code this way. Using aggregation compares almost directly to using multiple inheritance. This is a much more sane way of providing similar functionality. You will read more about this method in the next section.

Aggregation Through Properties

While Visual Basic does not support aggregation directly, it supports yet another way of reusing code. In the earlier days of Visual Basic, it was not possible to have properties that were objects. Of course, this is fairly common now.

The font property is a good example. At first, the font properties appeared as several different properties in each control that had a font. Now, of course, the font property contains all of those font properties within a font object. That font object is exposed through a font property.

This is not delegation, nor is it aggregation as aggregation is defined. It certainly bears more of a resemblance to aggregation, while the old way of handling these properties seemed more like delegation.

COM

Component Object Model (COM) has, for many years, been the mainstay of Microsoft's component programming model. Has Microsoft abandoned this type of programming?

COM will be around for a long time. The principles that it was built on will be around even longer. If you have managed to work with or even master COM programming, it will serve you well in .NET. As stated before, the objects created in COM programming and .NET work very much the same way. In fact, if you register a Windows-based .NET object in the system registry, it becomes a COM object.

This section will discuss COM, while keeping focus on what you're trying to accomplish— making you comfortable in the world of C, C++, and C# in support of your Visual Basic skills.

Interfaces

Interfaces are the means of communication in COM. What is an interface really? In its rawest form, stripped of all rhetoric and expressed in terms of C++, an interface is an abstract C++ class with pure virtual functions. This boils down to a pointer to a structure holding pointers to functions.

When you start designing interfaces, there are several rules to keep in mind. Some of these rules will live on in objects that are written for newer systems, such as .NET. All the following rules apply to COM:

- All interfaces derive from IUnknown.
- As much as possible, interfaces should be "remotable."
- Interfaces must have a unique identifier.
- Interfaces are immutable. Once published, they don't change.
- Functions should return HRESULTs.
- Strings should be UNICODE.

IUnknown

IUnknown is the base interface for all interfaces. The following code shows how IUnknown looks. In reality, you will probably implement your interface and IUnknown together.

```
interface IUnknown
{
    HRESULT QueryInterface(IID& iid, void **ppv);
    ULONG   AddRef(void);
    ULONG   Release(void);
}
```

QueryInterface

QueryInterface must be implemented for an object to qualify as a COM object. The following code shows how you might implement QueryInterface. This listing assumes that you use a main object that implements IUnknown and two friend classes that implement two interfaces.

These interfaces are instantiated during initialization and hold a pointer to the interface. You return a pointer to these variables in `QueryInterface`, which provides the pointer to the pointer to the implementation of the interface.

```
STDMETHODIMP OurMainObject::QueryInterface(REFIID riid, PPVOID ppv)
{
    *ppv=NULL;
    //IUnknown comes from our main object
    if (IID_IUnknown==riid)
        *ppv=this;
    //Other interfaces come from interface implementations.
    if (IID_IOurFirstInterface==riid)
        *ppv=m_pImpIOurFirstInterface;
    if (IID_IOurSecondInterface==riid)
        *ppv=m_pImpIOurSecondInterface;
    if (NULL==*ppv)
        return ResultFromScode(E_NOINTERFACE);
    ((LPUNKNOWN)*ppv)->AddRef();
    return NOERROR;
}
```

This code uses single inheritance.

NOTE

Unless the interfaces in question have methods that are named the same, using multiple inheritance is a way to save a lot of code—in fact, this is a popular way to implement interfaces.

You could go through complete code listings here, but I think the point is made. In reality, it is recommended that you use ATL or some other development system that will handle this code for you.

IDL and ODL Source Files and the MIDL Compiler

The Interface Description Language (IDL) source files are where you express the structure of a COM object and any interface that it has. Up to now, you've represented these interfaces in C++ code. The way the rest of the world sees the interface is up to the type library.

IDL is the way that you "program" the type library. IDL is somewhat different from procedural languages in that it is simply a definition language. There is no real executable code (proxy/stub code is produced from the MIDL compiler, but that is actually C code).

Object Definition Language (ODL) is Microsoft's version of IDL. MKTYPLIB was used on ODL source code to compile it into type libraries. Microsoft has released its own version of

IDL, which includes the features of ODL and the MIDL 3.0 compiler to generate type libraries and proxy/stub code.

Wizards generate much of the IDL or ODL code you use. It is possible to write it from scratch, but usually you don't. You need to be able to recognize the main parts of the IDL code, so you'll read about those first.

The `Library` Statement

The `Library` statement defines the type library that will be generated for your component. It typically contains the `coClass` statement at a minimum. Listing 9.1 shows a typical `Library` statement.

LISTING 9.1   IDL `Library` Statement

```
[
    uuid(2D17E2A7-979F-11D2-8D97-00105A0CAC96),
    version(1.0),
    helpstring("A Sample Type Library")
]
library MYSAMPLELib
{
    importlib("stdole32.tlb");
    importlib("stdole2.tlb");

    [
        uuid(2D17E2B4-979F-11D2-8D97-00105A0CAC96),
        helpstring("The co Class")
    ]
    coclass mySampleClass
    {
        [default] interface IMyinterface;
        [default, source] dispinterface _IMyEventInterface;
    };
};
```

At the start of the listing, in square brackets, are attributes that affect the statement following the closing square bracket (the `Library` statement in this case). The attributes have the `uuid`, the version, an, the help string. It is possible to have other attributes, but these are quite common.

The two import statements are typically always required for generating the type library.

Next you find another set of attributes, this time they belong to the `coClass` statement. In this case, you have the `uuid` and the help string again.

Then comes the `coClass` statement. This statement lists the interfaces that this object will support. This doesn't mean that the object can't support more interfaces—these are simply the interfaces that have type libraries and are marshaled.

Remember that in the previous section you read about proxy/stub code and how the MIDL compiler will build that code if the IDL is written to do so. Notice in Listing 9.1 that the definitions for the interfaces used in the `coClass` statement don't appear inside the function statement. The definitions for the interfaces will appear somewhere outside the library statement. When the IDL is written in this manner, it will generate proxy/stub code for those interfaces.

When ATL generates the IDL file for your object, it will place the interface definitions inside the library statements. This causes the MIDL compiler to generate the type library, but no proxy/stub code. This means that an object with an IDL file generated by ATL would be marshaled by the system at runtime.

Your best recourse is to modify the IDL file generated by ATL and move the interface definitions outside the library statement. This is not difficult to do and will result in the recommended procedure for marshaling your object.

Types and Interfaces in IDL

There is some IDL code that you might see outside that library statement. Listing 9.2 shows how these interfaces might look. You would use the same technique in either type of object.

LISTING 9.2   IDL Code for Interfaces

```
import "oaidl.idl";
import "ocidl.idl";
#include "olectl.h"

typedef enum
{
    [helpstring("Left")] bc_LeftAlignment=0,
    [helpstring("Right")] bc_RightAlignment=1,
    [helpstring("Center")] bc_CenterAlignment=2,
}enumAlignment;

typedef enum{
    [helpstring("Top")] bc_LeftVAlign=0,
    [helpstring("Bottom")] bc_RightVAlign=1,
    [helpstring("Center")] bc_CenterVAlign=2,
}enumVAlignment;

    [
```

LISTING 9.2   Continued

```
        object,
        uuid(2D17E2B3-979F-11D2-8D97-00105A0CAC96),
        dual,
        helpstring("Imyinterface Interface"),
        pointer_default(unique)
    ]
    interface IMyinterface : IDispatch
    {
        [propput, id(17)] HRESULT Alignment([in] enumAlignment newVal);
        [propget, id(17)] HRESULT Alignment([out, retval] enumAlignment *pVal);
        [propput, id(18)] HRESULT VAlignment([in] enumVAlignment newVal);
        [propget, id(18)] HRESULT VAlignment([out, retval] enumVAlignment
        *pVal);
    };


    [
        uuid(2D17E2B5-979F-11D2-8D97-00105A0CAC96),
        helpstring("_IbcstateEvents Interface")
    ]
    dispinterface IMyEventInterface
    {
        properties:
            //Event interface has no properties
        methods:
            [id(1), helpcontext(Change)] void Change();
        };
```

There are several things to notice about this IDL file. Almost everything in IDL source code can be prefaced with an attribute. Notice that even the elements of the enum definitions have attributes that declare a help string.

One interface is a normal interface that derives from IDispatch. The other is a dispinterface. The IDispatch interfaces of the two interfaces here work similarly. The difference is that the interface deriving from IDispatch is a dual interface, and the dispinterface is not dual. Also, the syntax for the dispinterface statement is slightly different from the interface statement.

The attributes for the IMyinterface include the object attribute, which identifies this as a COM interface. The uuid of the interface is next, then dual, which declares this interface as dual having both a vtable interface and an IDispatch interface. The last attribute, pointer_default, is for pointer declarations. It might not always be used, but will not hurt anything by being there.

Notice that the property declarations inside the interface use two definitions for one property. A propput attribute is required on one, and the propget is required on the other. In the propput, you pass an *[in]* variable by value. In the propget, a pointer to a variable is passed as an *[out]* parameter. You can provide read-only or write-only properties by providing only one definition. There is also a propputref that may be needed with interface pointers, such as a font property.

The dispinterface (commonly used for event interfaces) doesn't require the object attribute, and you can't use the dual attribute (obviously) on a dispinterface. Also, the property statements are quite a bit different. Event interfaces do not have properties, so there are no properties shown in this interface. The difference is that properties in the dispinterface syntax only use one statement to define the property, while the interface syntax can use one, two, or three statements to define the property.

In ATL, the interfaces will be maintained for you through wizards. However, I've never completed a control without manipulating the IDL directly. For example, using an enum as a type is one thing that you would have to do by directly manipulating the IDL file. The sample in Listing 9.2 declares two enums and types the properties using them.

NOTE

In .NET C++, you have the option of doing "attribute" programming, which means that you simply include the attributes that you see in the IDL file within the actual source code. This is similar to the way these features are obtained within managed code with C#. This might be easier for you and should produce the same results. Chapter 11 has a control written in C# that uses attributes.

You will apply these techniques when you get to the section on writing an ATL control. There will be a general section discussion on controls before that.

Custom Controls

The basis of this book has been to transition you (the Visual Basic programmer) to the C programming family of languages (C, C++, and C#). In doing so, the book hasn't tried to eliminate Visual Basic from your programs, but rather to support the VB program with the C/C++ code from this book.

Continuing with that objective, the intent in this section will be to cover custom controls that can be used in Visual Basic. Controls are the program building blocks that Visual Basic programmers use to construct programs. As a VB programmer, you no doubt have used many, whether they were custom controls or controls that are intrinsic to VB.

In using those controls, you probably encountered times when the control that you had to use didn't exactly fit your requirements. You may have worked around the limitations, maybe found a different control or perhaps you wrote a control in Visual Basic. This section will help take that next step and develop the control in C++ using ATL.

Before stepping off that ledge, you'll read briefly about the development technologies available to you today for control development.

- VBXs are 16-bit DLLs used in Visual Basic 1, 2, and 3, and they are fairly simple to write if you know C. These early DLLs are where the concept of controls began. The technologies have changed and the names have changed, but the basic idea of a user interface component was born with a VBX.

- OLE Controls were introduced with the first version of 32-bit Visual Basic. Visual Basic 4 also gave programmers 16-bit OLE Controls, but they never became prevalent. OLE Controls were written in C++ and typically based on the COleControl class in MFC (the Microsoft Foundation Class, a library delivered with Visual C++). All controls based on MFC carried the extra weight added on by the MFC support libraries.

- ActiveX was really a name change from OLE controls made by Microsoft in an attempt to popularize ActiveX controls for Internet applications. The ActiveX specification included some Internet technologies. The Active Template Library (ATL), a library delivered with Visual C++, became a popular technology to use in developing these controls, but there are plenty of controls around based on MFC that carry the ActiveX nomenclature.

- Win Forms Controls are a new type of control introduced by Visual Studio.NET. They are targeted at WIN32 programming, just like OLE and ActiveX controls. The differences from ActiveX controls are subtle. The differences in the way that you develop Win Forms Controls are not subtle.

- Web Forms Controls are a type of control also introduced by Visual Studio.NET. This is the first control that has been targeted solely at Internet technologies. This type of control runs on the Web server and delivers the UI to the client through HTML.

Methods Used to Build Controls

In this section, you'll learn about current methodologies used to develop controls. There will be a brief introduction to Visual Basic controls, MFC-based controls, and .NET controls. Later in the section, you will visit ATL type controls in depth. ATL controls are written only in C++.

> **NOTE**
>
> MFC, while still current, is less ideal for control development. MFC-based controls carry a lot of extra code in the MFC support libraries, and these libraries must either be distributed with your control or statically linked to it.
>
> Visual Basic 5/6 controls also require a large runtime and have been superceded by .NET controls. Consequently, VB and MFC controls will be touched on very lightly.

Visual Basic 5 and 6

Visual Basic 5 introduced the Control Development version of Visual Basic, marking the first time Visual Basic programmers had the chance to do true control development. The way in which that control development is accomplished in Visual Basic is very different from methods used in C++.

One of the really nice things about the controls in Visual Basic is that you can use any intrinsic or ActiveX control as a constituent (a *constituent* control is a control that is placed on the UserControl, the base for ActiveX controls in VB). This may give you a substantial head start on a control.

There are negatives, however. If you use Visual Basic 5 or 6 to write controls that are not based on existing controls, you must handle every aspect of the control yourself. C++ is a better choice for this type of control.

Visual Basic is not very good at a lot of the things that you need to do in a control that is written from the ground up, so writing anything more than simple controls in this way is not recommended.

Lastly, any Visual Basic 5 or 6 control must carry along the Visual Basic runtime files. This will cause a substantial hit in the distribution of a control.

MFC

C++/MFC was the predominant technology used to create OLE Controls. `COleControl` is the class in MFC that is used to develop a control. C++/MFC controls was the first step up from VBX development, in part because it supplied a great deal of code for control developers.

MFC was the only real option for the first 32-bit controls being developed. One other non-MFC approach existed, but it was difficult to use and required one to write a great deal of code that was already provided in MFC.

To write a control in MFC (there's a wizard to do most of the dirty work), you create a class based on `COleControl`, put in your properties, methods, and events with the provided wizards, and fill in your code.

MFC provides fairly good performance, but distribution of the controls requires either distributing the MFC runtimes as well, or statically linking them.

> **TIP**
>
> In my experience, statically linked MFC controls will be much larger, something like 350-500KB larger than non-statically linked controls. The MFC runtimes are over 1MB in size, so if you have just a few controls, it may make sense to link the run times.
>
> In addition, if you use the MFC runtimes, rather than statically linking them, you may find that you encounter versioning issues with those runtime files. While a good installation program goes a long way in solving this issue, you cannot control what happens to those files when other programs are installed.

Visual Studio.NET

The latest version of Visual Studio introduces a new type of control. You produce a control that can be used just like any control discussed up to now. In addition, these controls can be used like source code classes. In other words, functions within the class of the control can be overridden and programmed if you base a derived class on one of these classes. As you create classes that are based on these new classes, the derived classes immediately have the functionality of the base class. In addition, there are virtual functions in the base class that can be overridden and programmed within your own code. Using implementation inheritance requires very strict code structure. This is the reason that binary components inherit interfaces only and gain implementation through aggregation and delegation. You looked at inheritance in some depth earlier in this chapter, in the "Components and Inheritance" section.

ATL Controls in Detail

ATL is typically the preferred method when building an ActiveX control. ATL is a current technology and is also delivered with .NET.

ATL will provide the best performance and the best distribution size. It is possible to build ATL controls that have no dependencies. This is also possible in MFC type controls if you link the MFC libraries statically. However, as already stated, this makes for a rather large control.

Thus, ATL is the ideal choice for commercial ActiveX controls and ActiveX controls that will be used within a WEB page.

> **TIP**
>
> Certainly there are some valid reasons for creating controls with either Visual Basic (5 or 6) or MFC, especially if they are to be used within a "closed" environment. (A closed environment is one in which you manage the distribution of the controls, and in which distribution can include the runtimes without much worry or penalty.) In an in-house WIN32 application, the recommendation is probably to choose Visual Basic for any controls.

In the sample, you will:

1. Create an Active control.
2. Add message and interface handlers.
3. Add properties methods and events.
4. Look at and discuss the interfaces supported in ATL.

Creating the Control Project

There are several steps required to create an ATL control. The actual steps will vary slightly, depending upon which version of Visual Studio you use. For the example here, you will use the .NET version. Visual C++ in Visual Studio 6 is very similar to this process.

First, you will create a basic ATL project, and then you will add a control class to the ATL project. At the end of this section, you will have a basic control, but it will not have properties, methods, or events. You will add those elements in the following sections.

ATL COM AppWizard

Building an Active Control begins with two wizards, the first of which is the New Project Wizard. This wizard generates a set of base files. No ATL object has been added yet, but there are some items of note in this step.

Visual Studio will create ATL DLLs, EXEs, and Services, however an Active Control is a DLL, so for your purposes in this chapter, the other settings do not matter. You will choose the ATL Project from the window shown in Figure 9.1.

After you name the project and choose Next, you are presented with a dialog that will allow you to set some project options. Click Application Settings and the dialog shown in Figure 9.2 will appear.

The first option you see here is Attributed. The sample you use in this chapter is not attributed, so you won't choose this. If you choose this option, you will not have an IDL file. Instead all of those settings, go in the include file as Attributes. Attributes in the include file of your C++ program will be similar to the IDL file, so it's not a difficult transition if you want to use them.

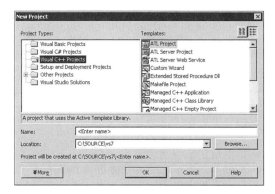

FIGURE 9.1
Visual C++ New Project Wizard.

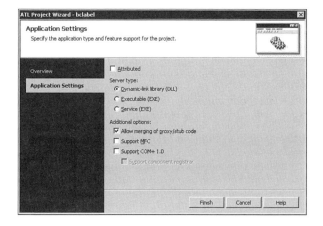

FIGURE 9.2
Visual C++ New Project Wizard.

The next option is the type of file, Dynamic Link Library (DLL), Executable (EXE), or Service (EXE). Because an ActiveX control is a Dynamic Link Library, that's what you'll choose to create.

The Allow Merging of Proxy/Stub Code allows the proxy/stub code to reside in your Active Control rather than in a separate DLL. Proxy/stub code is required to marshal an interface. There are times when your interfaces need to be marshaled and it is recommended to link this into the DLL, so you'll check this box.

The Support MFC option includes the MFC headers and defeats the whole purpose of writing in ATL at all. If you check this, just stop now and go back and write the control in MFC. It will take less time to write, and you'll be happier.

The Support MTS Setting changes the way an ATL control will register to be more compatible with MTS. It keeps you from having to reregister the component with MTS each time you change it. It really doesn't apply to Active Controls because they are written for Visual Basic and controls don't have a lot to do with MTS.

The last option is whether to support COM+. This is not useful for custom controls, so don't select it.

ATL Object Wizard

Next, you must insert an ATL control object. This is done by selecting Add Class from the Project menu. This dialog, shown in Figure 9.3 offers several choices. You'll choose ATL Control, which displays the wizard shown in Figure 9.4.

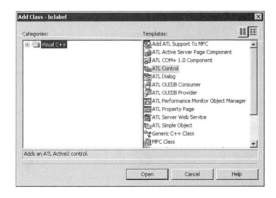

FIGURE 9.3
Visual C++ Add Class dialog.

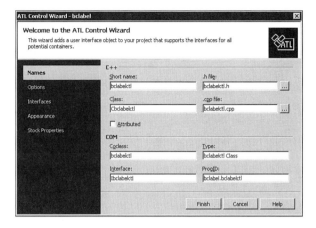

FIGURE 9.4

Visual C++ ATL Control Wizard —Names.

The first tab of the ATL Control wizard (Names, shown in Figure 9.4) allows you to name the files, classes, and interfaces involved with your control. You can place a name in the Short Name field and the wizard will fill in the rest for you. You cannot use the same name as the base project, because this would produce files with conflicting names. What I typically do is add ctl to the base name, indicating that these files are the control files rather than the base project files.

The next tab of the ATL Control Wizard (Options, shown in Figure 9.5) allows the configuration of several basic options for the control. One option allows you to select the type of control. Your choices are Standard Control, Composite Control, or DHTML Control. The Minimal setting allows you to create a light version of any one of these types of controls.

NOTE

The standard control is the type of control that you will explore in depth. This is typically the kind of control that you would create when you are writing a custom control for Visual Basic. The Standard Control is used for any type of control that exists as a single window (rather than multiple controls).

You would create a Composite Control if your custom control consists of several different windows. For example, if your control had several edit windows and a few buttons on it, the Composite Control would be the way to write that control. The Composite Control is also the only type of ATL control that will allow the use of other ActiveX controls in the project. You will learn more about Composite Controls later in this chapter.

The DHTML Control uses HTML to render the UI and interacts with the browser through special interfaces to interact with the HTML UI. While this is an interesting type of control, you will not explore it in this chapter.

The light version of any one of these controls eliminates certain interfaces from the control. The interfaces and the effects of removing them are discussed later in the chapter.

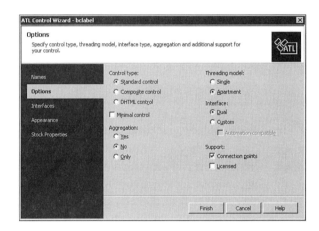

FIGURE 9.5

Visual C++ ATL Control Wizard —Options.

Next, you can choose whether the control can be aggregated or not. You can choose Yes, No, or Only. Only should not be chosen for an ActiveX Control written for Visual Basic, because it will not work properly. Either Yes or No can be chosen. Choosing Yes will allow some flexibility in the way a container works with the control. This is not important for controls used in Visual Basic, but it might be in other containers.

Another option that can be set is the threading model, the choices include Single and Apartment Threading. It is widely accepted today that Apartment Threading is the threading model required by Visual Basic components. (Threading is a very rich subject, but a full discussion is beyond the scope of this chapter.) Single threading would only be useful for a container that couldn't handle Apartment Threading. Choose Apartment Threading for this example.

You can also choose the Interface type, either Dual or Custom. Choosing a dual interface will make the control compatible with more containers and Visual Basic can handle dual interfaces, so this is what you'll choose for your sample control.

You should choose to Support Connection Points. You need them with Visual Basic, even if you don't have events. Connection points will notify Visual Basic about changes in property values, which is important for bound properties and the design environment of Visual Basic. You absolutely must have them to support events.

The next tab in the ATL Object Wizard (Interfaces, shown in Figure 9.6) is a new tab for the .NET version of Visual Studio. I'm not sure that this tab is terribly useful. Adding an interface usually consists of adding two lines to the `include` file, so it's pretty easy to add or remove interfaces later in the development of the control. Also, the list provided in this dialog is not exhaustive. There are other interfaces that you'll be interested in, and these are discussed as you apply them throughout the chapter.

In the sample, the only interface listed here that you do not need is `IserviceProvider`. You can place the rest of them in the Supported list.

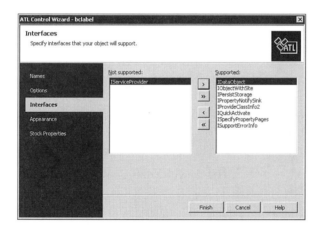

FIGURE 9.6
Visual C++ ATL Control Wizard—Interfaces.

On the next tab (Appearance, shown in Figure 9.7), there are several choices that are pertinent to the specific type of control you might be writing. You can choose to make the control opaque and use a solid background. These choices affect the way the control draws itself, but if you override `OnDraw` and draw the control yourself, these settings aren't terribly important. The biggest effect on your code could possibly be whether the control uses the `WM_ERASEBKGND` or not. Opaque controls would send this message; transparent controls would not.

In addition, the Appearance tab is where you can choose to base your control on a Windows base control (for example, `TextBox` or `CommandButton`). You will learn about writing a control based on a Windows control later in this chapter.

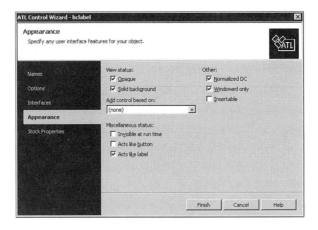

FIGURE 9.7
Visual C++ ATL Control Wizard—Appearance.

You can choose several Misc status bits here. The OLEMISC status bits are used by a container (like Visual Basic) to determine features that a control supports. To support these features usually require code in the control as well as the container. Many of the Misc status bits cannot be set from this wizard. Three of them can, Invisible at Runtime, Acts Like a Button, and Acts Like a Label.

Invisible at Runtime is self-explanatory and this actually requires no coding support in the control, Visual Basic handles this status bit. However, a control of this type will NOT have a valid window handle at runtime, even if you've selected the feature that the control is always supposed to have a valid window handle.

The Acts Like a Button status bit allows the container to handle a default button setting with the control. The Acts Like a Label will cause the container to handle a mnemonic with the control and set the focus to the control after it in the tab order.

Also choose a Normalized DC. This makes the control draw a little slower, but saves the DC state before drawing and restores it afterward.

Insertable is also available on this tab, but is not usually done for an Active control, so don't choose it. You may want to use the Insertable option if the control will be used in other containers, such as in Excel or Word. It will not adversely affect the control to choose this option.

Windowed Only is also on this tab. Setting this will guarantee the control will have a valid window handle.

> **TIP**
>
> It has been my experience when coding complex controls that you should use a windowed control and, in particular, with a control based on a Windows-base control, this is mandatory. Just remember that if you do not select this, you can't depend on having a valid window handle, and some things will be more difficult to do.

The last tab is Stock Properties, shown in Figure 9.8. These are properties that are supported by ATL without any additional coding on your part. This property page in Visual Studio 6 was not as useful as the one in .NET. The property names have been changed to more standard choices, and the spaces in the names have been removed. Using the properties on this page can save a lot of effort in a new control.

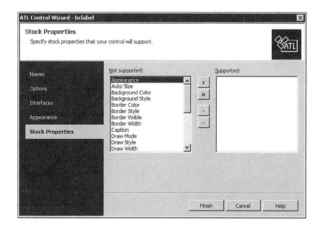

FIGURE 9.8
Visual C++ ATL Control Wizard—Stock Properties.

Now that you have set the options in the ATL Object Wizard, you can choose Finish to build the project. This builds your base project and now you can add properties, methods, and events to the project.

Most of the ATL sample code shown in this section can be found in the sample `bclabel`. This sample code is available on the Web site.

Adding Properties

You can either add properties manually or though the wizard interface. Using the wizard is pretty straightforward. The Add Property Wizard is accessed from the class view by right-clicking the main interface of the control. Figure 9.9 shows the Names tab where the property is added. Figure 9.10 shows the IDL Attributes tab.

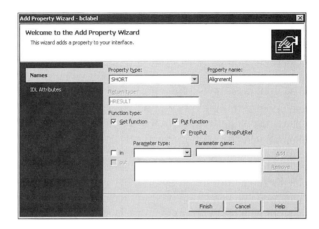

FIGURE 9.9
Visual C++ Add Property Wizard—Names.

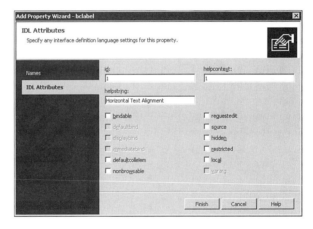

FIGURE 9.10
Visual C++ Add Property Wizard—IDL Attributes.

Now, you'll examine the result of using the wizard to add a property and see what changes are made to the files when properties are added.

When adding a property, there is an addition to the IDL file, the H file, and the C file. Look at the additions and the way they are interconnected. It is assumed, for this sample, that you've added a property named Alignment and that you'll initially make this property type short.

Because you have to update several files, it might make sense to use the wizard when adding a property. In Visual Basic, creating a property for a control or object is accomplished by changing one file, so a wizard is not really that much of an advantage.

The IDL file contains the interface definition. This is the source file that will generate the type library so other programs can discover the contents of the interface. This type information is generated automatically in Visual Basic for files that require it, so VB programmers will not be familiar with an IDL file. You have seen their format and use earlier in this chapter.

The additions are shown next. The `id` is an important aspect of the interface definitions. Later in the chapter, you'll change this to use a constant, which will be defined earlier in the IDL file. This `id` must be used in a few places within the code, and using a constant can be a much better experience than using the literal number.

Notice that the variable type is a `short`. Later, you will change this to a declared type.

```
[id(1), propget] HRESULT Alignment([out, retval] short* );
[id(1), propput] HRESULT Alignment([in] short );
```

The `include` file holds the prototypes for these functions. The additions to that file are shown next. Here, you see the Get and Set prototypes for the property. These prototypes appear within the class definition of the control, in a public section. This means that the functions will be publicly accessible. The type library, generated from the IDL file, is the mechanism that makes the routines discoverable through an interface to external programs.

```
STDMETHOD (get_Alignment)(/*[out, retval]*/ short* );
STDMETHOD (put_Alignment)(/*[in]*/ short );
```

The following code shows what happens to the implementation file. The implementation file has the routines where the actual code will be placed (`.CPP`). At this point, all you'll have is the skeleton of the functions. You'll have to add the implementation ourselves.

```
STDMETHODIMP Cbclabel::get_Alignment(/*[out, retval]*/ short* pVal)
{
}

STDMETHODIMP Cbclabel::put_Alignment(/*[in]*/ short newVal)
{
}
```

The following code shows the same code within a Visual Basic control. This is all the code that is required to implement the skeleton of the property. The Get does the same work as the `get_` in the C++ code, and the Let is the same as the `put_` in the C++ code.

```
Public Property Get Alignment() As Integer

End Property
```

```
Public Property Let Alignment(ByVal newVal As Integer)

End Property
```

In many circumstances, a property is supported by adding a member variable and then placing code within the put_ and get_ routines to interact with the member variable. Again, this is very similar to what you might do in Visual Basic control, use a member variable to store the property value.

Usually on the get_, all that is necessary is to return the value of the member variable. In the put_, however, is where you would typically place code to implement the property. How much work is done there depends on the use of the property within the control. If the property is used within the drawing code, it is usually sufficient to set the member variable and cause the control to repaint.

The next code snippet shows the addition of the member variable within the Public section of the class. This variable will hold the value of the alignment property for an instance of the control.

```
short   m_alignment;
```

The following code shows the addition of a member variable within the Declaration section of a class in Visual Basic. This variable will hold the value of the alignment property for an instance of the VB control.

```
Dim m_alignment As Integer
```

Listing 9.3 shows the implementation for the put_Alignment that you have done.

LISTING 9.3   Property put_ Changes

```
STDMETHODIMP Cbclabel::put_Alignment(short newVal)
{
if (m_alignment == newVal) return S_OK;

if (FireOnRequestEdit(DISPID_ALIGNMENT) == S_FALSE)
return S_FALSE;
m_alignment = newVal; // Save new alignment
m_bRequiresSave = TRUE; // Set dirty flag
//    if (!m_nFreezeEvents) // Notify container
FireOnChanged(DISPID_ALIGNMENT);
FireViewChange(); // Request redraw
SendOnDataChanged(NULL); // Notify advise sinks
return S_OK;
}
```

Listing 9.3.2 shows a comparable implementation for the `Alignment` property in a Visual Basic control.

LISTING 9.3.2 Property `Let` in VB

```
Public Property Let Alignment(ByVal newVal As Integer)

    If m_alignment <> newVal Then
        m_alignment = newVal   ' Save new alignment
    End If

End Property
```

Listing 9.3 shows some typical things that you might do in a property put. If the value is not changing, one thing you can do is short-circuit the routine. There is no use going through the motions if you aren't going to have an effect. Next, you can check to see if you can change the property by calling `FireOnRequestEdit`.

After you find that you can change the property, you set the new value into the member variable. Then you dirty the control by setting the `m_bRequiresSave` to `TRUE`.

`FireOnChanged` notifies any `IPropertyNotifySink` interface of the change in the property. `IPropertyNotifySink` is usually used to update the property browser or data binding.

> **NOTE**
>
> Notice that the `m_nFreezeEvents` is commented out. Some texts will tell you to use this to ensure that you don't send events back to the container while events are frozen. In my experience, doing this check at this point causes the Visual Basic container to miss these property change notifications, and the property window will not update properly. I've never had a problem just leaving this check out.

`FireViewChange` will cause the control to repaint, eventually. The actual repaint will occur when the next paint message comes through. This means that you can call `FireViewChange` for several different properties, and the control will probably just repaint once. `FireViewChange` will handle windowed and windowless controls and should be called if the control needs to be repainted after a property change.

The above items are standard for a control property that would affect the visual aspects of the control. There are several other types of properties that you may have to handle, and each one has its own requirements and attributes.

Runtime-only properties, for example, can be coded using a couple of methods: First you can leave the property off any of your property pages. Then, by making a change in the IDL file and adding the nonbrowseable attribute to the property there, the Visual Basic property browser will not see the property either. This combination effectively renders the property to runtime only. The following code shows how to change the IDL file to make a property non-browsable.

```
[propput, id(1), nonbrowseable] HRESULT Alignment([in] short newVal);
[propget, id(1) , nonbrowseable] HRESULT Alignment([out, retval] short *pVal);
```

> **NOTE**
>
> There are several attributes that you can use on properties. All these attributes are set in the IDL file.

If you want to be certain that a property is runtime only, you can check the User mode with GetAmbientUserMode. This will allow you to return an error in design mode and allow the property to change in run mode. Listing 9.4 shows how to use GetAmbientUserMode to make sure the property is set only at runtime.

LISTING 9.4   Runtime-Only Property

```
STDMETHODIMP Cbclabel::put_Alignment(short newVal)
{
    BOOL bMode=FALSE;

    GetAmbientUserMode(bMode);
    if (!bMode)
            return Error(_T("Runtime only set."),CLSID_CFrame,0x800A7D01);
        if (m_alignment == newVal) return S_OK;

        if (FireOnRequestEdit(DISPID_ALIGNMENT) == S_FALSE)
            return S_FALSE;
        m_alignment = newVal; // Save new alignment
        m_bRequiresSave = TRUE; // Set dirty flag
//    if (!m_nFreezeEvents) // Notify container
        FireOnChanged(DISPID_ALIGNMENT); FireViewChange(); // Request redraw
        SendOnDataChanged(NULL); // Notify advise sinks
        return S_OK;
}
```

Listing 9.4 returns an error when in design mode. We'll talk more about errors a little later in this section.

Design-time properties, too, are unique. When implementing a design time-only property, the User Mode is your only means of protecting that property from being set at runtime. Checking the User mode and returning an error is the way to block setting properties at runtime. Listing 9.5 shows how to code a design-time only property.

> **NOTE**
>
> Try to avoid building controls with design-time only properties if at all possible. It is much nicer to be able to set properties at runtime, if for no other reason than to document the changes to the control. Unlike VC++, ActiveX Controls built in Visual Basic cannot expose design time-only properties from your control when it is used as a constituent control.

LISTING 9.5   Design Time-Only Property

```
STDMETHODIMP Cbclabel::put_Alignment(short newVal)
{
    BOOL bMode=FALSE;

    GetAmbientUserMode(bMode);
    if (bMode)
            return Error(_T("Alignment property cannot be set at
    runtime"),CLSID_Cbclabel,0x800A017E);

    if (m_alignment == newVal) return S_OK;

    if (FireOnRequestEdit(DISPID_ALIGNMENT) == S_FALSE)
            return S_FALSE;
    m_alignment = newVal; // Save new alignment
    m_bRequiresSave = TRUE; // Set dirty flag
    if (!m_nFreezeEvents) // Notify container
        FireOnChanged(DISPID_ALIGNMENT);
        FireViewChange(); // Request redraw
        SendOnDataChanged(NULL); // Notify advise sinks
        return S_OK;
}
```

Array properties are fairly simple to implement. They are simply a property with a parameter. Normally, array properties should be runtime-only properties; Visual Basic will not show properties that have parameters within its property browser anyway. Typically, you use property arrays for certain sorts of lists, such as the strings in a list box. The parameter holds the Index to the property array, and the code merely returns or sets the proper item in the array.

The following code demonstrates an array property. This example was taken from a different production control, because the label control you are using does not demonstrate an array property.

```
[propget, id(68)] HRESULT DayArr([in] short Index, [out, retval] short *pVal);
[propput, id(68)] HRESULT DayArr([in] short Index, [in] short newVal);

STDMETHOD (get_DayArr)(/*[in]*/ short Index, /*[out, retval]*/ short *pVal);
STDMETHOD (put_DayArr)(/*[in]*/ short Index, /*[in]*/ short newVal);

STDMETHODIMP Ccal::get_DayArr(short Index, short *pVal)
{
    *pVal = m_lpselected[Index];
    return S_OK;
}
STDMETHODIMP Ccal::put_DayArr(short Index, short newVal)
{
    m_lpselected[Index] = newVal;
    return S_OK;
}
```

Read-only or write-only properties can be implemented by taking out the appropriate property get_ or put_ routine. Remove it from the IDL file, the H file, and the C file to set the property up properly. The hwnd property is an example of a read-only property.

Adding Methods

Adding methods to a control is similar to the way you added properties—even the code is somewhat similar. For example, methods can have parameters.

The Add Method Wizard is accessed from the same place as the Add Property Wizard, by right-clicking the control's interface. Figure 9.11 shows the Names tab of the Add Method Wizard, and Figure 9.12 shows the Attribute tab of the Add Method Wizard.

When adding a method, The wizard will make an addition to the IDL file, the H file, and the C file. Look at the additions and the way they are interconnected. The following line of code shows the code added to the IDL file.

```
[id(2)] HRESULT Refresh();
```

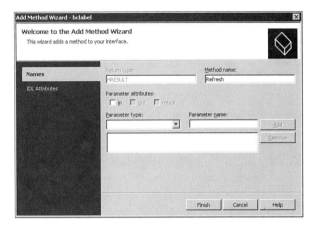

FIGURE 9.11
Visual C++ Add Method Wizard—Names.

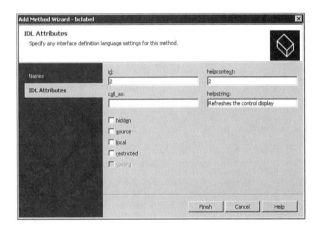

FIGURE 9.12
Visual C++ Add Method Wizard—IDL Attributes.

The method is in the same place as the properties for the control. Methods are part of the same interface as the properties.

The next code snippet shows the addition made by the wizard to the `include` file and, just as in the case with the properties, places a prototype of the method. Of course, the get and set prefixes are not there, just the method name.

```
STDMETHOD (Refresh)();
```

The next code snippet shows the implementation in the CPP file for the method. When the wizard adds it, the method is only the skeleton. Here, for the sake of brevity, the code has been added to that skeleton.

```
STDMETHODIMP Cbclabel::Refresh()
{
    FireViewChange();
    return S_OK;
}
```

In Visual Basic, you create a method simply by adding a `Public Sub` procedure to the control. The following code demonstrates this:

```
Public Sub Refresh()
    UserControl.Refresh
End Sub
```

Methods are runtime only and, as such, never appear in a property browser. As a result, there is no need to do a runtime check in a method, because unless the code calls it explicitly, it will never be called in design mode.

Implementing Events

Back when you first generated your ATL control, you chose to implement connection points—doing so allowed you to provide events for your control. You will learn the subsequent steps involved in implementing events in this section.

To implement an event in an ATL control, you first add methods to the event interface. This is done with a wizard that is very similar to one used for properties and methods added to the control interface. This wizard looks just like the one in Figure 9.11 that you've already reviewed. Event interfaces do not use properties, you add only methods to event interfaces.

A method when added to the event interface becomes an event for the control. You can check the IDL file, by looking under the event interface, to make sure these events go in the correct location. The following code shows how the event addition to the IDL might look. At this point, there have been no additions to the CPP or H file.

```
dispinterface _IbclabelEvents
    {
        properties:
        methods:
            [id(1), helpstring("Click Event")] void Click();
        };
```

Next, generate the type library (TLB) file. The TLB file is built when the IDL file is compiled. You can do this by compiling the project or just the IDL file. This is a little foreign to a Visual Basic programmer, because the type library information is handled internally by Visual Basic.

After you have compiled the IDL, you can then generate the code that implements the ICconnectionPoint interface. This is done with a wizard from C++. The wizard adds the proxy event class used to fire the events and exposes the IConnectionPointContainer interface from the control.

Windows Message Maps

Adding a Windows Message Handler is made much easier with VC++. This is done with a wizard from the environment. It is good to know what happens underneath, though. The message map in the header file comes into play here.

Handling Windows messages is where VC++ holds an advantage over Visual Basic Controls. In VB, there is no intrinsic way of handling messages at this level.

NOTE

You can use third-party controls to intercept messages in Visual Basic, or you can use AddressOf to intercept them as well. Both methods involve subclassing the window in question. However, neither of these methods lead to solid coding practices in the resultant program.

Handling messages at this level typically requires casting a pointer somewhere, which Visual Basic cannot do. This means that you usually end up doing a memory copy from one type of variable to another to make up for this fact. This is quite inefficient, especially if you are handling a message that occurs a lot, such as a mouse message.

In addition, AddressOf—according to Microsoft—may not react correctly to normal debugging procedures. In my experience, I've found that when you enter the subclass procedure, you must exit normally or bad things happen.

ATL message maps in the control's header file can have message handlers, command handlers, and notify handlers—these and many, many more.

The entry within the MESSAGE_MAP is what routes the message to a particular routine. You can route messages to a single routine or route each message to a different routine. I usually find it helpful to route all the different mouse messages to one single routine, because there is usually a lot of similar code to be executed. Listing 9.6 shows how a typical message map might look.

LISTING 9.6   Message Map

```
BEGIN_MSG_MAP(Cbclabel)
    CHAIN_MSG_MAP(CComControl<Cbclabel>)
    DEFAULT_REFLECTION_HANDLER()
    MESSAGE_HANDLER(WM_LBUTTONDBLCLK, OnMMessage)
```

LISTING 9.6   Continued

```
    MESSAGE_HANDLER(WM_LBUTTONDOWN, OnMMessage)
    MESSAGE_HANDLER(WM_LBUTTONUP, OnMMessage)
    MESSAGE_HANDLER(WM_MOUSEMOVE, OnMMessage)
    MESSAGE_HANDLER(WM_RBUTTONDBLCLK, OnMMessage)
    MESSAGE_HANDLER(WM_RBUTTONDOWN, OnMMessage)
    MESSAGE_HANDLER(WM_RBUTTONUP, OnMMessage)
    MESSAGE_HANDLER(WM_SETCURSOR, OnSetCursor)
    MESSAGE_HANDLER(WM_TIMER, OnTimer)
    MESSAGE_HANDLER(WM_NCHITTEST, OnMMessage)
    MESSAGE_HANDLER(WM_ERASEBKGND, OnEraseBK)
    MESSAGE_HANDLER(WM_CREATE, OnCreate)
    MESSAGE_HANDLER(WM_KEYDOWN, OnKey)
END_MSG_MAP()
```

The first entry chains a generic message map. The CHAIN_MSG_MAP adds a different series of messages to the message map. The MESSAGE_HANDLER macros direct your messages to the proper handlers.

Of course, the routine that you direct the messages to must exist. So you have the prototype of the routine within the Public section of the class. The implementation can be either in there or in the CPP file. The following is how the prototype will look:

```
LRESULT OnMMessage(UINT uMsg, WPARAM wParam, LPARAM lParam, BOOL& bHandled);
```

Handling the Mouse

Dealing with the mouse in a custom control can be straightforward, as in the case of firing the mouse events, or fairly complex, such as mouse enter and exit events, interactive drawing with the mouse, sizing areas on the screen and handling zooming. It depends on what the control is trying to accomplish. You'll first take on the "normal" handling of the mouse and then a few of the more complex issues.

Implementing Simple Mouse Events

Listing 9.7 shows the implementation for a typical set of mouse messages. Notice at the top of the function that you call routines that convert from pixels to container coordinates. This is pretty normal for handling the mouse. Mouse messages come from the system in device coordinates, you have to convert them to more useful coordinates, if that is required.

LISTING 9.7   Mouse Messages in an ATL Control

```
LRESULT Cbclabel::OnMMessage(UINT uMsg,
➡WPARAM wParam, LPARAM lParam, BOOL& bHandled)
```

LISTING 9.7   Continued

```
{
    USES_CONVERSION;
    short     button;
    short     shift = GetShiftState();
    float     X;
    float     Y;
    SIZEL     tsize;
    POINTF    psize;
    BSTR      cbstrscale;

    cbstrscale = SysAllocString((const OLECHAR *)_T("Twip"));
    GetAmbientScaleUnits((BSTR&)cbstrscale);
        //these lines can be used for twips if that's all you need
    //X = (float) XPixelsToTwips((int) (short) LOWORD(lParam), NULL);
    //Y = (float) YPixelsToTwips((int) (short) HIWORD(lParam), NULL);
    tsize.cx=(int) (short) LOWORD(lParam);
    tsize.cy=(int) (short) HIWORD(lParam);
    psize.x=0;
    psize.y=0;

    BCPixeltoContainerPos(m_polecontrolsite, &tsize, &psize,
➥OLE2T(cbstrscale));
    SysFreeString(cbstrscale);
    X=psize.x;
    Y=psize.y;
        switch (uMsg)
    {
    case WM_LBUTTONDBLCLK:
        Fire_DblClick();
        break;
    case WM_LBUTTONDOWN:
        button = 1;
        m_sButton = 1;
        Fire_MouseDown((LONG) &button, (LONG) &shift, (LONG) &X, (LONG) &Y);
        SetCapture();
        break;
    case WM_LBUTTONUP:
        button = 1;
        m_sButton = 1;
        ReleaseCapture();
        Fire_MouseUp((LONG) &button, (LONG)  &shift, (LONG) &X, (LONG) &Y);
        Fire_Click();
        break;
    case WM_MOUSEMOVE:
```

9

COMPONENTS AND
CONTROLS

LISTING 9.7   Continued

```
        if (!m_overcontrol)
            ::PostMessage(m_hWnd,WM_TIMER,0,0L);
        button = m_sButton;
        Fire_MouseMove((LONG) &button, (LONG) &shift, (LONG) &X, (LONG) &Y);
        break;
    case WM_RBUTTONDOWN:
        button = 2;
        m_sButton = 2;
        Fire_MouseDown((LONG) &button, (LONG) &shift, (LONG) &X, (LONG) &Y);
        SetCapture();
        break;
    case WM_RBUTTONUP:
        button = 2;
        m_sButton = 2;
        ReleaseCapture();
        Fire_MouseUp((LONG) &button, (LONG) &shift, (LONG) &X, (LONG) &Y);
        break;
    case WM_NCHITTEST:
        {
        BOOL bMode=FALSE;

        GetAmbientUserMode(bMode);

        if (bMode)
            if (!m_overcontrol)
                ::PostMessage(m_hWnd,WM_TIMER,0,0L);
        break;
        }
    }
    bHandled = FALSE;
    return 0;
}
```

Listing 9.7 has some routines that convert to Twips. Those routines are commented out. Twips will work fine as long as you leave the containing form in Twips scale mode. This is a little faster, but your control is not as robust. If you change the scale mode from Twips for the container of this label control, this control will also change its coordinate system and the top, left, width, and height will be expressed in the scale mode of the container.

Take a look at the conversion of the mouse coordinates. Listing 9.8 shows the code in the conversion routine. The conversion relies on two built-in functions to do the work—AtlPixeltoHiMetric and TransformCoods. Between these two routines, you can convert from pixels to any container coordinates.

LISTING 9.8   Convert Pixels to Container Coordinates

```
void BCPixeltoContainerPos(LPOLECONTROLSITE pcs, LPSIZEL inpix,
➥LPPOINTF incont, LPTSTR scalemode)
{
    SIZEL    tsize;
    POINTL   psize;

    AtlPixelToHiMetric( inpix, &tsize );
    psize.x = tsize.cx;
    psize.y = tsize.cy;

pcs->TransformCoords(&psize, incont,XFORMCOORDS_POSITION |
➥XFORMCOORDS_HIMETRICTOCONTAINER);

    if ((0==lstrcmp("Twip", scalemode)) || (0==lstrcmp("Pixel", scalemode)))
    {
        //round to even number
        incont->x = (float) (long) (incont->x + (float).5);
        incont->y = (float) (long) (incont->y + (float).5);
    }
}
```

What you've covered in this section will handle the "normal" mouse events. What about that timer message in Listing 9.8 and the m_overcontrol flag in that same routine? These have to do with the custom events MouseEnter and MouseExit.

Implementing Mouse Custom Events

MouseEnter and MouseExit routines can come in very handy. The mouse enter is pretty easy to handle. In the mouse move message, you simply check your flag (m_overcontrol). If it is cleared, you fire the event and set the flag. Of course, unless you can clear the flag, the event would only fire once.

You would clear your flag on the mouse exit, but that's the problematic part of the code. If your code will never run on WIN95 systems, you can use the TrackMouseEvent to track the mouse and tell when it leaves the window. If your code is to be functional on WIN95 systems though, your choices are limited to using a timer to tell when the mouse is no longer over your window.

What you do in each timer message is check to see if you're over the window. If your over flag is cleared, but now you are over the window, you set the timer, set the flag, and fire the mouse enter routine.

In the same timer event, you can clear your flag, fire the mouse exit routine, and kill the timer when you leave the window. You "seed" your timer routine by posting a timer message from

9

the mouse down message so that the logic will be in one place—in the timer routine. Listing 9.9 demonstrates how you manage the MouseEnter and MouseExit events.

LISTING 9.9   MouseEnter and MouseExit Events

```
LRESULT Cbclabel::OnTimer(UINT uMsg, WPARAM wp, LPARAM lp, BOOL& bHandled)
{
    POINT     Point;
    BOOL inrect;
    RECT    wrect;
    BOOL bMode=FALSE;
    GetAmbientUserMode(bMode);

    //no tip unless in run mode
    if (!bMode)           // if not run mode...
        return 0;
    //if window is disabled then return!
    if (!m_enabled)
        return 0;
    GetCursorPos( &Point);
    //get our screen rect
    GetWindowRect(&wrect);
    //if we're in it set to true and fire event
    if ((Point.x >= wrect.left) &&
        (Point.x <= wrect.right) &&
        (Point.y >= wrect.top) &&
        (Point.y <= wrect.bottom))
        inrect=TRUE;
    if (TRUE == inrect)
    {
        if (!m_overcontrol)
        {
            m_overcontrol = TRUE;
            Fire_MouseEnter();
            FireViewChange();
            ::SetTimer(m_hWnd,1,200,NULL);
        }
    }
    else
    {
        if (m_overcontrol)
        {
            m_overcontrol = FALSE;
            Fire_MouseExit();
            FireViewChange();
            ::KillTimer(m_hWnd,1);
```

LISTING 9.9   Continued

```
        }
    }
    return 0;


}
```

Setting the Mouse Cursor

Another area that you must address is the mouse cursor. Again, this is something that typically worked without any intervention in Visual Basic controls. In ATL controls, you need to handle the cursor setting. Listing 9.10 shows how to handle the different mouse cursor settings.

LISTING 9.10   Handling the Mouse Cursor

```
LRESULT Cbclabel::OnSetCursor(UINT uMsg, WPARAM wParam,
➥LPARAM lParam, BOOL& bHandled)
{
    POINT ptMouse;
    HCURSOR hCursor = NULL;
    HINSTANCE hInstance = NULL;
    BOOL bMode=FALSE;

    GetAmbientUserMode(bMode);

    // If the MousePointer property does not indicate the default
    // cursor and we're in run mode

    if (m_mousepointer && bMode)
    {
        // If the mouse cursor is over the client area
        if (((HWND)wParam == m_hWnd) && (LOWORD(lParam) == HTCLIENT))
        {
            GetCursorPos(&ptMouse);
            ::ScreenToClient(m_hWnd, &ptMouse);

            // If the MousePointer property indicates a custom
            //cursor is not to be used, set the mouse cursor to a
            //stock bitmap.
            // Otherwise, use the bitmap indicated by the MouseIcon
            // property.
            if ((m_mousepointer != CUSTOM_CURSOR) && (m_mousepointer != 16))
            {
                hCursor = LoadCursor(hInstance, idCursor[m_mousepointer]);
            }
```

9

LISTING 9.10   Continued

```
            else if (m_pmouseicon)
            {
                CComQIPtr<IPicture,&IID_IPicture> pPic(m_pmouseicon);
                if (pPic)
                {
                    pPic->get_Handle((OLE_HANDLE *)&hCursor);
                }
            }
            // If the bitmap exists, use it to set the mouse cursor
            if (hCursor)
                SetCursor(hCursor);
        return 0;
        }
    }
    bHandled=FALSE;
    return 0;
}
```

As you can see, after loading the appropriate bitmap, you use `SetCursor` to put that cursor into use.

Handling the Keyboard

Because your sample control is a label control, it cannot receive focus and, therefore, has no keyboard interaction. However, because many controls *will* have to handle the keyboard, you'll learn about some of the things that you might have to do using code cut out of other production controls.

First, to get all the keystrokes that you want, you might have to override `TranslateAccelerator`. Without doing this, your key down and key up routines probably would not receive messages that represent things like arrow keys, page keys, Tab, and enter. In other words, keys that might be used for navigation and control might not make it to your control. For example, an edit control may need arrow keys for navigation and the Enter key for new lines. Listing 9.11 shows how to override and use the `TranslateAccelerator`.

LISTING 9.11   Override `TranslateAccelerator`

```
STDMETHOD(TranslateAccelerator)(LPMSG pMsg)
    {
        BOOL    bHandled=FALSE;
        if ((pMsg->message == WM_KEYDOWN) || (pMsg->message == WM_KEYUP)
            OnKey(pMsg->message, pMsg->wParam, pMsg->lParam, bHandled);
```

LISTING 9.11   Continued

```
        if (!bHandled)
            return
IOleInPlaceActiveObjectImpl<Ccal>::TranslateAccelerator(pMsg);
        else
            return 0;
    }
```

When your control is receiving the keystrokes that you need, you'll probably need to place some code in the key events to handle those keystrokes. At the very least, you'll want to fire the keyboard events and block action on keystrokes that you really don't want that might have been enabled in your override of `TranslateAccelerator`. Listing 9.12 shows the code necessary to fire the Key events.

LISTING 9.12   Key Event Handler

```
LRESULT Ccal::OnKey(UINT msg, WPARAM wp, LPARAM lp, BOOL& bHandled)
{
    short    shift = GetShiftState();
    short    sKey=wp;
    switch(msg)
    {
        case WM_CHAR:
            Fire_KeyPress((LONG) &sKey);
            bHandled=FALSE;
            return 0;
        case WM_KEYUP:
            Fire_KeyUp((LONG) &sKey, (LONG) &shift);
            bHandled=FALSE;
            return 0;
        case WM_KEYDOWN:
            Fire_KeyDown((LONG) &sKey, (LONG) &shift);
            bHandled=FALSE;
            switch(wp)
            {
                //this switch statement can handle
                //individual keystroke reactions
                case VK_LEFT:
                    break;
                case VK_RIGHT:
                    break;
                case VK_DOWN:
                    break;
                case VK_UP:
```

LISTING 9.12   Continued

```
                    break;
                case VK_PRIOR:
                    break;
                case VK_NEXT:
                    break;
                case VK_SPACE:
                    break;
                default:
                    break;
            }
        }
    return 0;
}
```

Notice that, like the mouse events, you route all the key events through one function. Based on the message, you fire the correct event. The switch statement in the key down event has no functionality built in, but is an example of how you can respond to different keys. The same type of switch statement can be placed in the key up or char cases. Notice that you are setting bHandled to false. If you want the default processing to not take place, set the bHandled to true and the control will "eat" the keystroke.

Your keyboard handling could be much more complex, especially if your control is an input control of some type. Code fashioned after these examples will handle most types of controls.

Property Pages

Now, you'll take a look at simple property pages done in ATL and Visual Basic. The property pages are connected to the property by the persistence macros. This works well, because it doesn't make much sense to have a property page for properties that are not persisted. You'll look at the actual connection mechanism in a little more detail when you work with the actual property page.

These property pages (either ATL or VB property pages) can be summoned (in the Visual Basic property browser) by clicking the ellipses placed next to the property. The property pages can also be accessed from the (Custom) property listed in the property browser. If you want to be able to bring up your property page with a right-click on your control in design mode, you have to do a little more work.

You must implement DoVerb, as shown in Listing 9.13. This adds the code that will respond to the right button click within the control at design time to bring up the property pages.

LISTING 9.13   Activate Property Page with Right Click

```
STDMETHOD(DoVerb)(LONG iVerb,LPMSG lpmsg, IOleClientSite *pActiveSite, _
➥LONG lindex, HWND hwndParent, LPCRECT lprcPosRect)
{
    if (iVerb == 1)
        return IOleObjectImpl<Cbclabel>::DoVerb(OLEIVERB_PROPERTIES, lpmsg,
                                        pActiveSite, lindex, hwndParent,
                                lprcPosRect);
    return IOleObjectImpl<Cbclabel>::DoVerb(iVerb, lpmsg,
                                        pActiveSite, lindex, hwndParent,
                                lprcPosRect);


}
```

Property pages provided through ATL are straightforward using a wizard. The property page is a scaled-down sample from a calendar control. The property page will have one text control on it that will set the date of the control. Call the property page testprop, and Date is the property you'll be setting.

You start by adding a property page to the custom control, just as you first added the full control. Set the information on the Names tab, the Options tab, and the Strings tab. This wizard is very similar to the wizard that you used to add the ATL Control with fewer choices to be made.

NOTE

Don't get hung up on deciding what needs to go on the Strings tab. Those items get added to your string table in your resource file, and you can change them at any time. However, you do want to be comfortable with the name of the class and files on the Names tab; it isn't so easy to change that information later.

After you have the property page added to the project, you need to add controls that you will use to set properties. In the sample, you'll add just one text control. In addition to the text control, you need to add a mapping for the text box change event. The following code shows the routine that is called for this text control's change notification. All you do is call SetDirty. You'll read more about that a little later in this section.

```
LRESULT OnChangeDate(WORD wNotifyCode, WORD wID, HWND hWndCtl, BOOL& bHandled)
{
    // TODO : Add Code for control notification handler.
    SetDirty(true);
    return 0;
}
```

After you've done this, you need to start adding code to make the property page work. This is where most documentation I've seen doesn't do a very good job. The Apply override is usually shown to you, but there are two more overrides that are important when using property pages.

The first override is SetObjects. Because you'll be setting the date property, you'll only allow one object to be set at a time. The following code shows the SetObjects override. Notice that you check for a single object and the correct interface. If you find that, you set the properties in the object.

```
STDMETHOD(SetObjects)(ULONG nObjects, IUnknown** ppUnk)
{
    HRESULT hr = E_INVALIDARG;
    if (nObjects == 1)
    {
        CComQIPtr<Ical> pDoc(ppUnk[0]);
        if (pDoc)
            hr = IPropertyPageImpl<Ctestprop>::SetObjects(nObjects, ppUnk);
    }
    return hr;
}
```

The next routine you'll need to handle is Activate. This is where you set the default values in the controls on the property page. Listing 9.14 shows the Activate override. This property page has only one text box control on it. You get the value for that control from the date property of the custom control to which this property page is attached. Again, you check for the proper interface first.

LISTING 9.14   The Activate Override

```
STDMETHOD(Activate)(HWND hWndParent, LPCRECT prc, BOOL bModal)
{
    USES_CONVERSION;
        // Call the base class implementation
    HRESULT hr = IPropertyPageImpl<Ctestprop>::Activate(hWndParent, prc,
➥bModal);
    if (FAILED(hr))
        return hr;
    // Get the Ical pointer
    CComQIPtr<Ical> pDoc(m_ppUnk[0]);
    if (!pDoc)
        return E_UNEXPECTED;
    // Get the FullName property
    CComBSTR bstr;
    hr = pDoc->get_Date(&bstr);
    if (FAILED(hr))
```

LISTING 9.14   The Activate Override

```
      return hr;
   // Set the text box so that the user can see the document name
⮕USES_CONVERSION;
   SetDlgItemText(IDC_DATE, W2CT(bstr));
   SetDirty(false);
   return hr;
}
```

The last override is `Apply`. This is where you take the values in the property page and apply them to the control. You get a pointer to the control's class and call the set function directly. The following code demonstrates the `Apply` override.

```
STDMETHOD(Apply)(void)
{
    USES_CONVERSION;
    for (UINT i = 0; i < m_nObjects; i++)
    {
        CComQIPtr<Ical, &IID_Ical> pPoly(m_ppUnk[i]);

        CComBSTR bstrDate;
        GetDlgItemText(IDC_DATE, bstrDate.m_str);
        if FAILED(pPoly->put_Date(bstrDate.m_str))
        {
            CComPtr<IErrorInfo> pError;
            CComBSTR          strError;
            GetErrorInfo(0, &pError);
            pError->GetDescription(&strError);
            MessageBox(OLE2T(strError), _T("Error"), MB_ICONEXCLAMATION);
            return E_FAIL;
        }
    }
    SetDirty(false);
    return S_OK;
}
```

The Apply button on the property pages is worth a closer look. This button on the property pages can be enabled or disabled through a method called `SetDirty` in the property page interface. This routine was mentioned before when you looked at the code for the text control change notification mapping earlier in this section.

Basically, you must call the `SetDirty` routine with a value of `true` whenever you change a value on one of the controls on the property page that affects a property in the custom control. You need to clear the dirty flag whenever you apply the changes to the control. So there is a call to `SetDirty` routine in the `Apply` function to set the dirty flag to `false`.

9

One last place you need to clear the dirty flag is in the `Activate` function. This isn't immediately obvious, but the change mappings for the controls on the property page will set the dirty flag as the controls initialize. Because the values have not yet been changed by the user of the property page, the dirty flag should be clear. So you clear it in the `Activate` function after initializing the controls. (This is the simplest of several ways to handle the initial state of the Apply button.)

Done in Visual Basic

Because property pages are simply an interface, they can be supplied from a separate COM object. You can provide property pages written in Visual Basic in a separate OCX and use them in an ATL control. You wouldn't normally want to do this, unless you are pretty sure your target audience has the Visual Basic runtime library.

To do a property page in VB, you must also do a control, although the control need not have any functionality.

The technique involves writing the property page in Visual Basic. You use standard automation to access the control properties through two of the property pages' events. `SelectionChanged` is generally where you load values from the control to the property page, and `ApplyChanges` is where you set the control's properties based on the values in the property page.

The property page cannot really be tested within the development environment with the actual control it will support. So it is best to run your property page's interface within the environment by either dummying a control in VB or running most of the code within the environment in the best way you can find. The actual code that can't be debugged this way is minimal.

After you have a functioning property page, compile the OCX in Visual Basic. Use the OLE/COM Object Viewer (found on the tools menu in Visual Studio) to look at the resulting type library. This tool will allow you to build an IDL file. Build this IDL file and add it to your ATL control project. Compile the IDL file and add the resultant H file to your header file.

Now you can reference the property page in the VB OCX from the `PROP_ENTRY` macros. This will allow you to bring the property page up from the Visual Basic browser when your custom control is on a form in Visual Basic.

The sample label control has a property that can be set from a property page written in this manner. Listing 9.15 shows the applicable routines in Visual Basic.

LISTING 9.15   Visual Basic Property Page

```
Private Sub PropertyPage_ApplyChanges()
    Dim c As Object
    For Each c In SelectedControls
```

LISTING 9.15 Continued

```
        c.FlashTime = Val(txtFlashTime.Text)
    Next
End Sub

Private Sub PropertyPage_SelectionChanged()
    txtFlashTime = CStr(SelectedControls(0).FlashTime)
    Changed = False
End Sub

Private Sub txtFlashTime_Change()
    Changed = True
End Sub
```

As you can see, the Visual Basic code is simpler and easier to write. After writing the code, just produce and compile the IDL file.

Hooking the Property to the Page

After you produce the property page, all that's left to do is to hook it to the associated property so that it can be displayed from an ellipses button next to the property. Either method of property page production results in an `include` file. You'll use this include file with your custom control.

Either method of writing a property page will produce an `include` file that has the property page identifiers in it.

Simply include the property page include file in your control's `include` file where your property persistence macros are located. Then put the CLSID of the property page in the last parameter of the macro. You can identify this ID in the `include` file, it is declared `EXTERN_C` and is a CLSID. The following two lines are samples of the CLSID definitions that you will find in the property page `include`.

```
EXTERN_C const CLSID CLSID_VCDCFlashProp;
```

```
EXTERN_C const CLSID CLSID_testprop;
```

The ID is placed in the PROP macro as follows:

```
PROP_ENTRY("FlashTime",DISPID_BC_FLASHTIME , CLSID_VCDCFlashProp)
```

Proper Property Persistence

Persistence in a custom control refers to saving property values that are set at design time so that they are available when the form is unloaded and reloaded. This makes the property values that are persisted accessible in run mode and design mode.

Handling persistence is very straightforward in an ATL control. However, there are a few details to take care of if you want to do it properly.

This is one of the few places that a Visual Basic control requires more code than ATL. In VB, you have to place two routines to persist a property. The following code demonstrates Visual Basic property persistence:

```
Private Sub UserControl_ReadProperties(PropBag As PropertyBag)
    m_EditButton = PropBag.ReadProperty("EditButton", m_def_EditButton)
End Sub

Private Sub UserControl_WriteProperties(PropBag As PropertyBag)
    Call PropBag.WriteProperty("EditButton", m_EditButton, m_def_EditButton)
End Sub
```

The `IPersistStreamInit` interface is used in ATL controls instead of `IPersistStream`, which is used in most other objects, including Visual Basic objects. In fact, the `IPersistStreamInit` interface is used by default in all ATL COM objects. You may be asking yourself why you might write a COM object that is not an Active control, but can persist itself. Objects like that are actually fairly common; the `stdPicture` and `stdFont` objects in Visual Basic are not active controls, but they know how to persist themselves. Any object that you use as a property should know how to persist itself.

NOTE

There is a curious bug in the persistence code of ATL (before the .NET version). It seems that the code would not save objects using `IPersistStreamInit`. This is not really important for Active Controls, but could have an impact in the previously outlined procedure where you write objects in ATL and use those objects within a control as a property.

If you write a self-persisting object in ATL and use it within an ATL control, the object would not persist properly, unless you make a change in the ATL source code. Listing 9.16 shows the changes necessary to make this persistence work. The changes are applied to `CComVariant::WriteToStream`.

The ATL code delivered with the .NET versions does not require this change. The problem has been fixed.

LISTING 9.16   ATL Persistence

```
//ATL source unchanged
case VT_DISPATCH:
{
```

LISTING 9.16 Continued

```
        CComPtr<IPersistStream> spStream;
        if (punkVal != NULL)
        {
            hr = punkVal->QueryInterface(IID_IPersistStream, (void**)&spStream);
            if (FAILED(hr))
                return hr;
        }
        if (spStream != NULL)
            return OleSaveToStream(spStream, pStream);
        else
            return WriteClassStm(pStream, CLSID_NULL);
}
//ATL source modified to handle IPersistStreamInit
case VT_DISPATCH:
{
    BOOL    usestreaminit=FALSE;
    CComPtr<IPersistStream> spStream;
    CComPtr<IPersistStreamInit> spStreamInit;
    if (punkVal != NULL)
    {
        hr = punkVal->QueryInterface(IID_IPersistStream, (void**)&spStream);
        if (FAILED(hr))
        {
            hr = punkVal->QueryInterface(IID_IPersistStreamInit,
(void**)&spStream);
            if (FAILED(hr))
                return hr;
        }
        if (spStream != NULL)
            return OleSaveToStream(spStream, pStream);
        else
            return WriteClassStm(pStream, CLSID_NULL);
    }
}
```

Proper persistence in controls means inheriting from another interface besides
IPersistStreamInit for persistence. This also brings up a problem in the persistence code in
the ATL source, which you'll read about in a moment. If you persist your properties with the
control as generated by the wizard, when the control is used within Visual Basic, the control's
properties all get shoved into the FRX file in binary form.

This doesn't really hurt anything in particular, it just doesn't seem professional when all the other controls are writing in ASCII form to the FRM file. What you need to do is include the property bag interface.

Place the following line of code within your class declaration:

```
public IPersistPropertyBagImpl<CMyTest>,
```

Place the following line of code within the BEGIN_COM_MAP block.

```
COM_INTERFACE_ENTRY(IPersistPropertyBag)
```

It is worth mentioning now that the COM_INTERFACE_ENTRY is for purposes of exposing the interface to the outside world. In this case, you are letting other objects know you support IPersistPropertyBag. The addition in the class declaration points to the implementation of that interface.

If you want your control to act properly in Visual Basic when persisting properties, you need to use the PROP_ENTRY or PROP_DATA_ENTRY macro to persist a property. The ATL Object Wizard adds the first two PROP_DATA_ ENTRY macros to a control's property map when it generates the initial source code. These entries cause ATL to save and restore the extent of the control.

You must explicitly add entries for any additional properties that the control needs to persist. The PROP_ENTRY macro causes ATL to save and restore the specified property by accessing the property using the default dispatch interface for the control. When persisted properties are described via a PROP_DATA_ENTRY macro, ATL accesses the member variable in the control directly.

CAUTION

Don't add a PROP_ENTRY macro that has a property name containing an embedded space character. Visual Basic provides an implementation of IPropertyBag::Write that cannot handle names with embedded spaces.

For properties described with the PROP_ENTRY and PROP_ENTRY_EX macros, the various persistence implementations query for the appropriate interface and call IDispatch::Invoke, specifying the DISPID from the property map entry to get and put the property. Using the PROP_DATA_ENTRY macro will set the member variable directly without going though the control's automation properties.

There is presently a bug in the ATL implementation of property bag persistence for properties described using the `PROP_DATA_ENTRY` macro. The problem is in the `AtlIPersistPropertyBag_Load` function. Listing 9.17 shows a code fragment from that function. Again, this is fixed in the .NET version.

LISTING 9.17   Property Bag Load Bug Fix

```
CComVariant var;

 if (pMap[i].dwSizeData != 0)
{
    void* pData = (void*) (pMap[i].dwOffsetData + (DWORD)pThis);
    // BUG FIX line added
    var.vt = pMap[i].vt;
    HRESULT hr = pPropBag->Read(pMap[i].szDesc,  &var, pErrorLog);
    if (SUCCEEDED(hr))
    {
        switch (pMap[i].vt)
        {
            case VT_UI4:
                *((long*)pData) = var.lVal;
                break;
        }
    }
}
```

The `CComVariant` constructor initializes `var` to `VT_EMPTY`. An empty input variant permits the `IPropertyBag::Read` method to coerce the value read to any appropriate type. Note, however, that the code copies the variant's value into the member variable of the control based on the type specified in the property map entry, regardless of the type contained in the variant.

When the `_cx` and `_cy` extents are small enough, the `Read` method initializes the variant to contain a `VT_I2` (short) value. However, the property map entry specifies that the member variable is `VT_UI4` type. In this case, the code sets the high-order 16 bits of the control's extents to bogus values. Initializing the variant type to the type contained in the property map fixes the problem.

There is also a small bug in the implementation of the `PROP_ENTRY` macro that causes Visual Basic to place an ellipsis button next to a property, even when you've declared the property as having no property page by placing the CLSID_NULL constant within the PROP_ENTRY macro. Visual Basic will still try to invoke a property page and return an error for such a property. The solution, shown in Listing 9.18, has to do with the IPerPropertyBrowsing interface. Override the MapPropertyToPage and return the proper code when the CLSID_NULL is encountered. Once again, this is not necessary in the .NET code.

LISTING 9.18   Fixing MapPropertytoPage

```
STDMETHODIMP Cframe::MapPropertyToPage (DISPID dispid, CLSID *pClsid)
{
    HRESULT hr = IPerPropertyBrowsingImpl<Cframe>::
            MapPropertyToPage(dispid, pClsid);
    if (SUCCEEDED(hr) && CLSID_NULL == *pClsid)
        hr = PERPROP_E_NOPAGEAVAILABLE;
    return hr;
}
```

Enumerated Properties

Enumerated properties are those that use an enumeration to define the possible values that the property can take on. This enumeration has two distinct attributes associated with it—a list of actual values and a description for each of those values. In ATL, you need to provide both when an enumeration is required.

A Visual Basic control provides the enumerated property in a much simpler manner than what you have to do in ATL to fully support that property. The following code shows how to support an enumerated property in a Visual Basic control:

```
'the enum declaration for the property
'use square brackets [] to enclose
'a property with spaces in the name
Public Enum enmFlashType
    [No Flash]
    Black
    Background
    Color
End Enum

Private m_eFlashType As enmFlashType

Public Property Get FlashType() As enmFlashType
    FlashType = m_eFlashType
End Property
```

```
Public Property Let FlashType(newVal As enmFlashType)
    m_eFlashType = FlashType
End Property
```

When using a control within Visual Basic's property browser, you would expect to see human readable forms of the possible values (such as the no flash with the space in it). The enumerated properties get their display strings and lists from the `IPerPropertyBrowsing` interface. When using a Visual Basic control within VB, the Visual Basic control supplies the display string from the enum as shown previously. In ATL, however, you must implement the interface yourself.

Implementing the Required Interface

The code that implements this is in the sample program. An important thing to note is that for properties that are not supported by enumerated lists, the code should return `E_NOTIMPL` from the functions in this interface.

This interface includes `GetPredefinedValue`, `GetPredefinedStrings`, and `GetDisplayString`. These are the procedures that have to be implemented to supply the readable form of the enumerated property.

Listing 9.19 shows a cut-down implementation of this interface, along with a couple of helper routines that deal with the lists. Only one enumerated property is shown in this code, whereas an actual control would probably have several.

LISTING 9.19   `IPerPropertyBrowsing`

```
CHAR szFlashType[]= "0 - No Flash\0"
               "1 - Black\0"
               "2 - Background\0"
               "3 - Color\0"
               "\0";

STDMETHODIMP Cbclabel::GetEnumList(CALPOLESTR *pCaStringsOut,
➥CADWORD *pCaCookiesOut, LPTSTR lpElements, short cOffset)
{
    //find the number of elements
    //walk lpElements until double 0
    //count 0's along the way
    LPTSTR    lpTemp = lpElements;
    short     cElems = 0;
    short     i;
    int cch = 5;
    LPOLESTR strTemp = NULL;
    do
```

LISTING 9.19   Continued

```
    {
        lpTemp++;
        if (*lpTemp==0)
        {
            cElems++;
            lpTemp++;
        }
    }
    while (*lpTemp!=0);
    // allocate memory for string array structure
    pCaStringsOut->pElems = (LPOLESTR*)CoTaskMemAlloc(sizeof(LPOLESTR) *
cElems);
    if (pCaStringsOut->pElems == NULL)
        return E_OUTOFMEMORY;
    // allocate memory for dword array structure
    pCaCookiesOut->pElems = (DWORD*)CoTaskMemAlloc(sizeof(DWORD*) * cElems);
    if (pCaCookiesOut->pElems == NULL)
    {
        CoTaskMemFree(pCaStringsOut->pElems);
        return E_OUTOFMEMORY;
    }
    pCaStringsOut->cElems = cElems;
    pCaCookiesOut->cElems = cElems;
    // fill dword array structure
    for (i=0;i<cElems;i++)
    {
        pCaCookiesOut->pElems[i] = i+cOffset;
    }
    // fill string array structure
    lpTemp = lpElements;

    i=0;
    do
    {
        cch = lstrlen(lpTemp) + 1;
        if ((strTemp = (LPOLESTR)CoTaskMemAlloc(cch * sizeof(OLECHAR))) !=
➥NULL)
            MultiByteToWideChar(CP_ACP, 0, lpTemp, -1, strTemp, cch);
        pCaStringsOut->pElems[i] = strTemp;
        i++;
        lpTemp += lstrlen(lpTemp) + 1;
    }
    while (*lpTemp!=0);
    return S_OK;
```

LISTING 9.19 Continued

```
}

STDMETHODIMP Cbclabel::GetEnumString(BSTR *pBstr,
➥LPTSTR lpElements, short svalue, short sOffset)
{
    LPTSTR     lpTemp = lpElements;
    short     i = sOffset;
    //go though the array to the value
    do
    {
        if (i == svalue)
            break;
        lpTemp++;
        if (*lpTemp==0)
        {
            i++;
            lpTemp++;
        }
    }
    while (*lpTemp!=0);
    *pBstr = A2BSTR(lpTemp);
    return S_OK;
}

STDMETHODIMP Cbclabel::GetDisplayString(DISPID dispID,BSTR *pBstr)
{
    switch (dispID)
    {
        case DISPID_BC_FLASHTYPE: //FlashType
            return GetEnumString(pBstr, szFlashType, m_flashtype,0);
        default:
            return E_NOTIMPL;
    }
    return S_OK;
}

STDMETHODIMP Cbclabel::GetPredefinedStrings(DISPID dispID,
➥CALPOLESTR *pCaStringsOut,CADWORD *pCaCookiesOut)
{
    if (pCaStringsOut && pCaCookiesOut)
    {
        switch (dispID)
        {
        case DISPID_BC_FLASHTYPE: //FlashType
```

LISTING 9.19   Continued

```
            return GetEnumList(pCaStringsOut, pCaCookiesOut, (LPTSTR)
szFlashType, 0);
        default:
            return E_NOTIMPL;
        }
    }
    return E_NOTIMPL;
}

STDMETHODIMP Cbclabel::GetPredefinedValue(DISPID dispID,
➥DWORD dwCookie, VARIANT* pVarOut)
{
    switch (dispID)
    {
        case DISPID_BC_FLASHTYPE: //FlashType
            VariantClear(pVarOut);
            V_VT(pVarOut) = VT_I2;
            V_I2(pVarOut) = (short)dwCookie;
            return S_OK;
        default:
            return E_NOTIMPL;
    }
}
```

Changes to the IDL file

In addition to the IPerPropertyBrowsing interface, the IDL file should declare an enum property type that corresponds to the property supported in IPerPropertyBrowsing. The properties involved should be declared in the IDL file as that type. This will allow the code completion feature in Visual Basic to work to present a list of possible property values to the programmer.

Listing 9.20 shows the applicable code from the IDL file. Again, many properties are removed for clarity.

LISTING 9.20   Enumerated Properties in the IDL File

```
import "oaidl.idl";
import "ocidl.idl";
#include "olectl.h"

typedef
enum {
    bc_NoneFlash = 0,
    bc_BlackFlash = 1,
```

LISTING 9.20 Continued

```
    bc_BackgroundFlash = 2,
    bc_ColorFlash = 3
} enumFlashType;

[
    uuid(263C7484-B4A7-11D2-8D97-00105A0CAC96),
    version(1.0),
    helpstring("VCDC Sample Label"),
    helpfile("bclabel.HLP"),
    control
]
library BCLABELLib
{
    importlib("stdole32.tlb");
    importlib("stdole2.tlb");
    [
        object,
        uuid(263C7491-B4A7-11D2-8D97-00105A0CAC96),
        dual,
        helpstring("Ibclabel Interface"),
        pointer_default(unique)
    ]
    interface Ibclabel : IDispatch
    {
    const int DISPID_BC_FLASHTYPE = 0x68030011;

    [id(DISPID_BC_FLASHTYPE), propget] HRESULT FlashType([out, retval]
➥enumFlashType* );
    [id(DISPID_BC_FLASHTYPE), propput] HRESULT FlashType([in] enumFlashType );

    const int DISPID_BC_CLICK = 2;
    };

    [
        uuid(263C7493-B4A7-11D2-8D97-00105A0CAC96),
        helpstring("_IbclabelEvents Interface")
    ]
    dispinterface _IbclabelEvents
    {
        properties:
        methods:
[id(DISPID_BC_CLICK)] void Click();
    };
```

LISTING 9.20   Continued

```
    [
        uuid(263C7492-B4A7-11D2-8D97-00105A0CAC96),
        helpstring("VCDC Sample Label")
    ]
    coclass bclabel
    {
        [default] interface Ibclabel;
        [default, source] dispinterface _IbclabelEvents;
    };
};
```

Categorizing Properties

Visual Basic provides a property view that displays the properties of a control on a form. The property view can display the properties on a control alphabetically or group them by arbitrary categories.

The Interface

A control must implement the ICategorizeProperties interface so that Visual Basic can display the control's properties in the appropriate categories in its property view. Unfortunately, this interface isn't presently defined in any system IDL or header file, and ATL provides no implementation class for the interface. This section discusses what you need to do to support it.

This interface is implemented like all interfaces in ATL; you derive your control class from ICategorizeProperties, add the interface entry to the control's interface map, and implement the two methods MapPropertyToCategory and GetCategoryName. Note that there are 11 predefined property categories with negative values. You can define your own custom categories, but be sure to assign them positive values.

The MapPropertyToCategory method returns the appropriate property category value for the specified property. The GetCategoryName method simply returns a BSTR containing the category name. You only need to support your custom category values within GetCategoryName because Visual Basic knows the names of the standard property categories.

Listing 9.21 shows the code for the ICategorizeProperties interface. The PROPCAT_ constants are defined in the IDL file, which is shown in Listing 9.22.

LISTING 9.21   Property Categories in the IDL File

```
STDMETHODIMP Cbclabel::MapPropertyToCategory
➥ (/*[in]*/ DISPID dispid, /*[out]*/ PROPCAT* ppropcat)
{
    if (NULL == ppropcat) return E_POINTER;
```

LISTING 9.21 Continued

```
    switch (dispid)
    {
        case DISPID_BC_ALIGNMENT:
        case DISPID_BC_VALIGNMENT:
        case DISPID_BC_BACKCOLOR:
        case DISPID_BC_BACKSTYLE:
        case DISPID_BC_BORDERCOLOR:
        case DISPID_BC_BORDERSTYLE:
        case DISPID_BC_BORDERSIZE:
        case DISPID_BC_FORECOLOR:
            *ppropcat = PROPCAT_Appearance;
            return S_OK;
        case DISPID_BC_WORDWRAP:
        case DISPID_BC_CAPTION:
            *ppropcat = PROPCAT_Text;
            return S_OK;
        case DISPID_BC_HELPCONTEXTID:
        case DISPID_BC_MOUSEICON:
        case DISPID_BC_MOUSEPOINTER:
        case DISPID_BC_ENABLED:
            *ppropcat = PROPCAT_Behavior;
            return S_OK;
        case DISPID_BC_FONT:
            *ppropcat = PROPCAT_Font;
            return S_OK;
        case DISPID_BC_FLASHTIME:
        case DISPID_BC_FLASHCOLOR:
        case DISPID_BC_FLASHTYPE:
            *ppropcat = PROPCAT_Flashing;
            return S_OK;
        default:
            return E_FAIL;
    }
}

STDMETHODIMP Cbclabel::GetCategoryName(/*[in]*/ PROPCAT propcat,
➥/*[in]*/ LCID lcid, /*[out]*/ BSTR* pbstrName)
{
    if(PROPCAT_Flashing == propcat)
    {
        *pbstrName = ::SysAllocString(L"Flashing");
        return S_OK;
    }
    return E_FAIL;
}
```

9

COMPONENTS AND
CONTROLS

The IDL Changes

Because ATL has no support for categorization of properties built in, you must also supply the interface code in the IDL file. Listing 9.22 shows the IDL definition for the ICategorizeProperties interface.

LISTING 9.22   Property Categories in the IDL File

```
[
    object, local,
    uuid(4D07FC10-F931-11CE-B001-00AA006884E5),
    helpstring("ICategorizeProperties Interface"),
    pointer_default(unique)
]
interface ICategorizeProperties : IUnknown
{
    typedef [public] int PROPCAT;
    const int PROPCAT_Nil        = -1;
    const int PROPCAT_Misc       = -2;
    const int PROPCAT_Font       = -3;
    const int PROPCAT_Position   = -4;
    const int PROPCAT_Appearance = -5;
    const int PROPCAT_Behavior   = -6;
    const int PROPCAT_Data       = -7;
    const int PROPCAT_List       = -8;
    const int PROPCAT_Text       = -9;
    const int PROPCAT_Scale      = -10;
    const int PROPCAT_DDE        = -11;
    const int PROPCAT_Flashing   = 1;
HRESULT MapPropertyToCategory([in] DISPID dispid, [out] PROPCAT* propcat);
HRESULT GetCategoryName([in]PROPCAT propcat,
➥ [in]LCID lcid,[out]BSTR* pbstrName);
}
```

Returning Errors

Back when you generated your control, you chose that it would support ISupportErrorInfo. This means that your control will return complex error information when requested by Visual Basic. The wizard that generated your control added a routine in the H file that tells Visual Basic that this interface is supported.

So now the question is, what do you do when you want to provide an error back to Visual Basic, as in the case of an Invalid Property Value (Basic error 380). The Error function will set up this structure and return the code to Visual Basic.

```
return Error(_T("Invalid property Value"),CLSID_BCAcal,0x800A017C);
```

This line of code returns an error of 380 (17C hex) to Visual Basic. The high word of the error code contains the Severity and Facility of the error. I routinely use hex 8 (1 in the high bit) as the severity (0 would mean success) and A as the facility code; A is for controls. The low word gets the actual error code.

The `CLSID` is the one for your control. The error code is pretty standard. You can use `MAKE_HRESULT` to build the error code, or simply put the error code within the function call. Better yet, just make a constant with that value. Looking at the code in hex, begin with a hex 8. This turns on the most significant bit and makes the code negative. The facility code goes in the 16–19 bits, shown in this code with the value of A. The actual error code goes in the low word and—don't forget—in hex.

Safe for Initialization and Scripting

What exactly does it mean for a control to be safe for scripting and safe for initialization? Essentially, this means that no one can use the control in an Internet environment to damage someone's system. (It is difficult to ensure that your control is safe for these things—indeed I have found many controls that are not safe for scripting, but are marked that way.)

You can use `IObjectSafety` and a certificate with your ATL control. ATL provides a default implementation of this interface in the `IObjectSafetyImpl` class. You specify, as a template parameter, the safety options supported by the control, and a container can use the `SetInterfaceSafetyOptions` method of this interface to selectively enable and disable each supported option. A control can determine its current safety level and potentially disable or enable unsafe functionality by checking the `m_dwCurrentSafety` member variable.

You also have an easier way out, if you want it—component categories. Registering a control as a member of the Safe for Initialization or Safe for Scripting component category is a static decision. You can't decide at runtime that the control is not safe. This can work for many applications. You still have to sign the control with a certificate. The following code shows the lines to add to your `include` file to use component categories in your control.

```
BEGIN_CATEGORY_MAP(Cframe)
    IMPLEMENTED_CATEGORY(CATID_ATLINTERNALS_SAMPLES)
    IMPLEMENTED_CATEGORY(CATID_SafeForScripting)
    IMPLEMENTED_CATEGORY(CATID_SafeForInitializing)
END_CATEGORY_MAP()
```

Licensing

This is a continuing struggle—trying to make a commercial control easily available for your licensed users, but stop people from stealing it. This section will not discuss the security methods, just the interface and code required to implement a simple scheme in an ATL control.

To provide licensing, you must change the class factory and implement a class. In your H file, replace the DECLARE_CLASSFACTORY with the following:

```
DECLARE_CLASSFACTORY2(BCLicense)
```

BCLicense specifies a class that implements the licensing scheme.

The class factory for the control will call the following functions to provide licensing:

```
static BOOL VerifyLicenseKey(BSTR bstr)
    static BOOL GetLicenseKey(DWORD dwReserved, BSTR* pBstr)
        static BOOL IsLicenseValid()
```

Different environments might do it different ways, but it appears that IsLicenseValid is always called before GetLicenseKey.

In Visual Basic 6, this is what happens. Going into design mode or run mode from the environment, IsLicenseValid is called—that's it. Building an EXE IsLicenseValid is called and then GetLicenseKey. The key returned by GetLicenseKey is embedded in the application. Running the EXE VerifyLicenseKey is called, passing the key embedded in the application.

Listing 9.23 shows a sample class that shows a simple implementation of licensing.

LISTING 9.23   Licensing a Custom Control

```
#define BC_LICSTRING "Some Control, CopyRight © 1998 by me."

class BCLicense
{
public:
    static BOOL VerifyLicenseKey(BSTR bstr)
    {
        USES_CONVERSION;
        //compare the string
        return !lstrcmp(OLE2T(bstr), BC_LICSTRING);
    }
    static BOOL IsLicenseValid()
    {
        // Presumably there would be some check of a license
        // before returning true, like a license file.
        return TRUE;
    }
    static BOOL GetLicenseKey(DWORD dwReserved, BSTR* pBstr)
    {
        USES_CONVERSION;
        *pBstr = SysAllocString(T2OLE(BC_LICSTRING));
        return TRUE;
    }
};
```

ISimpleFrame

ISimpleFrame is an interface supported by only a few ActiveX control containers. Visual Basic is one of those containers that supports it. This interface was brought about by the need for a simple frame type control (hence the name). The idea of this interface was to allow a control to contain other controls, but not implement the full OLE hosting for those controls.

Visual Basic User controls (controls created within Visual Basic) can support this interface. ATL controls, on the other hand, did not have this feature built into them, so it's completely up to the programmer to provide support. There are several distinct steps that must be performed to write a control that will be a container in ATL.

This section will take a look at what an ATL control must do differently to define itself as an ISimpleFrame type of control.

- The control must report itself as being a Simple Frame control. This is done with the OLEMiscStatus bits.
- Then the control must obtain a pointer to the ISimpleFrame interface.
- It must use that pointer to call two functions—a PreMessageFilter before the control's wndproc and PostMessageFilter after the control's wndproc.

That's it for the basics. The implementation details are somewhat more complex.

In an ATL control, you can modify what is reported through the OLEMiscStatus by modifying a registry entry. You do this by modifying the .RGS file generated by the wizard. The following code shows the status value as it appears in the .RGS file. Simply add 65536 to the value there, and this control will report itself as a simple frame control. In this case, the value becomes 221585. Make that change and save that file.

```
'MiscStatus' = s '0'
{
    '1' = s '156049'
}
```

Now things start to get a little messy. It was stated earlier that you need to call PreMessageFilter before the control's default window procedure and PostMessageFilter after it. Normally, you would simply override the required function, call your procedures at the proper time, and call the base implementation in between these two procedures. The problem that you run into is that the procedure you need to override (ProcessWindowMessage) has already been overridden.

This fact is disguised within a macro. The message map overrides this function. This makes sense, because the message map has to take Window messages and connect them to the function that will handle those messages in your code. So how are you going to get in the middle of those macros? One solution is to write a new set of macros to replace BEGIN_MSG_MAP and END_MSG_MAP. This allows you to call the required functions to allow the simple frame to work.

Listing 9.24 shows a set of macros written to take a class and the function name as parameters to the macro and handle the call to the functions. You use these macros in place of the BEGIN_MSG_MAP and END_MSG_MAP macros. One thing to remember is that the wizard that handles updating the message map won't work properly any more.

LISTING 9.24   Message Map Macros for Simple Frame

```
#define BEGIN_MSG_MAP_FRAME(theClass, prefunc) \
public: \
BOOL ProcessWindowMessage(HWND hWnd, UINT uMsg,
➥WPARAM wParam, LPARAM lParam, LRESULT& lResult, \
    DWORD dwMsgMapID = 0) \
{ \
    HRESULT hResult = S_OK; \
    BOOL bHandled = TRUE; \
    hWnd; \
    uMsg; \
    wParam; \
    lParam; \
    lResult; \
    bHandled; \
    hResult = prefunc((UINT) uMsg, (WPARAM)wParam, (LPARAM)lParam); \
    if (S_OK == hResult) \
    { \
        switch(dwMsgMapID) \
        { \
        case 0:

#define END_MSG_MAP_FRAME(postfunc) \
            break; \
        default: \
            ATLTRACE2(atlTraceWindowing, 0, _T("Invalid message map (%i)\n"),
dwMsgMapID); \
            ATLASSERT(FALSE); \
            break; \
        } \
        hResult = postfunc((UINT) uMsg, (WPARAM)wParam, (LPARAM)lParam); \
    } \
    return FALSE; \
}
```

Now you need to add your pre-function and the post-function to the code. Listing 9.25 shows how the functions look. Notice that the functions handle some messages differently. Messages that require reflection do not get handled properly if they go through the pre- and post-message filters.

You can see the results of this by taking those case statements out. This results in certain controls not setting their BackColor properly.

LISTING 9.25 ISimpleFrame Pre and Post Functions

```
HRESULT PreProcessforFrame(UINT uMsg, WPARAM wParam, LPARAM lParam)
{
    HRESULT hResult=S_OK;
    LRESULT lResult;
    BOOL    bHandled=1;
    switch(uMsg)
    {
    case WM_COMMAND:
    case WM_NOTIFY:
    case WM_PARENTNOTIFY:
    case WM_DRAWITEM:
    case WM_MEASUREITEM:
    case WM_COMPAREITEM:
    case WM_DELETEITEM:
    case WM_VKEYTOITEM:
    case WM_CHARTOITEM:
    case WM_HSCROLL:
    case WM_VSCROLL:
    case WM_CTLCOLORBTN:
    case WM_CTLCOLORDLG:
    case WM_CTLCOLOREDIT:
    case WM_CTLCOLORLISTBOX:
    case WM_CTLCOLORMSGBOX:
    case WM_CTLCOLORSCROLLBAR:
    case WM_CTLCOLORSTATIC:
        break;
    default:
        // Give the simple frame site the opportunity to filter the message
        if (m_psimpleframesite != NULL)
            hResult = m_psimpleframesite->PreMessageFilter(m_hWnd, uMsg,
➥wParam, lParam, \
                &lResult, &m_dwCookie);
    }
    return hResult;
}

HRESULT PostProcessforFrame(UINT uMsg, WPARAM wParam, LPARAM lParam)
{
    LRESULT lResult;
    // Simple frame site may have been cleared...
    // check before calling again.
```

9

LISTING 9.25   Continued

```
BOOL     bHandled=1;
switch(uMsg)
{
case WM_COMMAND:
case WM_NOTIFY:
case WM_PARENTNOTIFY:
case WM_DRAWITEM:
case WM_MEASUREITEM:
case WM_COMPAREITEM:
case WM_DELETEITEM:
case WM_VKEYTOITEM:
case WM_CHARTOITEM:
case WM_HSCROLL:
case WM_VSCROLL:
case WM_CTLCOLORBTN:
case WM_CTLCOLORDLG:
case WM_CTLCOLOREDIT:
case WM_CTLCOLORLISTBOX:
case WM_CTLCOLORMSGBOX:
case WM_CTLCOLORSCROLLBAR:
case WM_CTLCOLORSTATIC:
    break;
default:
    if (m_psimpleframesite != NULL)
        m_psimpleframesite->PostMessageFilter(m_hWnd, uMsg, wParam, lParam, \
➥&lResult, \
        m_dwCookie);
}
return S_OK;
}
```

That does it. You've written a container control. Now all you have to do is get more containers to support it. IE does not support ISimpleFrame, so don't bother with this for an Internet-based control. .NET supports containers in a different way, so it's best to write container controls for it in managed code in .NET.

Basing a Control on a Windows Control

The control you've been working with until now has been "built from scratch." In other words, the window you use for this control is not based on any other Windows control. You can write ActiveX controls that obtain much of their functionality from Windows base controls, such as buttons, edit controls, and list boxes. (These base Windows controls are discussed in Chapter 4, "C++ Basics.")

An ATL control based on a Windows control contains a child window that is based on the Windows control. This is different from a simple ATL control that has just a single window. Most of the things that you've read about in the sample you built are still valid for a control of this type.

- Adding properties and methods remain the same.
- Property pages, property persistence, property categories, and enumerated properties remain the same.
- Adding events are the same, but firing them might be different.
- The way you do the message map will probably change.
- You probably wouldn't use the ISimpleFrame interface with a control of this type.

Because you've covered most of these topics, just the differences will be discussed here. First you'll learn about some of the basic changes to the include file and some things that have to be done to let the control be based on a Windows control.

The following code shows the declaration of a member variable of type CContainedWindow. This is the window that will be based on a Windows control. After you declare the variable, you initialize the variable, indicating what type of control you are superclassing ("EDIT"), where the message map is (this, which indicates you supply the message map), and which alternate message map to use (1). You'll show the message map next, and this code will become more clear.

```
CContainedWindow m_EditControl;

CAtlEdit() : m_EditControl(_T("EDIT"), this, 1)
{
    //makes sure there is always a valid window handle
    m_bWindowOnly = TRUE;
}
```

Notice that you set the member variable that forces the control to always have a valid window handle to true. Because any Windows control has a window handle, it follows that any control based on a Windows control needs to have a valid window handle.

To handle messages from either your control window or the superclass window, you use a different message map than what you used for your label control. The following code shows the modified message map:

```
BEGIN_MSG_MAP(CCVBEdit)
    MESSAGE_HANDLER(WM_CREATE, OnCreate)
    MESSAGE_HANDLER(WM_CTLCOLOREDIT, OnCtlColorEdit)
ALT_MSG_MAP(1)
    MESSAGE_HANDLER(WM_CHAR, OnChar)
END_MSG_MAP()
```

9

COMPONENTS AND
CONTROLS

Notice that you have an alternate message map. This is where you can map messages from your superclass window. You can map messages from the control's "base window" in the message map section above the ALT_MSG_MAP macro.

The messages you override for the superclassed control depends on your coding needs. You might want to provide events for mouse and keyboard messages. The following code shows the function that maps WM_CHAR and the resulting message handler in OnChar. This function fires an event and then calls default processing on the character.

```
LRESULT OnChar(UINT uMsg, WPARAM wParam, LPARAM lParam, BOOL& bHandled)
{
    Fire_KeyPress(wParam);
    m_EditControl.DefWindowProc(WM_CHAR, wParam, lParam);
    return 0;
}
```

There are a couple of messages that you need to map from the base control. The WM_CREATE message needs to be mapped; this is where you actually create the superclassed control. Listing 9.26 shows the creation of the window.

LISTING 9.26   OnCreate for Superclass Control

```
LRESULT OnCreate(UINT uMsg, WPARAM wParam, LPARAM lParam, BOOL& bHandled)
{
    RECT rc;
    GetWindowRect(&rc);
    rc.right -= rc.left;
    rc.bottom -= rc.top;
    rc.top = rc.left = 0;
    m_EditControl.Create(m_hWnd, rc, _T("CVBEdit"), WS_CHILD | WS_VISIBLE );
    return 0;
}
```

You can map the WM_CTLCOLOREDIT and provide a way to set the background and text color of the edit control. When you build a control from the ground up, you usually have complete control over the painting of your control. However, when you use a Windows control, you don't. You can set certain aspects of the painting process, including the colors. The following code shows how to use member variables to set the colors. These member variables can be set through properties.

```
LRESULT OnCtlColorEdit(UINT uMsg, WPARAM wParam, LPARAM lParam, BOOL& bHandled)
{
    ::SetTextColor((HDC)wParam, m_forecolor);
    ::SetBkColor((HDC)wParam,m_backcolor);
    return (LRESULT)::CreatePen(PS_SOLID,1,m_backcolor);
}
```

Because the control drawing is handled by Windows, you do not have to map the WM_PAINT message. However, you should override the OnDraw function and return S_OK without drawing anything. The default OnDraw draws something in the Window, which is not necessary.

Finally, you need to override the SetObjectRects function. In this function, you keep your child control sized to the parent control. Listing 9.27 shows how to do this.

LISTING 9.27   Sizing a Superclass Control

```
STDMETHOD(SetObjectRects)(LPCRECT prcPos,LPCRECT prcClip)
{
    IOleInPlaceObjectWindowlessImpl<CAtlEdit>::SetObjectRects(prcPos, prcClip);
    int cx, cy;
    cx = prcPos->right - prcPos->left;
    cy = prcPos->bottom - prcPos->top;
    ::SetWindowPos(m_EditControl.m_hWnd, NULL, 0, 0, cx, cy, SWP_NOZORDER |
➥SWP_NOACTIVATE);
    return S_OK;
}
```

Notice in this case that you are not using message mapping here but are overriding a virtual routine of IoleInplaceObject.

Beyond these items, a superclassed control is programmed like any other. In fact, it is many times easier to write a control of this type, because drawing the control is typically one of the more time-consuming aspects of writing a complex control. With a superclassed control, all the drawing is done for you.

Composite Controls

Composite controls are ActiveX controls that use a dialog box for a presentation space. This type of control is very similar to the way that Visual Basic controls are developed using the UserControl. In VB, you create a UserControl and then add controls to it.

In ATL, you create the control in the manner described earlier in this chapter. At this point, you can use the dialog editor to add controls to the dialog.

One of the advantages of the composite control compared to the superclassed control is that you can use other ActiveX controls within the composite control. For this reason, you might actually want to create a composite control with only one ActiveX control on the dialog. This would allow you to extend the ActiveX control through the composite control. This is essentially the way that a UserControl in Visual Basic with one control on it works. Of course, most of the time, your composite control contains more than one child control on it.

- Again, many of the things already discussed in a regular control will work in a composite control.

- Adding properties and methods remain the same.

- Adding events are the same, but firing them will be different.

- The message map is the same as a simple control.

- Property pages, property persistence, property categories, and enumerated properties remain the same.

- The messages you map and program change.

- How you get the events from the child controls is different. If you use controls that have events, you may want to sink those events; this is not something discussed at this point.

First, notice that in the class declaration you derive from CComCompositeControl, instead of CComControl. This gives you your dialog and handles much of the work going on around that dialog box.

It follows that one of the first messages that you might like to map would be the WM_INITDIA-LOG. In this procedure, one of the most useful things you can do is set a member variable equal to each control on the dialog. Listing 9.28 shows how this looks.

LISTING 9.28   InitDialog

```
LRESULT OnInitDialog(UINT uMsg, WPARAM wParam, LPARAM lParam, BOOL& bHandled)
{
    GetDlgControl(IDC_LISTVIEWCTRL1,IID_IListView,(VOID**) &m_listview);
    m_hwndEdit = GetDlgItem(IDC_EDIT1);
    bHandled = FALSE;
    return 0;
}
```

Notice that you are dealing with one ActiveX control and one Windows base control in this listing. With the ActiveX control, you use GetDlgControl to get a reference to the dispatch interface for the control. Because a Windows base control wouldn't have a dispatch interface, you simply retrieve the window handle for it. That will let you handle any aspects of these controls.

With the base edit control, you can simply use SendMessage and any Windows API that will control the edit control. These include many regular WM_ messages and also the EM_ messages that are specifically for the edit control.

The ActiveX control is a little more difficult to deal with. You need to have a C++ wrapper for the interface to make this work. In fact, that wrapper has to be there to set up the member variable that is used in this routine.

You have a command that will handle generating a C++ wrapper for a type library with very little work on your part. This is the #import directive, discussed in Chapter 3, "C Programming." It will generate the required code from the type library.

In this case, you are using the listview control contained in MSCOMCTL.OCX. The following import directive is used to build the wrappers you need.

```
#import "C:\WINDOWS\SYSTEM\MSCOMCTL.OCX" raw_interfaces_only,
➥raw_native_types, no_namespace, named_guids
```

Of course, MSCOMCTL.OCX would be required to use your control, because it is using a control from this OCX. With these wrappers in place, you can now call procedures on the contained ActiveX control.

One of the complications of using an ActiveX control within a composite control is sinking the events. You set up an event sink map, very similar to a message map. Listing 9.29 shows how this event sink looks.

LISTING 9.29 Event Sink Map

```
BEGIN_SINK_MAP(Cowlistview)
    SINK_ENTRY(IDC_LISTVIEWCTRL1, DISPID_CLICK, OnClickListviewctrl1)
    SINK_ENTRY(IDC_LISTVIEWCTRL1, 0x4, OnItemClickListviewctrl1)
    SINK_ENTRY(IDC_LISTVIEWCTRL1, DISPID_DBLCLICK, OnDblClickListviewctrl1)
    SINK_ENTRY(IDC_LISTVIEWCTRL1, 0x3, OnColumnClick1)
    SINK_ENTRY(IDC_LISTVIEWCTRL1, 0xfffffda3, OnMouseDown1)
    SINK_ENTRY(IDC_LISTVIEWCTRL1, 0xfffffda2, OnMouseMove1)
    SINK_ENTRY(IDC_LISTVIEWCTRL1, 0xfffffda1, OnMouseUp1)
END_SINK_MAP()
```

The SINK_ENTRY macro takes three parameters, the ID of the control, the ID of the event, and a function name. The ID of the control is assigned when you put the control on the dialog. The ID of the event is determined by the control with which you are working. You can look at the type library in the OLE/COM Object Viewer to find the ID of an event. After you have the sink map, you can fire your events or do whatever you need done with those events.

When you use a Windows base control, like an edit control, things are somewhat simpler. In this case, you can program the controls and the dialog like a standard dialog. You get the events back from the controls in WM_COMMAND and WM_NOTIFY messages.

A few things will work like a superclassed control does. For example, setting the background color and the text color of a Windows control would work the same way (using WM_CTLCOLOR messages). Also, you may want to override the SetObjectRects routine and control the size of the child controls.

C# Basics

IN THIS CHAPTER

C# represents a modern object-oriented language that was designed to allow for the expressiveness of C++ with RAD-style development found in 4GLs, such as Microsoft Visual Basic. This section explores the C# language, semantics, and the grammar that comprises the language. I've already covered C and C++, which accounts for a lot of the syntax and grammar used in C#.

Visual C++ has always maintained compatibility with C code and C++ was an extension to the C language. C#, while in some ways an extension to C++, is also somewhat of a departure from C and C++. Most of the departure from C and C++ occurs in the way classes are handled in C#. I'll explore these departures as I proceed through the chapter.

It is important to cover some basic topics before diving into the language itself. First and foremost, is that almost everything in C# is an object. Unlike procedural languages, the C# language does not allow for global data or global functions. All data and methods must be contained within either a struct or a class. This is a key concept in any object-oriented (OO) language, although most OO languages (including this one) have ways around that. All data and all methods that operate on that data should be packaged as a functional unit. These functional units are reusable objects that are self-contained and self-describing.

Although it is not the goal of this text to cover OO design patterns and software engineering, it is important to understand the key concepts of OO design and implementation that I covered in Chapters 5, "C++ Classes," and 9, "Components and Controls." C# will allow both advanced and new developers to implement solid code with minimal effort.

The C# Type System

In the .NET framework, a common type system is used to allow all languages targeted at the .NET environment to interoperate with each other. C# uses this underlying type system. As I stated before, almost everything in C# is an object. Primitive data types are not objects and the reason for this is performance. Because objects are allocated on the heap and managed by the GC (garbage collector), this would introduce a significant amount of overhead to deal with basic types such as int and char. For this reason, C# implements primitive types as structs, which are considered value types. In C#, a value type is allocated on the stack as opposed to being allocated on the heap and managed by the GC. Because value types are allocated on the stack, their lifetime is limited to the scope in which they were declared.

Table 10.1 presents a listing of the available types within C#.

TABLE 10.1   C# Types

Type	Description
object	Base class of all objects in C#
string	Unicode sequence of characters

TABLE 10.1   Continued

Type	Description
sbyte	8-bit signed integral
short	16-bit signed integral
int	32-bit signed integral
long	64-bit signed integral
byte	8-bit unsigned integral
ushort	16-bit unsigned integral
uint	32-bit unsigned integral
ulong	64-bit unsigned integral
float	Single-precision floating point
double	Double-precision floating point
bool	Boolean—true or false
char	A Unicode character
decimal	28 significant digit decimal type

With the exception of the string type, all types represented within Table 10.1 are implemented as a struct. The string type is special in the fact that its implementation is actually a sealed class. A *sealed class* is a class that cannot be inherited from and thus terminates the inheritance chain.

Value Types in Action

When a primitive type is declared, C# requires that the variable is initialized before any attempt is made to use that variable. In C++, the value of an uninitialized variable is undefined; the same rule applies in C#. The difference is that in C++, the variable can be used with unknown results.

The following are examples of variable declarations:

```
int _999;      //valid, begins with an underscore
int a_var;     //valid
int 123_go;    //invalid, begins with a number
```

NOTE

C# allows for the // and /*...*/ comment markers. The // denotes that all text to the right on the current line is a comment. The /*...*/ marker is used for multiline comments.

C# also enforces strict type checking and assignment. This means no fudging! In C++, it was possible to declare an unsigned integer and then assign the value of –1 to the variable. The C# compiler will quickly catch the assignment and produce a compiler error pointing out the invalid assignment:

```
unsigned int cpp_fudge = -1;        //valid C++
uint csharp_fudge = -1;        //error in C#
```

The error produced by the C# compiler will declare that the constant value of –1 cannot be converted to an unsigned integer.

NOTE

C# cannot make the conversion from a negative number to an unsigned number intrinsically like C++ can. In fact you cannot even cast the negative number to the unsigned number. For me, this is bit too much hand-holding since there is no real danger in a statement that assigns –1 to an unsigned integer. C# provides a way to work around this difference in the compiler.

The unchecked keyword will allow a block of code to handle this conversion:

```
unchecked {uint csharp_fudge = (uint) -1;}
```

The struct

In C/C++, it was not possible to create a primitive type. The primitive types were like little magic entities that just existed—their meaning known, their implementation a mystery. C# implements primitive types as simple `struct`s. This means that it is possible for you to create types that are treated in the same manner as the C# primitive types.

When creating a `struct`, it is important to keep the implementation to a bare minimum. After all, if additional functionality is required in its implementation, it would be better to implement the entity as a full-blown object. `struct`s are often used to represent small pieces of data that generally have a restricted lifetime and tend to be inexpensive to manage in terms of memory requirements.

A `struct` in C# cannot inherit from another `struct` or class, however a `struct` can implement one or more interfaces. `struct`s may contain data members and methods. A `struct` cannot define a parameter-less constructor. All `struct`s contain an implicit constructor that is responsible for initializing all data members to their default values. However, a `struct` can define a construct that accepts parameters. A construct in C# is the same as a constructor in C++. The big difference between a `struct` and a class is, of course, that `struct`s are value-types that are allocated on the stack and not reference counted.

The following is the syntax for declaring a `struct`:

```
struct name {
    [access-modifier] members;
}
```

The syntax is similar to C++ with respect to the declaration and construction. Member visibility defaults to private in C#. Members of a `struct` can have the following access modifiers applied to them: public, private, or internal. Because a `struct` cannot serve as the base from which another `struct` can inherit, the protected modifier has no place; if used, the C# compiler will quickly point out the error.

Listing 10.1 shows the declaration of a `struct` named Fraction. Notice that the member access is achieved by use of the dot operator. In C#, all member access is through the dot operator regardless if it is a `struct` or class.

LISTING 10.1   A Simple struct

```
//Purpose    :Declare a simple struct
struct Fraction
{
    public int numerator;
    public int denominator;
}
public class StructTest
{
    public static void Main( )
    {
        Fraction f;
        f.numerator   = 5;
        f.denominator = 10;
    }
}
```

Value types also have a built-in assignment operator that performs a copy of all data members. In C++, this functionality was achieved by implementing the assignment operator and providing the code necessary to copy the data members. Listing 10.2 uses C# built-in assignment operators to copy the value of one `struct` to another `struct` of the same type.

LISTING 10.2   struct Assignment

```
//Purpose    :Declare a simple struct

  using System;
```

Listing 10.2 Continues

```
struct Fraction
{
    public int numerator;
    public int denominator;

    public void Print( )
    {
        Console.WriteLine( "{0}/{1}", numerator, denominator );
    }
}


public class StructTest
{
    public static void Main( )
    {
        Fraction f;
        f.numerator   = 5;
        f.denominator = 10;
        f.Print( );
        Fraction f2 = f;
        f2.Print( );
        //modify struct instance f2
        f2.numerator = 1;
        f.Print( );
        f2.Print( );
    }
}
```

Listing 10.2 extends the implementation of the Fraction struct by implementing the Print method. The Print method uses the Console.WriteLine method to display the current value of the Fraction.

To demonstrate the assignment operator provided by C# for structs, two instances of the Fraction are declared. You declare a variable f2 which is initialized with the previous Fraction variable f. When f2.Print() is invoked, the same 5/10 output will be displayed as the call to f.Print().

It is important to realize that a copy has occurred and not a reference assignment of f to f2. When f2 is modified on line 29, the following Print method invocations display two different values. The call to f.Print() will still produce the 5/10 output, whereas the call to f2.Print() will now output 1/10.

Reference Types

C# can be a difficult language to describe. It seems that to discuss one aspect of the language, knowledge of a different aspect of the language is necessary. To this end, a brief discussion of reference types is necessary to grasp the remaining topics.

A class construct is an example of a reference type in C#. Reference counting means that any reference type will exist so long as there remains some active reference to the entity. In classic COM, referencing counting was visible in the `AddRef` and `Release` methods of a COM object. When the final reference was released on the instance of the object, the object took the necessary steps to clean up.

Fortunately, C# has abstracted away all the gory details of referencing counting. The GC (garbage collector) is responsible for cleaning up memory being used by unreferenced classes and interfaces. When an object's reference count reaches zero, the GC will invoke the `Finalize` method on the object, reclaim the memory, and return it to the general application heap. The `Finalize` method is similar to the destructor concept in C++, but there is no deterministic finalization in C#. Basically, there is no way to know when an object will expire.

> **NOTE**
>
> C# has a garbage collector that will reclaim unused objects. As stated, the programmer does not know when the GC might release an object.
>
> With most objects you can call the `finalize` method yourself, and in fact Microsoft recommends this with objects that consume a lot of resources.
>
> I expect that you'll see a lot of code where `Finalize` is used, just like Visual Basic programmers see objects set to Nothing to make sure VB turns loose of the object.

A reference is acquired in one of two ways: when an instance of a reference type is created and when an assignment takes place. Remember that when the assignment operator was used in conjunction with value types, a copy of the value type was created. This is not the case when the assignment operator is used with reference types. Changing the `Fraction` struct to a `class` changes the behavior of the assignment operator, as shown in Listing 10.3.

LISTING 10.3 Reference Types

```
using System;
//A class represents a reference type in C#
class Fraction
{
```

LISTING 10.3   Continued

```
    public int numerator;
    public int denominator;
    public void Print( )
    {
        Console.WriteLine( "{0}/{1}", numerator, denominator );
    }
}

public class ReferenceTest
{
    public static void Main( )
    {
        Fraction f = new Fraction( );
        f.numerator   = 5;
        f.denominator = 10;
        f.Print( );
        Fraction f2 = f;     //f2 is a reference to f and not a copy!!!
        f2.Print( );
        //modify instance f2. Note that f is also effected.
        f2.numerator = 1;
        f.Print( );
        f2.Print( );
    }
}
```

There are only two changes made to Listing 10.2 to create Listing 10.3. The first change was declaring the Fraction to be a class instead of a struct. This small change means that instead of the Fraction being allocated on the stack, it will now be created on the heap and reference counted.

The next change to the code involves the way an instance of Fraction is created. To create an instance of a reference type, the new keyword must be used. Now, an instance of the Fraction class must be created to declare the variable f. Without using the proper declaration, the variable f would be considered an uninitialized variable.

The changes to Listing 10.2 impact the overall semantics of the code in Listing 10.3. Notice that the declaration of the variable f2 is now considered a reference to the variable f. This means that the variable f2 is the same as variable f—f2 is not a copy. This is the fundamental difference between value types and reference types. When f2 is modified, that same modification is apparent in the variable f.

The invocation of f.Print() and f2.Print() will always produce the same output. When a change is made to f2.numerator, it is the same as changing f.numerator. In C++, it was possible to define an assignment operator and to control the behavior of that operator. This ability does not exist in C#. The assignment operator cannot be overloaded or reimplemented by the developer.

> **NOTE**
>
> I'll discuss operators a little later in the chapter, but a few points about assignments should be made here.
>
> Visual Basic requires a `Set` operator on assignments involving objects. C# and VB.NET has done away with the `Set` operator, but in doing so placed some extra restrictions on VB and C++ programmers.
>
> C# took away the assignment overload from C++ programmers. It also took away default properties from VB programmers.

All assignments on C# classes result in a reference to the object rather than a copy of the object. Copying an object in C# is done essentially the same way a Visual Basic programmer would do it. Either provide a copy method or create a new object and do a manual member by member copy.

Boxing and Unboxing

The concept of boxing (unique to C#) allows for treating a value type as a reference type. There exist times when it is necessary for a value type to be treated as an object, such as storing values in an array or some other collection.

When a value type is boxed, an object instance is created on the heap and the value of the value type is copied into the object. When this happens, the boxed object and the value type are two different entities. The object is not a reference to the original value type. Any change to the value type is not reflected in the object and vice versa.

Boxing a value type can be done with an implicit assignment. An *implicit assignment* is an assignment that does not require a type cast, as shown in the following:

```
int i = 10;
object o = i;
```

The value type variable *i* is implicitly cast to that of type object. When the value type *i* is boxed into object o, an instance of type object is created on the heap and the type information and value of the right side of the expression is copied into the object.

To unbox an object, an explicit conversion is required, as shown in the following:

```
int i = 10;
object o = i;
int j = (int)o;    //explicit conversion from object to int
```

The integer variable *j* now holds the value that was held by the object o. It is important to understand that the variables *i*, *o*, and *j* are all independent of each other and not merely references to the same memory space.

Programming Concepts

There is a very small learning curve involved in moving from C++ to C#. The syntax and productions found in the language are very similar to those found in C++. The truth of the matter is that C# was designed to be simple to learn and powerful enough to be extremely expressive.

The learning curve for Visual Basic programmers is somewhat higher, but certainly not exponentially so. C# is a language that has the syntax of C, but the "feel" of Visual Basic.

Namespaces

In recent years the prevalence of namespaces has come to play a major role in software engineering and component development. Namespaces provide for isolation and packaging of related classes, interfaces, and structs into a logical unit. I covered namespaces in C++; however, C# is slightly different and depends on them much more heavily than C++, so further discussion is warranted.

The .NET framework uses nested namespaces stemming from the System namespace. Microsoft has also provided classes and interfaces located under the Microsoft namespace for Windows-specific functionality. When developing components for the .NET platform, you should use your company name as the outer namespace in which to contain all of your classes, interfaces, and component code.

A namespace declaration should precede any code you develop, although it is not required. The syntax for declaring a namespace is as follows:

```
namespace some-namespace-name {
        //classes, interfaces, structs, and so on
}
```

Making use of entities within a namespace can be accomplished two different ways. The easiest way to access entities within a namespace is to use the using directive. Consider the System namespace, which has been used in every example presented so far. The first line of code in the previous examples is the line

```
using System;
```

This directive instructs the compiler to use the System namespace to locate the names of classes used in the code body. This is roughly equivalent to adding a reference to an object in Visual Basic. This functionality also allowed for the removal of the #include directive from C.

The second option is to make use of the fully qualified name of a particular entity. For example, the Console class exists within the System namespace. Rather than making use of the using directive, it is possible to use the fully qualified name instead, as shown in the following:

```
System.Console.WriteLine("Fully Qualified Name Access");
```

Let's see namespaces in action. The sample code in Listing 10.4 implements two namespaces. Each namespace contains a Money class. It is important to understand that the two Money classes are not the same as far as C# is concerned. Even though the Money class is identical in declaration and implementation, C# sees two distinct classes distinguished by namespace.

LISTING 10.4   Namespaces

```
//Purpose      :Demonstrate Namespaces

using System;


namespace Foo
{

    public class Money {

        private double m_Amount;

        public Money( )
        {
            Init( 0.0 );
        }

        public Money( double Amount )
        {
            Init( Amount );
        }


        public void Print( )
        {
            Console.WriteLine("Foo.Money.Print  {0}", m_Amount );
        }
```

LISTING 10.4   Continued

```csharp
        private void Init( double Amount )
        {
            m_Amount = Amount;
        }
    }
}

namespace Bar
{

    public class Money
    {

        private double m_Amount;

        public Money( )
        {
            Init( 0.0 );
        }

        public Money( double Amount )
        {
            Init( Amount );
        }

        public void Print( ) {
            Console.WriteLine("Bar.Money.Print  {0}", m_Amount );
        }

        private void Init( double Amount ) {
            m_Amount = Amount;
        }
    }
}


 public class NamespaceTest {

    public static void Main( ) {

        Foo.Money fm = new Foo.Money(5.00);
        Bar.Money bm = new Bar.Money(5.00);


        fm.Print( );
```

LISTING 10.4   Continued

```
        bm.Print( );


    }
}
```

The code in Listing 10.4 declares two namespaces—Foo and Bar. A Money class exists within each namespace. To make use of each Money class, the Main method creates an instance of each Money class by using the fully qualified name. One caveat to note is the using statement, there does not exist a keyword to unuse a namespace. Therefore, if you have two objects with the same name residing in different namespace, be sure to use qualified names rather than the using directive.

Statements

Chapter 3, "C Basics," covered flow control and looping constructs while discussing C programming. Most of that discussion still applies here. I'll try to point out the differences introduced by C#. Most of these differences are created by stricter type checking.

if

One of the most basic control statements is the if statement. Simply stated, the if statement evaluates a Boolean expression. The result of the Boolean expression determines whether or not a given line of code or a code segment will be executed. When the result of the Boolean expression is true, any code within the control body of the if statement is executed. When the condition expression is false, the code contained within the control body of the if statement is not executed.

As previously stated, C# enforces strict type checking, and this means that the expression used within an if construct must evaluate to a Boolean result. For example, the following line of code must be written to produce a Boolean result:

```
if( (i % 2) == 0 )
```

In C and C++, the line of code could have been written as

```
 if( i % 2 )
```

However, the expression i % 2 produces an integer result and not a Boolean result. For this reason, C# will reject the statement and issue an error.

goto

Yes, the goto statement still survives. I've covered the goto statement in sufficient detail in Chapter 3, and there are no real surprises using the goto in C#.

switch

The `switch` statement was discussed in Chapter 3. I didn't go over it for C++ because there weren't any significant differences in C++. C# introduces a significant difference.

Unlike C and C++, C# does not allow for one case to fall through into another case. To accomplish fall-through style execution, the `goto` keyword can be used to transfer control to another case. Listing 10.5 shows the basic use of the `switch` statement.

LISTING 10.5   The `switch` Statement

```
//Purpose   :The switch statement
using System;

public class SwitchTest
{
  public static void Main( )
  {

    Console.WriteLine("Please make your selection");
    Console.WriteLine("1 Hamburger");
    Console.WriteLine("2 Cheese Burger");
    Console.WriteLine("3 Fish");

    int Selection = int.Parse( Console.ReadLine( ) );

    switch( Selection )
    {
      case 1:
        Console.WriteLine("Hamburger");
        break;

      case 2:
        Console.WriteLine("Cheese Burger");
        break;

      case 3:
        Console.WriteLine("Fish");
        break;

      default:
        Console.WriteLine("Unknown choice");
        break;
    }
  }
}
```

Listing 10.5 presents an example of the switch statement in action. Each case expression is represented by some constant integral value. Notice that the break jump statement separates each case.

Because C# does not allow for case fall-through (that is, execution cannot continue from one case to another), the goto statement can be used to transfer control to another case or the default case. Listing 10.6 uses the goto statement to transfer control from one case statement to another.

LISTING 10.6   Using the goto Inside a Case Statement

```
//Purpose   :The switch statement and the use of goto

using System;

public class SwitchTest
{

  public static void Main( )
  {

    Console.WriteLine("Please make your selection");
    Console.WriteLine("1 Hamburger");
    Console.WriteLine("2 Cheese Burger");
    Console.WriteLine("3 Fish");
    Selection = int.Parse( Console.ReadLine( ) );

    switch( Selection )
    {
      case 1:
        Console.WriteLine("Hamburger");
        goto case 4;
      case 2:
        Console.WriteLine("Cheese Burger");
        goto case 4;
      case 3:
        Console.WriteLine("Fish");
        break;
      case 4:
        Console.WriteLine("Transferred to case 4");
        Console.WriteLine("Transferring to default case");
        goto default;
      default:
        Console.WriteLine("Unknown choice");
        break;
```

10

C# BASICS

LISTING 10.6   Continued

```
    }
  }
}
```

Listing 10.6 is a modification of the code found in Listing 10.5. Cases 1, 2, and 4 make use of the goto statement to transfer control from the current case to another case. Again, the goto statement can be used to transfer control to another case label or to the default case label.

for

Like C and C++, the for statement consists of an initialization, conditional expression, and an iteration statement.

while

I've covered the while statement in sufficient detail in Chapter 3, and there are no significant differences using the while statement in C#, except for the strict enforcement of Boolean expressions that I discussed before.

do...while

A similar construct to the while statement is the do...while statement. Unlike the while statement, the body of the do...while statement will always execute at least one iteration. This is due to the fact that the conditional expression is tested at the end of each loop rather than at the beginning.

foreach

The foreach statement will be familiar from Visual Basic. Essentially, the foreach statement allows for iteration over the elements within an array or any collection that implements the IEnumerable interface. Interfaces will be covered in more detail later in this section.

Every collection provides some method for iterating through the contents of the container. Anyone who has had the pleasure of implementing the IEnumVARIANT interface will appreciate the ease of implementing the IEnumerable interface along with providing an IEnumerator interface available in the .NET framework.

Listing 10.7 uses the foreach statement to iterate over the contents of an integer array.

LISTING 10.7   The foreach Statement

```
//Purpose:Using the foreach statement
using System;
public class ArrayListing
{
```

LISTING 10.7 Continued

```
public static void Main( )
{
   int[] whole_numbers = {1,2,3,4,5,6,7,8,9,10};
   //Display each element in the whole_numbers array
   foreach( int value in whole_numbers )
      Console.WriteLine( "value = {0}", value );
}
}
```

There is not a lot of code in Listing 10.7 because the focus is on putting the `foreach` statement to work. When you look under the covers of the `foreach` statement, lines 5 and 6 are equivalent to the following code segment in Listing 10.8.

LISTING 10.8 Expanding the `foreach` Statement

```
1: IEnumerator iterator = whole_numbers.GetEnumerator( );
2: while( iterator.MoveNext( ) ) {
3:    int value = (int)iterator.Current;
4:    Console.WriteLine( "value = {0}", value );
5: }
```

As you can see, the expanded code uses the `IEnumerator` interface and the `GetEnumerator()` method provided by the `System.Array` type. Next, a `while` statement is used to enumerate the elements of the array. The current element is accessed and cast to the proper type. When the type requested is a primitive type, this step requires unboxing the element from the object type and placing the value into the appropriate primitive type.

Operators

Table 10.2 contains the available operators found in C#. Most of them are comparable to operators in C++ and Visual Basic.

TABLE 10.2 C# Operators

Operator Category	Operator
Arithmetic	+, -, *, /, %,
Logical (Boolean and Bitwise)	&, |, ^, !, ~, &&, ||, true, false
Increment, Decrement	++, —
Shift	>>, <<

10

TABLE 10.2   Continued

Operator Category	Operator
Relational	==, !=, <, >, <=, >=
Assignment	=, +=, -=, *=, /=, %=, !=,
	^=, <<=, >>=
Type Information	is
Casting	(Type)Variable, as

The C# reference contains a full listing of not only unary and binary operators, but also index-ing, member access, indirect access, expanded type information, and casting. The operators in Table 10.2 will be familiar to programmers of most languages with the exception of is and as. These two operators need some further explanation; each operator accomplishes similar, but slightly different tasks.

The is Operator

The is operator tests whether an entity is of a certain type. C# supports very robust runtime type information and the is operator uses this type information to determine if the given entity is of the requested type. Visual Basic has a similar operator called TypeOf.

The is operator evaluates to a Boolean result and can be used as a conditional expression. The is operator will return true if the following conditions are met:

- The expression is not null.
- The expression can be safely cast to the type. The cast assumes an explicit cast in the form of (type)(expression).

If both of these conditions are satisfied, the is operator will return a Boolean true; otherwise, the is operator will return false. Listing 10.9 demonstrates the use of the is operator.

LISTING 10.9   The is Operator

```
//Purpose    :Demonstrate the 'is' operator
using System;

//Create two empty classes.  We only need their declaration for
//the purpose of demonstrating the is keyword

class Square
{
}
```

LISTING 10.9   Continued

```
class Circle
{
}


public class IsDemo
{
    public static void Main( )
    {
        Square mySquare = new Square( );
        Circle myCircle = new Circle( );
        int i = 10;

        WhatIsIt(mySquare);
        WhatIsIt(myCircle);
        WhatIsIt(i);
    }

    public static void WhatIsIt( object o )
    {
        if( o is Square )
            Console.WriteLine("It is a square");
        else if( o is Circle )
            Console.WriteLine("It is a circle");
        else
            Console.WriteLine("I don't know what it is");
    }
}
```

The is example in Listing 10.9 actually introduces two concepts not yet discussed. The first is the creation of a static method WhatIsIt in the IsDemo class. A static method can be used like a standalone function because no object instance is required. Static methods will be covered in detail when classes are covered later in this section.

The next item of interest is the parameter being passed to the static WhatIsIt method. Notice that the formal parameter is object. In C#, all classes implicitly inherit from the base class object and all value types can be boxed as object. Because this is the case, object can be used as a generic type that accepts anything.

The actual use of the is operator is fairly straightforward. Within each if statement, the is operator is used to determine the runtime type information of the object passed in. Depending on the results of the is expression, the appropriate response will be displayed to the console.

The following is the output of Listing 10.9:

```
It is a square
It is a circle
I don't know what it is
```

The as Operator

Like the `is` operator, the as operator uses runtime type information in an attempt to cast a given expression to the requested type. The normal casting operator—$(T)e$, where T is the type and e is the expression—generates an `InvalidCastException` when there is no valid cast. The as operator does not throw an exception; instead, the result returned is null.

> **NOTE**
>
> In Visual Basic the as operator is used to define the type of a variable at the point that the variable is introduced:
>
> ```
> Dim s As String
> ```
>
> This has no relation to the as operator in C#. And in fact there is no real counterpart to the C# as operator in Visual Basic.

The as operator uses the same syntax as the `is` operator:

```
expression as type
```

The as syntax can be formally expanded into the following:

```
expression is type ? (type)expression : (type)null
```

The as operator is therefore merely shorthand notation for using both the `is` operator and the conditional operator. The benefit of the as operator is its ease of use and the fact that no exception is thrown in the event that a type-safe cast does not exist.

Arrays

In C#, arrays are a special entity. All arrays implicitly inherit from the `System.Array` type. The `System.Array` base class provides various methods used during the manipulation of arrays. Arrays are also index checked; that is, any attempt to access an invalid index, such as an index out of range, will generate an exception. In C and C++, simple arrays were not range checked and it was possible to overwrite the stack space or the heap; not so in C#.

This of course is what Visual Basic programmers are used to, so you'll feel right at home with these arrays.

The declaration of an array might seem slightly odd at first, but when you analyze the syntax, it actually makes much more sense than the C and C++ declaration for arrays.

The following syntax is used to allocate an array of Rank 1:

```
array-type[] var = new array-type[size]
```

Notice that the array brackets are next to the array type and not the variable name. This syntax actually makes more sense than placing the brackets next to the variable name. After all, the array is the type, and type declarations precede the variable name.

Arrays in C# use zero-based indexing. Languages such as COBOL use one-based indexing. Visual Basic allows you to define the default array indexing base value, but the default is 0. The odd thing in Visual Basic is that the size determines the upper bound, whether you start at 0 or 1. Listing 10.10 uses a single dimension array and some of the methods the System.Array type provides.

LISTING 10.10 Single Dimension Array

```
//Purpose :Demonstrate C# arrays
using System;
public class ArrayTest
{
  public static void Main( )
  {
    //Declare a single dim array of ints
    int[] array_1 = new int[5];
    //Fill the array
    for(int i = array_1.GetLowerBound(0);i <= array_1.GetUpperBound(0);i++)
      array_1[i] = i+1;
    //Display the contents of the array
    for(int j = array_1.GetLowerBound(0);j <= array_1.GetUpperBound(0);j++)
      Console.WriteLine("array_1[{0}] = {1}", j, array_1[j]);
    Console.WriteLine("\n****** Phase II ******\n");
    //Declare an array and initialize the values
    int[] array_2 = new int[] { 25, 10, 4, 7, 15, 2, 1 };
    //Sort the array
    System.Array.Sort( array_2 );
    //Display the sorted values
    for(int k = array_2.GetLowerBound(0); k <= array_2.GetUpperBound(0);k++)
      Console.WriteLine("array_2[{0}] = {1}", k, array_2[k] );
  }
}
```

10

C# BASICS

Listing 10.10 uses the System.Array methods GetLowerBound and GetUpperBound. The method GetLowerBound takes an integer argument that specifies the Rank for which to get the lower index value. GetUpperBound also takes an integer argument that specifies the Rank to get the largest index value.

The System.Array class also provides the static method Sort. The Sort method can be used to sort intrinsic types or any type that implements the IComparable interface.

C# arrays are not restricted to a single dimension. Declaring arrays of rank greater than one merely requires specifying the lengths of each rank. It is also important to note that arrays do not have to be rectangular. Each rank can have a different upper bound (see Listing 10.11).

LISTING 10.11   Multidimensional Arrays

```
//Purpose :Arrays with a Rank greater than 1
using System;
public class ArrayTest
{
    public static void Main( )
    {
        int[,] grid = new int[3,3] { {1,2,3}, {4,5,6}, {7,8,9} };
        //Display the contents of the grid
        for( int i = 0; i < 3; i++ )
        {
            for( int j = 0; j < 3; j++ )
            {
                Console.Write("{0} ", grid[i,j] );
            }
            Console.WriteLine("");
        }
    }
}
```

The declaration for the array variable grid follows the same syntax and initialization as an array of rank 1. The only difference is the number of dimensions is now 2; the rank of the array is 2. Notice that the indexers for the array are separated with a comma. This syntax will be familiar to Visual Basic programmers, but to C and C++ developers, the syntax is different from what you are used to seeing.

Listing 10.11 also uses an initialization list when declaring the grid array.

struct

Early on in this section, there was a discussion of value types and reference types. In C#, a struct is considered a value type and, as such, is managed on the stack rather than the heap. C# implements primitive types such as int and char as structs.

structs are best used for simple data types or mementos for object serialization and object state. structs can contain data members, methods, properties, and constructors. In most ways, a struct is similar to a class. However, a struct cannot inherit from a class or another struct, but can implement one or more interfaces. structs cannot contain constructors without parameters, and the compiler will issue an error if you attempt to define one.

The default protection level for struct members is private. In C++, the only real difference between a struct and a class was the default protection level. Not so in C#. It is important to know that in C#, structs and classes are not interchangeable. Remember that a struct is considered a value type and a class is considered a reference type. Listing 10.12 implements a simple struct to represent a Point.

LISTING 10.12   Declaring and Using a struct

```
using System;
public struct Point {
    public int x;
    public int y;
}
public class StructTest
{
    public static void Main( )
    {
        Point p;
        p.x = 5;
        p.y = 10;
        Point p2 = p;
        PrintPoint( p );
        PrintPoint( p2 );
    }
    public static void PrintPoint( Point p )
    {
        Console.WriteLine( "x = {0}, y = {1}", p.x, p.y );
    }
}
```

Listing 10.12 demonstrates how to define and use a C# struct. The struct Point contains two public data members—x and y. Notice that on line 14 the variable p2 is assigned the value of variable p. When dealing with value types, the default assignment operator will copy the contents of the right side to the variable on the left side. This is in sharp contrast to the way in which reference types work. Remember that when dealing with reference types, the assignment operator will act as a reference and not a copy, as with value types.

There are some interesting points to note when dealing with structs. A struct cannot be used until all the values within the struct have been initialized. Every struct has a synthesized default constructor that initializes the data members to their respective default values. However, when a `struct` contains a private data member, the default constructor will not initialize it without an explicit invocation of the default constructor. To accomplish this, the `struct` must be created using the new operator. This is a bit confusing because the `struct` is still created on the stack and not on the heap, as would be expected by the use of the new operator. Listing 10.13 demonstrates the warning issued by the compiler when attempting to use a `struct` that contains uninitialized members.

LISTING 10.13   struct Member Initialization

```
using System;
public struct Simple
{
    public  int i;
    private string s;
    public void init( )
    {
        i = 10;
        s = "Hello";
    }
}
public class T
{
    public static void Main( )
    {
        Simple simple;
        simple.init( );
    }
}
```

When Listing 10.13 is compiled, the C# compiler will issue the following error.

```
Microsoft (R) Visual C# Compiler Version 7.00.9030 [CLR version 1.00.2204.21]
Copyright (C) Microsoft Corp 2000. All rights reserved.
struct_02.cs(25,3): error CS0165: Use of unassigned local variable 'simple'
```

The error issued by the C# compiler is somewhat misleading at first because it complains about the use of an unassigned local variable simple. This error is due to the fact that the private data member s is uninitialized. To have private data members initialized, an instance of the `struct` must be declared using the new operator (see Listing 10.14).

LISTING 10.14   Revision of Listing 10.13

```
using System;
public struct Simple
{
```

LISTING 10.14 Continued

```
    public  int i;
    private string s;
    public void init( )
    {
        i = 10;
        s = "Hello";
    }
    public void show( )
    {
        Console.WriteLine("i = {0}", i);
        Console.WriteLine("s = {0}", s);
    }
}
public class T
{
    public static void Main( )
    {
        Simple simple = new Simple( );
        simple.init( );
    }
}
```

Revising the previous listing and making two changes now allows for a clean compile and the expected behavior. The first change involves the addition of the show method, which uses the data member s. This change satisfies the compiler's complaint about the unused private data member.

Notice that the declaration now uses the new operator. Again, it is important to understand that a struct is a value type and, as such, will still exist on the stack. The usage of the new operator forces the invocation of the default constructor and initializes the private data members.

Because C# provides a synthesized parameter-less constructor, any attempt to implement such a construct for a value type will cause the compiler to issue an error.

Classes

A class represents the encapsulation of data and methods that act on that data. In C#, classes are considered reference types and, as such, instances of classes are allocated on the heap and managed by the GC. When an instance of a class is created, memory is allocated on the heap and the object is reference counted. When the reference count for the object reaches zero, the GC will reclaim the memory area being used by the object and return that memory to the available memory pool.

10

C# BASICS

Classes can contain fields, methods, events, properties, and nested classes. Classes also have the ability to inherit from another class and implement multiple interfaces. C# classes combine some of the best features from both Visual Basic and C++: inheritance, from C++ classes, but properties, methods, and events from Visual Basic.

Like structs, the default protection level for class members is private. Classes can declare members to be public, protected, private, internal, or protected internal.

Declaring a class consists of specifying the following:

```
[attributes] [access modifier] class class-name [: [base-class], [interface]*]
{
    body
}
```

The square brackets indicate optional specifiers and are not required to declare a class. Listing 10.15 presents a simple class representation for a Circle type.

LISTING 10.15   A Simple Class

```
using System;

public class Circle {
   //Fields
   protected int x, y, r;
   //Constructor
   public Circle( int xr, int yr, int rr )
   {
      x = xr;
      y = yr;
      r = rr;
   }
   //Methods
   public void Draw( )
   {
       //we'll put in actual drawing code later
      Console.WriteLine("x = {0}", x);
      Console.WriteLine("y = {0}", y);
      Console.WriteLine("r = {0}", r);
   }
}
public class Simple
{
    public static void Main( )
    {
        Circle cir = new Circle( 100,100,50 );
        cir.Draw( );
```

LISTING 10.15   Continued

```
    }
}
```

The `Circle` class in Listing 10.15 demonstrates the basics of defining and implementing a class in C#. The class contains a private field, a parameter-based constructor, and a single method. Unlike a `struct`, the `new` operator must be used to create an instance of the class. The `Main` function shows the creating of a new instance of the `Circle` class and uses the parameter constructor to initialize the object.

As a brief note on access modifiers, Table 10.3 presents the access modifiers and how they affect class members.

TABLE 10.3   Member Access Modifiers

Access Modifier	Definition
public	Visible to all code
protected	Visible to current class and derived classes
private	Visible only to current class
internal	Visible to current assembly only
protected internal	Visible to current assembly or types derived from the class

Object

Every class in C# implicitly derives from the base class `System.Object`. Because all classes derive from a common base class, the ability to create generic collection classes becomes a trivial point. Every instance of a class can be treated as if it were a `System.Object` instance.

The `System.Object` class also provides a few basic services that other classes in the .NET framework use. For example, the `Console.Write` method will use the `ToString` method of a class to display the class to the console. Any C# class can thus override the behavior of `ToString` and provide a custom implementation specific to the class. Table 10.4 lists some of the basic `Object` methods.

TABLE 10.4   The `System.Object` Class

Method	Purpose
Equals(`Object`)	Boolean comparison
Finalize	Similar to a C++ destructor
ToString	Convert class to string representation

The System.Object base class also provides additional methods for type information, reflection, and cloning. These topics are outside the scope of this conversation, but their exploration is well worth the time spent.

Methods

In OO terminology, a method represents an object message. Methods can be either instance or static in nature. An instance method requires an instance of the object and generally acts on the data members of the current object. Static methods do not require an instance of an object and, therefore, cannot access the data members of the current class.

Methods, like data members, can also have an access modifier applied to them. Public methods allow any user of the object to invoke that method; it is the public contract, so to speak. Protected methods are only to be used by the object itself or any object that derives from the object. Private methods can only be accessed by the class declaring the method. Derived classes cannot make use of any private methods found in the base class.

Listing 10.16 demonstrates the use of instance verses static methods.

LISTING 10.16 Instance and Static Methods

```
using System;
public class MyMath
{
    //instance method
    public long Factorial( long l )
    {
        return l <= 0 ? 1 : l * Factorial( l - 1 );
    }
    //static method
    public static long SFactorial( long l )
    {
        return l <= 0 ? 1 : l * SFactorial( l - 1 );
    }
}
public class Methods
{
    public static void Main ( )
    {
        //Use the static method
        Console.WriteLine("5 Factorial = {0}", MyMath.SFactorial( 5 ) );
        //Use the instance method
        MyMath m = new MyMath( );
        Console.WriteLine("5 Factorial = {0}", m.Factorial( 5 ) );
    }
}
```

To access a static method, the method name needs to be qualified with the name of the class. The `SFactorial` method of the `MyMath` class is invoked in this manner. C# has unified member, method, and scooping access to the dot operator. In C++, it was necessary to use the pointer access operator, the dot operator, or the scope resolution operator, depending on the situation. Not so in C#, where only the dot operator is necessary to perform all access.

Instance methods require an object to invoke them. The `Factorial` method is such a method because the static modifier has not been applied to the method. Notice that the same dot operator is used to access the instance method the same way that access to the static method is specified.

Parameter Passing

Depending on the language you are familiar with, there exists specific syntax for defining whether a parameter is passed by value—a copy of the parameter is placed on the call stack—or by reference—an alias to the variable is placed on the call stack. In C and C++, you can pass a parameter by value or pass a pointer. In Visual Basic, parameters are passed by reference or by value. In traditional VB the default was by reference, whereas in .NET the default is by value.

C# offers not only support by-value and by-reference parameter passing, but it also allows for additional marshaling instructions, such as in and out.

In C#, value types, such as primitive types and `structs`, are passed by value unless otherwise specified. When a parameter is passed by value, a copy of the value type is created. The method receiving the parameter can use the copy and even modify its value. However, the parameter is not in any way related to the outside world. If a method modifies a value passed by value, the effects of that modification only exist within the scope of that method.

Reference types—any class or interface—are passed by reference and cannot be passed by value. To pass a value type by reference, the `ref` keyword must be used. When a parameter is passed by reference to a method, the method can modify the parameter, and the modifications will affect the actual parameter, thus producing a side effect. Listing 10.17 demonstrates parameter passing available in C#.

LISTING 10.17 Parameter Passing

```
using System;

//Create a value type
public struct Point {

    public int x;
    public int y;
}
```

LISTING 10.17 Continued

```
//Create a Reference type
public class MyObject {
    public int i;
}

public class Pass
{
    public static void Main( )
    {
        //Create a primitive type and pass to the various methods
        int i = 100;
        Console.WriteLine("Value of i before PassByValue Method is {0}", i );
        PassByValue( i );
        Console.WriteLine("Value of i after PassByValue Method is {0}", i );
        Console.WriteLine("");

        Console.WriteLine("Value of i before PassByRef Method is {0}", i );
        PassByRef( ref i );
        Console.WriteLine("Value of i before PassByRef Method is {0}", i );
        Console.WriteLine("");

        //Create an the Point type
        Point p; p.x = 10; p.y = 15;
        Console.WriteLine("Value of p before is x={0}, y={1}", p.x,p.y);
        PassByValue( p );
        Console.WriteLine("Value of p after PassByValue is x={0}, y={1}",
p.x,p.y);
        Console.WriteLine("");

        Console.WriteLine("Value of p before PassByRef is x={0}, y={1}",
p.x,p.y);
        PassByRef( ref p );
        Console.WriteLine("Value of p after PassByRef is x={0}, y={1}",
p.x,p.y);
        Console.WriteLine("");

        //Create an object instance
        MyObject o = new MyObject( );
        o.i = 10;
        Console.WriteLine("Value of o.i before PassReferenceType is {0}", o.i
);
        PassReferenceType( o );
        Console.WriteLine("Value of o.i after PassReferenceType is {0}", o.i );
    }
```

LISTING 10.17   Continued

```csharp
    public static void PassByValue( Point p )
    {
        Console.WriteLine("Entering public static void PassByvalue( Point p )"
➥);
        Console.WriteLine("Value of Point.x = {0} : Point.y = {1}", p.x, p.y );
        p.x++; p.y++;
        Console.WriteLine("New Value of Point.x = {0} : Point.y = {1}", p.x,
➥p.y );
        Console.WriteLine("Exiting public static void PassByvalue( Point p )"
➥);
    }

    public static void PassByValue( int i )
    {
        Console.WriteLine("Entering public static void PassByValue( int i )" );
        Console.WriteLine("Value of i = {0}", i );
        i++;
        Console.WriteLine("New Value of i = {0}", i );
        Console.WriteLine("Exiting public static void PassByValue( int i )" );
    }

    public static void PassByRef( ref Point p )
    {
        Console.WriteLine("Entering public static void PassByRef( ref Point p
➥)" );
        Console.WriteLine("Value of Point.x = {0} : Point.y = {1}", p.x, p.y );
        p.x++; p.y++;
        Console.WriteLine("New Value of Point.x = {0} : Point.y = {1}", p.x,
➥p.y );
        Console.WriteLine("Exiting public static void PassByRef( ref Point p )"
➥);
    }

    public static void PassByRef( ref int i )
    {
        Console.WriteLine("Entering public static void PassByRef( ref int i )"
➥);
        Console.WriteLine("Value of i = {0}", i );
        i++;
        Console.WriteLine("New Value of i = {0}", i );
        Console.WriteLine("Exiting public static void PassByRef( ref int i )"
➥);
    }

    public static void PassReferenceType( MyObject o )
```

LISTING 10.17   Continued

```
    {
        Console.WriteLine("Entering public static PassReferenceType(MyObject
o)" );
        Console.WriteLine("Value of MyObject.i = {0}", o.i);
        o.i++;
        Console.WriteLine("New Value of MyObject.i = {0}", o.i);

        Console.WriteLine("Exiting public static PassReferenceType(MyObject o)"
);
    }
}
```

The parameter passing in Listing 10.17 presents cases for passing primitive types, structs, and reference types to methods by value and by reference.

Properties

In the C++ and COM world, properties are nothing more than a simple semantic for assessor and setter methods. In COM, the methods would be put_T and get_T where T is the property name. Visual Basic programmers will be immediately familiar with the concept of properties, because there exists a parallel among the entities.

C# allows for properties to be either read only, write only, or read/write.

Properties provide a simple syntax for accessing elements within a class while still allowing for a level of abstraction as to the actual property implementation. Listing 10.18 takes the Circle example and adds three properties to it—CenterX, CenterY, and Radius.

LISTING 10.18   Using Properties

```
using System;

public class Circle {
    //Fields
    protected int x, y, r;
    //Constructor
    public Circle( int xr, int yr, int rr )
    {
        x = xr;
        y = yr;
        r = rr;
    }
    public int CenterX
```

LISTING 10.18 Continued

```
    {
        get { return x;}
        set {x=value;}
    }
    public int CenterY
    {
        get { return y;}
        set {y=value;}
    }
    public int Radius
    {
        get { return r;}
        set {r=value;}
    }
    //Methods
    public void Draw( )
    {
        //we'll put in actual drawing code later
        Console.WriteLine("x = {0}", x);
        Console.WriteLine("y = {0}", y);
        Console.WriteLine("r = {0}", r);
    }
}
public class Simple
{
    public static void Main( )
    {
        Circle cir = new Circle( 100,100,50 );
        cir.Draw( );
    }
}
```

The purpose of properties is to allow for a natural semantic for accessing data members but still allowing for a layer of abstraction. Within the implementation of the property accessor or setter, the developer is free to implement validation, conversion, and any other logic necessary. From the user's point of view, all the implementation detail has been abstracted away, and a clean semantic for accessing data elements is provided.

Operators

C# provides the facility for user-defined operators. Any struct or class can provide a specific implementation of a given operator, such as addition, subtraction, or casting from one type to another. The ability to create a new type and define operator semantics for it allows for the development of new value types as well as reference types.

In earlier discussions, the assignment operator was discussed and how it differs from value types and reference types. C# does not allow for the implementation of an assignment operator. This restriction is due to reference counting verses copying. Another consideration is the .NET platform is meant for languages to interoperate with each other in ways never before possible. To make a copy of a reference type, most reference types provide a Copy method. When developing classes, you should follow the same guidelines.

C# requires that all operators be static methods. Again, this makes sense to a language purist. Operators pertain to a type and not an instance, which is just one of the details that was not overlooked in the design of C#.

To gain an understanding of operator overloading, the Fraction class, Listing 10.19 demonstrates implementing the arithmetic operators + and -.

LISTING 10.19   Operator Overloading

```
//Purpose     :Demonstrate operator overloading
using System;
public class Fraction
{
    //data members
    private int    m_numerator;
    private int    m_denominator;
    //Properties
    public int Numerator
    {
        get { return m_numerator; }
        set { m_numerator = value; }
    }
    public int Denominator
    {
        get { return m_denominator; }
        set { m_denominator = value; }
    }
    //Constructors
    public Fraction( ) { m_numerator = 0; m_denominator = 0; }
    public Fraction( int iNumerator, int iDenominator )
    {
            m_numerator = iNumerator;
            m_denominator = iDenominator;
    }
    //Arithmetic operators +,-,/,*
    public static Fraction operator+(Fraction f1, Fraction f2)
    {
        Fraction Result = new Fraction( );
```

LISTING 10.19   Continued

```
        //In order to add fractions, the denominators need to be the same
        //the fastest way is to multiply them together and adjust the
numerators
        if( f1.Denominator != f2.Denominator )
        {
            Result.Denominator = f1.Denominator * f2.Denominator;

Result.Numerator=(f1.Numerator*f2.Denominator)+(f2.Numerator*f1.Denominator);
        }
        else
        {
            Result.Denominator = f1.Denominator;
            Result.Numerator   = f1.Numerator + f2.Numerator;
        }
        return Result;
    }

    public static Fraction operator-(Fraction f1, Fraction f2)
    {
        Fraction Result = new Fraction( );
        //In order to subtract fractions, the denominators need to be the same
        //the fastest way is to multiply them together and adjust the
numerators
        if( f1.Denominator != f2.Denominator )
        {
            Result.Denominator = f1.Denominator * f2.Denominator;
            Result.Numerator=(f1.Numerator*f2.Denominator)-
(f2.Numerator*f1.Denominator);
        }
        else
        {
            Result.Denominator = f1.Denominator;
            Result.Numerator   = f1.Numerator - f2.Numerator;
        }
        return Result;
    }
}

public class OperatorTest
{
    public static void Main( )
    {
        Fraction f1 = new Fraction( 1, 5 );
        Fraction f2 = new Fraction( 2, 5 );
```

LISTING 10.19   Continued

```
        //Add the Fractions
        Fraction f3 = f1 + f2;
        //Display the result
        Console.WriteLine("f1 + f2 = {0}/{1}", f3.Numerator, f3.Denominator );
        //Subtract f2 from f3 should get f1
        f3 = f3 - f2;
        Console.WriteLine("f3 - f2 = {0}/{1}", f3.Numerator, f3.Denominator );
    }
}
```

The Fraction class implements both the + and – operators. The general form for overloading an operator can be expressed as follows:

```
public static return-type operator T(param p [,param p1])
```

The return-type specifies the result of the operator, T is the actual operator to overload, and the number of parameters depends on the operator being overloaded.

In addition to standard arithmetic operators, C# provides the ability to overload relational operators and casting operators. Relational operators often come in pairs. For example, when overloading the equality operator ==, the inequality operator != must also be defined. Relational operators have the same semantic for overloading as the operators presented so far.

Casting operators have a slightly different semantic than regular operators. When implementing a casting operator, the decision of implicit or explicit must be made. Remember, an implicit cast does not require the type to be specified, whereas an explicit cast does.

```
Fraction f = new Fraction( 1, 5 );
double d = f;              //implicit cast
double dd = (double)f;        //explicit cast
```

The decision about implicit verses explicit will need to be determined by the use case in mind. The syntax for overloading a casting operator is as follows:

```
public static [implicit|explicit] operator Return-Type( Type T )
```

Again, the Return-Type denotes to what the Type T is being cast or converted. Extending the previous operator example, the Fraction class has been extended to implement an explicit cast to double and the relational operators == and !=. When compiling the code in Listing 10.20, the compiler will issue two warnings CS660 and CS661. The warning stems from the overloaded operators == and != and the requirement that any class overloading these operators must also provide an implementation of Object.Equals and Object.GetHashCode. For now you can dismiss the warnings. However when creating production code be sure to implement the necessary Equals and GetHashCode methods in order to satisfy the rule that says any two objects that are considered equal by Equals or by the overloaded == and != operators should have the same hash code.

LISTING 10.20   Extend the Fraction Class

```
//Purpose      :Demonstrate operator overloading

using System;

public class Fraction
{
    //data members
    private int    m_numerator;
    private int    m_denominator;


    //Properties
    public int Numerator
    {
        get { return m_numerator; }
        set { m_numerator = value; }
    }
    public int Denominator
    {
        get { return m_denominator; }
        set { m_denominator = value; }
    }


    //Constructors
    public Fraction( ) { m_numerator = 0; m_denominator = 0; }

    public Fraction( int iNumerator, int iDenominator )
    {
            m_numerator = iNumerator;
            m_denominator = iDenominator;
    }

    //Arithmetic operators +,-,/,*

    public static Fraction operator+(Fraction f1, Fraction f2)
    {
        Fraction Result = new Fraction( );
        //In order to add fractions, the denominators need to be the same
        //the fastest way is to multiply them together and adjust the
numerators
```

LISTING 10.20   Continued

```
            if( f1.Denominator != f2.Denominator )
            {
                Result.Denominator = f1.Denominator * f2.Denominator;
                Result.Numerator=(f1.Numerator*f2.Denominator)+(f2.Numerator*f1.
➡Denominator);
            }
            else
            {
                Result.Denominator = f1.Denominator;
                Result.Numerator  = f1.Numerator + f2.Numerator;
            }
            return Result;
        }

    public static Fraction operator-(Fraction f1, Fraction f2)
        {
            Fraction Result = new Fraction( );
            //To subtract fractions, the denominators need to be the same
            //the fastest way is to multiply them together and adjust the
numerators
            if( f1.Denominator != f2.Denominator )
            {
                Result.Denominator = f1.Denominator * f2.Denominator;
                Result.Numerator=(f1.Numerator*f2.Denominator)-
➡(f2.Numerator*f1.Denominator);
            }
            else
            {
                Result.Denominator = f1.Denominator;
                Result.Numerator  = f1.Numerator - f2.Numerator;
            }
            return Result;
        }

    //add an explicit casting operator from fraction to double
    public static explicit operator double(Fraction f)
        {
            double dResult = ((double)f.Numerator / (double)f.Denominator);
            return dResult;
        }

    public static bool operator==(Fraction f1, Fraction f2)
        {
            //TODO: Implement comparison of f1 to f2
            return true;
```

LISTING 10.20 Continued

```csharp
    }
    public static bool operator!=(Fraction f1, Fraction f2)
    {
        return !(f1 == f2);
    }


}


public class OperatorTest
{
    public static void Main( )
    {
        Fraction f1 = new Fraction( 1, 5 );
        Fraction f2 = new Fraction( 2, 5 );

        //Add the Fractions
        Fraction f3 = f1 + f2;

        //Display the result
        Console.WriteLine("f1 + f2 = {0}/{1}", f3.Numerator, f3.Denominator );

        //Substract f2 from f3 should get f1
        f3 = f3 - f2;
        Console.WriteLine("f3 - f2 = {0}/{1}", f3.Numerator, f3.Denominator );

        //Print f3 as a double
        Console.WriteLine("f3 as a double = {0}", (double)f3);
    }
}
```

Inheritance

Inheritance is a key concept in OO design and languages. Inheritance allows for common functionality and attributes to reside in a base class, and specialized classes can inherit the functionality provided by the base class. C# supports single inheritance only. C++ provides for multiple inheritances and, when used correctly, is a truly powerful paradigm. However, multiple inheritance has proven to be difficult to maintain and somewhat hard to follow. This is one reason that C# only implements single inheritance.

I explored single and multiple inheritance in C++. The sample in Listing 10.21 is the same sample that you used in the C++ chapter, modified for C#. A circle class is available that will draw a circle with GDI+ statements and a derived class of ArcPie that draws an arc.

LISTING 10.21   Inheritance

```csharp
//chap5.cs
using System;
using System.Drawing;

namespace vbcbook
{
    public class Circle
    {
        protected int x,y,r;
        public System.Drawing.Color lineColor;

        public Circle()     {}
        public Circle(int xr, int yr, int rr)
        {
            x=xr;
            y=yr;
            r=rr;
        }

        public int CenterX
        {
            get { return x;}
            set {x=value;}
        }
        public int CenterY
        {
            get { return y;}
            set {y=value;}
        }
        public int Radius
        {
            get { return r;}
            set {r=value;}
        }

        public virtual void Draw(System.Drawing.Graphics g)
        {
            Pen pen = new Pen(lineColor, 1);
            g.DrawEllipse(pen, x-r, y-r, r*2, r*2);
        }
    }
    public class ArcPie : Circle
    {
        protected float s, e;
```

LISTING 10.21   Continued

```csharp
        public ArcPie(int xr, int yr, int rr, float sr, float er)
        {
            x=xr;
            y=yr;
            r=rr;
            s=sr;
            e=er;
        }
        public override void Draw(System.Drawing.Graphics g)
        {
            Pen pen = new Pen(lineColor, 1);
            g.DrawPie(pen,x-r,y-r,2*r,2*r,s,e);
        }
        public float Start
        {
            get { return s;}
            set {s=value;}
        }
        public float Sweep
        {
            get { return e;}
            set {e=value;}
        }

    }
}
//place this code in a C# form
protected override void OnPaint(PaintEventArgs e)
{
    //use the circle base class
    vbcbook.Circle cir = new vbcbook.Circle(200,200,50);
    cir.lineColor=System.Drawing.Color.Red;
    cir.Draw(e.Graphics);

    //use the arcpie derived class
    vbcbook.ArcPie pie = new vbcbook.ArcPie(100,100,50,30,120);
    pie.lineColor=System.Drawing.Color.Red;
    pie.Draw(e.Graphics);
}
```

In this sample, `ArcPie` is a derived class using `Circle` as the base class. The derived class uses the protected members of the base class. The properties of the base class are available for use as well. The `Draw` method is overridden and the derived class provides its own drawing code.

Also worth mentioning is the way the code that calls the `Circle` and `ArcPie` class is written. Notice that you place the code in an override in a Form. C++ programmers might not be surprised by this because many class libraries would require the same type of code. Visual Basic programmers might find this a little strange, though. In VB you can call drawing code from almost anywhere. In .NET this becomes more difficult because you have to have a drawing object to use. Using the `OnPaint` override is the best way to get this drawing object.

Remember that C# only supports single inheritance, so it is not possible to create a derived class that specifies more than one base class. The syntax to inherit from a base class is to place the name of the base class to the right of a colon following the name of the derived class, as shown in the following:

```
class Bar : Foo { }
```

In this case, `Bar` is the derived class and `Foo` is the base class.

Interfaces

Interfaces provide a powerful abstraction to component-based development. Interfaces provide a public contract that allows components to work together. The alarm clock next to your bed implements several interfaces—the `Alarm` interface, the `Clock` interface, and possibly the `Radio` interface.

Figure 10.1 depicts an `AlarmClock` component that supports an `Alarm` interface, a `Clock` interface, and a `Radio` interface. Figure 10.1 is know as a box-spoon diagram; the spoons are the lines with circles at the end sticking out of the box.

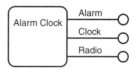

FIGURE 10.1

The `AlarmClock` component and supported interfaces.

An interface is not a class and, as such, does not contain any implementation code. An interface contains members and method signatures, all of which must be public. C# allows for both a `struct` and a class to implement one or more interfaces. This is different from inheritance. Inheritance involves implementation from a base class, whereas interface implementation only states that the class implementing a particular interface guarantees to fulfill the interface contract.

C# uses the `interface` keyword to denote the declaration of an interface, as follows:

```
interface name {
    body;
}
```

A class or `struct` can implement an interface by declaring the interface during declaration, as shown in the following:

```
public class AlarmClock : IAlarm, IClock, IRadio {
//implementation
}
```

> **NOTE**
>
> A standard naming convention for interfaces states that an interface name should begin with the capital letter *I*. This naming convention allows for consistency and makes it easy to spot an interface with respect to a class or `struct` definition.

The .NET framework makes heavy use of interfaces. In fact, to take full advantage of the services provided by .NET, understanding interface development and implementation is a must. Listing 10.22 implements an `AlarmClock` class.

LISTING 10.22   The `AlarmClock`

```
//Purpose    :Interfaces
using System;
//Define the IAlarm interface
interface IAlarm
{
    bool On { get; set; }
    void Snooze( );
}
//Define the IClock interface
interface IClock
{
    void SetTime( );
}
//Define the IRadio interface
interface IRadio
{
    void SetStation( double station_id );
}
```

LISTING 10.22   Continued

```
//Create an alarm clock that implements IAlarm, IClock and IRadio
public class AlarmClock : IAlarm, IClock, IRadio {

    //Data members
    private bool    m_bOnOff;

    //The IAlarm interface implementation
    public bool On { get { return m_bOnOff; } set { m_bOnOff = value; } }
    public     void Snooze( ) { Console.WriteLine("IAlarm.Snooze"); }

    //The IClock Interface
    public     void SetTime( ) { Console.WriteLine("IClock.SetTime"); }

    //The IRadio interface
    public     void SetStation( double station_id )
➨{ Console.WriteLine("IRadio.SetStation( {0} )", station_id ); }
}
public class InterfaceTest {
    public static void Main( ) {
        AlarmClock a = new AlarmClock( );
        //Get the IAlarm Interface
        IAlarm ialarm = (IAlarm)a;
        ialarm.On = false;
        ialarm.Snooze( );
        //Get the IClock interface
        IClock iclock = (IClock)a;
        iclock.SetTime( );
        //Get the IRadio interface
        IRadio iradio = (IRadio)a;
        iradio.SetStation( 95.5 );
    }
}
```

Figure 10.1 has been implemented in Listing 10.22. The casting operator is used to obtain a requested interface. The IAlarm interface is requested from the AlarmClock instance. In the event that the AlarmClock does not support the IAlarm interface, an InvalidCastException will be thrown. If the interface does exist, a reference to the interface will be returned. As a quick aside, there are now two references to the alarm clock—one reference for the AlarmClock variable and one reference for the IAlarm interface. Both of these references must be released before the GC will collect the AlarmClock instance.

Delegates

Delegates are the ultimate function pointer. Developers familiar with C and C++ are very familiar with function pointers and their lack of instance-based knowledge. A delegate can be thought of as a call-back mechanism, essentially saying, "Please invoke this method for me when the time is right." I will take a closer look at delegates in the next chapter.

I would encourage any developer to explore delegates in detail because their use in .NET is prolific, especially in Windows Forms development.

Summary

By now you should have an idea of the power and simplicity that C# offers. Interface-based development has been a prominent theme in recent years, and C# delivers on this theme with simple and consistent model of development. With the addition of instance-based delegates, a powerful subject/observer model is built into the language.

Applying C#

IN THIS CHAPTER

The objective in this chapter will be to talk about controls that can be used with VB.NET or C#, written in C#. (You have already read about several types of custom controls in previous chapters.) The discussion of WinForm controls here will include adding and programming properties, events, design time support, and drawing on the screen.

C# WinForm Controls

You have read about .NET WinForm Controls before in Chapter 9, "Componenets and Controls." These are controls written in managed code to run on WIN32 systems. .NET also has WebForms Controls that are written in .NET to run on a Web server. These controls can be written in any language that is supported in .NET.

WinForm controls can be based on several different classes in .NET. They can be based on any class that will allow inheritance that also inherits from `Object/MarshalbyRefObject/MarshalbyRefComponent/Control`. This includes the `Control`, `RichControl`, and `UserControl` classes.

Writing controls in .NET is more like writing a control in Visual Basic 5 or 6 than writing an ATL control. Although the language you'll be working in is C, or C# to be more specific, the way you create WinForm controls in .NET is not at all like C++/ATL controls. As a Visual Basic programmer, you will probably be fairly comfortable with the way you develop controls in .NET.

You will also find this section much smaller than the discussion on ATL controls, due mostly to the fact that it is just easier to create controls in .NET than in ATL, which is good news.

Creating the Control Project

This section briefly covers creating the control project and how to construct the control.

The control project is created in the same manner as any other project in .NET. This was covered this in Chapter 9, "Components and Controls." You should choose to create a Windows Control Library. This creates a WinForm Control based on `UserControl`. To test your control, you will probably create a Windows Application project and add it to this same solution. This allows you to test your control without having to load a different project.

After creating the control project, you may want to add constituent controls to the UserControl. *Constituent controls* are child controls that you use in the construction of your control. Any type of WinForm control can be used as a constituent control. You can use properties and methods that you add to your control to manipulate properties and methods in the constituent controls. Further, you can sink events from the constituent controls and raise events out of your control in those event sinks.

The wizard bases the new control on the `UserControl`. You can change that to any control class that you like. Right after creating the project is a good time to do that.

> **NOTE**
>
> There are two ways to use a .NET control —as a constituent control, as just described, or as a base class. While any control could be used as a constituent control, not all controls can be used as a base class. Inheriting from a class that represents a control is very different from using a control as a constituent.
>
> We talked about implementation inheritance in Chapter 5, "C++ Classes." Let's contrast implementation inheritance briefly with delegation, which is basically what you use with constituent controls.
>
> Most Visual Basic programmers are familiar with the `Implements` key word. Using `Implements` is a form of inheritance. However, this type of inheritance ends up using delegation, not implementation inheritance. The difference comes from the way that you obtain the functionality for your component.
>
> With implementation inheritance, your component gets most of its functionality simply by inheriting from the base class. Initially, all the functionality of the base class is available. You can override functions or add functions to change functionality.
>
> In contrast, when building controls with constituent controls, you inherit no functionality. You must program the functionality. You can use the capabilities of the constituent controls, but you do not have any of those features unless you specifically use those properties or methods.
>
> For example, say you use a text control as a constituent on a user control and, without any further coding, you build and use the custom control. The control will work and will display the text control. However, you will not be able to access the control programmatically, because none of the text control's properties are exposed through the user control.
>
> In contrast, if you build a control by inheriting from a text rather than user control, not only will the control work, but you can access all the properties of the control because implementation inheritance allows you to do so.

Coding the Control

Our sample, called `netLabel`, is the same label control that you created in the chapter on ATL. The source for it is on the Web site and is shown in Listing 11.1.

LISTING 11.1   netLabel Control

```
namespace netLabel
{
  using System;
  using System.Collections;
  using System.ComponentModel;
  using System.Drawing;
  using System.Data;
  using System.Windows.Forms;
  using System.ComponentModel.Design;
  using System.Diagnostics;
  using System.Drawing.Drawing2D;
  using System.Drawing.Design;
  using System.Windows.Forms.Design;

  /// <summary>
  ///  This declares a delegate which is used in an event.
  /// </summary>
  public delegate void TickTimerHandler(object sender, TickTimerEventArgs e);
  /// <summary>
  ///  an exception class to throw an error
  /// </summary>
  public class InvalidPropertyValueException : Exception
  {
    private readonly string message="Invalid property Value";
    public InvalidPropertyValueException() {}
    public InvalidPropertyValueException(string message) {  }

    new public string Message
    {
      get
      {
        return message;
      }
    }
  }

  /// <summary>
  ///          everything is a class
  ///          this is the arguments for a custom event
/// </summary>
  public class TickTimerEventArgs : EventArgs
  {
    //a cancel parameter to stop the flashing
private bool bCancel = false;
```

LISTING 11.1   Continued

```csharp
      //the border color
      private Color cBorderColor = System.Drawing.SystemColors.WindowFrame;
      //event args constructor
      public TickTimerEventArgs(bool bCancel, Color cBorderColor) {}

      //these are properties that set the member variables
      public bool Cancel
      {
        get
        {
          return bCancel;
        }
        set
        {
          bCancel = value;
        }
      }
      public Color BorderColor
      {
        get
        {
          return cBorderColor;
        }
        set
        {
          cBorderColor=value;
        }
      }
    }
    //property types
    public enum enumAlignment
    {
      Left,
      Center,
      Right
    };
    public enum enumBorderStyle
    {
      No_Border=0,
      ThreeD_Border=1,
      Single_Color_Border=2
    };
    public enum enumBackStyle
    {
```

LISTING 11.1   Continued

```
  Transparent = 0,
  Opaque = 1
};
public enum enumFlashType
{
  NoneFlash = 0,
  BlackFlash = 1,
  BackgroundFlash = 2,
  ColorFlash = 3
};
public enum enumVAlignment
{
  Top,
  Center,
  Bottom
};
//ah, finally the Control
/// <summary>
///    Summary description for nLabel.
/// </summary>
public class nLabel : System.Windows.Forms.UserControl
{
  private System.ComponentModel.IContainer components;

  /// <summary>
  /// </summary>
  private enumAlignment      m_alignment;
  private enumVAlignment     m_valignment;
  private enumBackStyle      m_backstyle;
  private Color              m_bordercolor;
  private enumBorderStyle    m_borderstyle;
  private int                            m_bordersize;
  private Color                     m_flashcolor;
  private enumFlashType      m_flashtype;
  private bool                      m_wordwrap;
  private int                        m_flashtime;
  private Color                     m_curflash;
  //supplies the timer that allows the
  //border to flash
  Timer                              m_timer;
  //the timer event that fires from this control
  private TickTimerHandler  m_eTimer;
  //properties
  //Alignment
```

LISTING 11.1 Continued

```
[
  Category("Appearance"),
  Description("Specifies the horizontal alignment of text."),
  Bindable(true),
  Browsable(true)
]
public enumAlignment Alignment
{
  get
  {
    return m_alignment;
  }
  set
  {
    m_alignment = value;
    //Invalidate invokes the OnPaint method
    Invalidate();
  }
}
//VAlignment
[
  Category("Appearance"),
  Description("Specifies the vertical alignment of text."),
  Browsable(true),
  DefaultValue(enumVAlignment.Top)
]
public enumVAlignment VAlignment
{
  get
  {
    return m_valignment;
  }
  set
  {
    m_valignment = value;
    //Invalidate invokes the OnPaint method
    Invalidate();
  }
}
//Caption
[
  Category("Appearance"),
  Description("Specifies the caption."),
]
```

LISTING 11.1   Continued

```
public string Caption
{
  get
  {
    return Text;
  }
  set
  {
    Text = value;
    //Invalidate invokes the OnPaint method
    Invalidate();
  }
}
//Text
[
  Browsable(false)
]
public override string Text
{
  get
  {
    return base.Text;
  }
  set
  {
    base.Text = value;
  }
}
//BackStyle
[
  Category("Appearance"),
  Description("Specifies the transparency of the control."),
Browsable(true),
  DefaultValue(enumBackStyle.Opaque)
]
public enumBackStyle BackStyle
{
  get
  {
    return m_backstyle;
  }
  set
  {
    m_backstyle = value;
```

LISTING 11.1   Continued

```
      //Invalidate invokes the OnPaint method
      Invalidate();
  }
}
//BorderColor
[
  Category("Appearance"),
  Description("Specifies the color of the border."),
  Browsable(true)
]
public Color BorderColor
{
  get
  {
    return m_bordercolor;
  }
  set
  {
    m_bordercolor = value;
    m_curflash = value;
    //Invalidate invokes the OnPaint method
    Invalidate();
  }
}
//BorderStyle
[
  Category("Appearance"),
  Description("Specifies the style of the border."),
  Browsable(true),
  DefaultValue(enumBorderStyle.Single_Color_Border)
]
public enumBorderStyle BorderStyle
{
  get
  {
    return m_borderstyle;
  }
  set
  {
    m_borderstyle = value;
    //Invalidate invokes the OnPaint method
    Invalidate();
  }
}
```

LISTING 11.1   Continued

```
//BorderSize
[
  Category("Appearance"),
  Description("Specifies the size of the border."),
  Browsable(true),
  DefaultValue(1)
]
public int BorderSize
{
  get
  {
    return m_bordersize;
  }
  set
  {
    if (value>10)
    {
      InvalidPropertyValueException ex=new InvalidPropertyValueException();
      throw ex;
    }
    m_bordersize = value;
    Invalidate();
  }
}
//FlashColor
[
  Category("Appearance"),
  Description("Specifies the color that flashes."),
  Browsable(true)
]
public Color FlashColor
{
  get
  {
    return m_flashcolor;
  }
  set
  {
    m_flashcolor = value;
    Invalidate();
  }
}
//FlashType
[
```

LISTING 11.1   Continued

```csharp
        Category("Appearance"),
        Description("Specifies the type of flashing."),
        Browsable(true),
        DesignerSerializationVisibility(DesignerSerializationVisibility.Visible),
        DefaultValue(enumFlashType.NoneFlash)
    ]
    public enumFlashType FlashType
    {
        get
        {
            return m_flashtype;
        }
        set
        {
            m_flashtype = value;
            if (m_flashtype>0)
            {
                if (m_flashtime>0)
                {
                    if (DesignMode==false)
                    {
                        m_timer.Start();
                    }
                }
            }
        }
    }
    //WordWrap
    [
        Category("Appearance"),
        Description("Determines if the text wraps or not."),
        Browsable(true),
        DefaultValue(true)
    ]
    public bool WordWrap
    {
        get
        {
            return m_wordwrap;
        }
        set
        {
            m_wordwrap = value;
            Invalidate();
```

LISTING 11.1   Continued

```
    }
  }
  //FlashTime
  [
    Category("Appearance"),
    Description("Specifies the time between flashes."),
    Browsable(true),
    DefaultValue(0)
  ]
  public int FlashTime
  {
    get
    {
      return m_flashtime;
    }
    set
    {
      if (m_flashtype!=enumFlashType.NoneFlash)
      {
        m_timer.Stop();
      }
      m_flashtime = value;
      if (value>0)
      {
        m_timer.Interval=value;
        if (m_flashtype>0)
        {
          if (DesignMode==false)
          {
            m_timer.Start();
          }
        }
      }
      Invalidate();
    }
  }

  //Timer Event
  [Description("Raised when the Timer message hits")]
  public event TickTimerHandler TickTimer
  {
    add
    {
      m_eTimer += value;
```

LISTING 11.1   Continued

```
    }
    remove
    {
      m_eTimer -= value;
    }
  }
  //this is where the event is actually fired
  //we could fire the event directly, without this
  //function, but using this virtual function
  //allows controls based on this class to override
  //this event
  protected virtual void OnTimer(TickTimerEventArgs e)
  {
    if (m_eTimer != null)
    m_eTimer(this, e);
  }
  public override void  Refresh()
  {
    Invalidate();
  }
  public nLabel()
  {
    InitializeComponent();
    // Add any initialization after the InitForm call
  }

  protected override void OnPaint(System.Windows.Forms.PaintEventArgs sa)
  {
    StringFormat style = new StringFormat();
    //provides left to right alignment
    switch (m_alignment)
    {
      case enumAlignment.Left:
        style.Alignment=System.Drawing.StringAlignment.Near;
        break;
      case enumAlignment.Center:
        style.Alignment=System.Drawing.StringAlignment.Center;
        break;
      case enumAlignment.Right:
        style.Alignment=System.Drawing.StringAlignment.Far;
        break;
      default:
        style.Alignment=System.Drawing.StringAlignment.Near;
        break;
```

LISTING 11.1 Continued

```
      }
      //provide top to bottom alignment
      switch (m_valignment)
      {
        case enumVAlignment.Top:
          style.LineAlignment=System.Drawing.StringAlignment.Near;
          break;
        case enumVAlignment.Center:
          style.LineAlignment=System.Drawing.StringAlignment.Center;
          break;
        case enumVAlignment.Bottom:
          style.LineAlignment=System.Drawing.StringAlignment.Far;
          break;
        default:
          style.LineAlignment=System.Drawing.StringAlignment.Near;
          break;
      }
sa.Graphics.DrawRectangle(new Pen(m_curflash,1),ClientRectangle.Top,
➥code lClientRectangle.Left,ClientRectangle.Width,
➥ClientRectangle.Height);
      sa.Graphics.DrawString(Text,Font,new SolidBrush(ForeColor),
➥ClientRectangle,style);
    }

    /// <summary>
    ///      Clean up any resources being used.
    /// </summary>
    public override void Dispose()
    {
      base.Dispose();
      components.Dispose();
    }

    /// <summary>
    ///      Required method for Designer support - do not modify
    ///      the contents of this method with the code editor.
    /// </summary>
    private void InitializeComponent()
    {
      this.components = new System.ComponentModel.Container();
      this.m_timer = new System.Windows.Forms.Timer(this.components);
      this.m_timer.Tick += new System.EventHandler(this.OnTimerEvent);
      this.AccessibleName = "netLabel";
```

LISTING 11.1 Continued

```
    this.Name = "nLabel";
    this.Size = new System.Drawing.Size(344, 80);
    this.Load += new System.EventHandler(this.nLabel_Load);
}

///<summary>
///   this is where we receive our timer event
///   we use this to flash the border
///</summary>
private void OnTimerEvent(object source, EventArgs e)
{
  //we create the arguments for our own event
  TickTimerEventArgs etick = new TickTimerEventArgs(false,m_curflash);
  //and fire our event
  OnTimer(etick);
  //if we weren't canceled in our event
  //then do the flash
  if (!etick.Cancel)
  {
    if (m_curflash==m_bordercolor)
    {
      m_curflash=m_flashcolor;
    }
    else
    {
      m_curflash=m_bordercolor;
    }
    Invalidate();
  }
}
  }
 }
}
```

Control Elements

The following sections will review this code a little at a time and show snippets from it while discussing different aspects of the control. The intent of this discussion is to cover typical pro-gramming constructs used in a .NET component, including:

- Namespaces—Group functionality into logical and functional groups.
- Properties and Methods—Define the main interface for any component, including a .NET component.

- Events—Are programmed very differently in .NET than in traditional Visual Basic or C++.
- Design Time Support—Has changed from property pages to designers.
- Drawing—Requires the GDI+ classes provided by .NET.

NameSpaces

Namespaces, first talked about in Chapter 4, are important to avoid conflicts between .NET objects.

In the example, I've placed the sample control and all the enums and classes associated with it in the netLabel namespace. The control uses other namespaces and some of those are listed in the using statements at the beginning of the code listing. Listing 11.2 shows the using statements from the control listing.

LISTING 11.2   netLabel Namespace

```
namespace netLabel
{
  using System;
  using System.Collections;
  using System.ComponentModel;
  using System.Drawing;
  using System.Data;
  using System.Windows.Forms;
  using System.ComponentModel.Design;
  using System.Diagnostics;
  using System.Drawing.Drawing2D;
  using System.Drawing.Design;
  using System.Windows.Forms.Design;

    //...other code

}
```

To use the control, the code will have to refer to that namespace either directly or with a using statement. The control class is nLabel, for example,

```
private netLabel.nLabel NLabel1;
```

This line declares a variable of netLabel.nLabel type. The following lines do the same thing with a using statement:

```
Using netLabel;
private nLabel NLabel1;
```

Namespaces are fairly simple to use, but very important in coding in C#. Most sample listings have using statements and all code is enclosed in a namespace. Namespaces in C# are as important as GUIDs were in COM programming.

Properties and Methods

This discussion goes right to the heart of the matter and shows you how to add properties and events by adding the code directly to the control. At the time of writing, no wizards were available for this purpose. It is perfectly okay to use wizards to add properties and methods, but it's important to understand the code. The wizard will only do so much, at some point you must manipulate the code to make the control behave as designed.

A typical property will set and return values in a member variable. If the property involves drawing, the property set will typically invalidate the control so that it will repaint. Listing 11.3 shows a typical property from the nLabel C# project.

LISTING 11.3   BorderColor Property

```
//BorderColor
[
  Category("Appearance"),
  Description("Specifies the color of the border."),
  Browsable(true),
  DefaultValue(System.Drawing.Color.Red)
]
public Color BorderColor
{
  get
  {
    return m_bordercolor;
  }
  set
  {
    m_bordercolor = value;
    m_curflash = value;
    //Invalidate invokes the OnPaint method
    Invalidate();
  }
}
```

Looking at Listing 11.3, the section contained within the square brackets before the actual property function consists of attributes. These attributes can control several aspects of the property. In many cases, what took a lot of code in ATL can now be added by simply specifying an attribute. In traditional VB, some of the features that can be specified with these attributes were not even available, and the ones that were available had to set through special wizards.

In this case, we set four attributes:

1. `Category`   The first attribute sets up a category that is used in the .NET property browser at design time.

2. `Description`   Next, set a description. Descriptions are typically used in design time property browsers.

3. `Browsable`   In the third attribute, set the browsable attribute to `true`, which will cause design time browsers to show and manipulate the property.

4. `DefaultValue`   Finally, set a default value for the property—in this case, the color red.

Following the attribute block is the public property declaration, which includes the type and the name of the property. Within the block defined by the property are the "getter" and "setter." In this case, you simply set the value into a member variable. Other property procedures could contain a lot of code to do their jobs—how much code depends on the property.

Some properties are enumerated. As we saw in the ATL control, they can be difficult to write. Enumerated properties in .NET are almost exactly like enumerated properties in traditional Visual Basic. You declare an enumeration of the proper type and then define your property with that type. This results in an enumerated property that shows in the browser as a drop-down list of choices. Listing 11.4 shows a property of this type.

LISTING 11.3   `BorderColor` Property

```
public enum enumAlignment
{
  Left,
  Center,
  Right
};

//... other enums
public class nLabel : System.Windows.Forms.UserControl
{
  //Alignment
  [
    Category("Appearance"),
    Description("Specifies the horizontal alignment of text."),
    Bindable(true),
    Browsable(true)
  ]
  public enumAlignment Alignment
  {
    get
    {
```

LISTING 11.3 Continued

```
          return m_alignment;
      }
      set
      {
        m_alignment = value;
        //Invalidate invokes the OnPaint method
        Invalidate();
      }
  }
//... other enums
```

With the plethora of default properties provided by most base classes that .NET provides for developing our own controls, you are faced with a new problem—the presence of unwanted properties. There could be a number of reasons for wanting to get rid of a property provided by a base class; it might not make sense for the particular control you are writing, or you may not want to provide that particular functionality. In reality, you can't get rid of public properties in .NET classes, but you can hide them from property browsers. Listing 11.4 shows how to do this.

LISTING 11.4 Hiding a Property

```
[
  Browsable(false),
]
public string Text
{
  override get
  {
    return base.Text;
  }
  override set
  {
    base.Text = value;
  }
}
```

Methods are a simple addition. They are simply a public function. Methods may or may not have parameters. Typically, you would make a method a void return, for example:

```
public void Refresh()
{
  Invalidate();
}
```

Events

Providing events in .NET using C# is a bit more bulky than working with the events in traditional Visual Basic code, which is fairly straightforward. You declare the event in the member area of the module and then raise the error within code. The parameters are placed in the declaration and handled as simple variables.

With C#, things are a bit more convoluted. You use an event argument class for the event arguments and there are several other steps required to make your event work. Let's take a look at the steps required for adding an event to your control. There are two basic ways to add an event to your control. One way is with no event parameters, which is discussed first. This is much simpler than using parameters, which will be the next discussion.

Before getting started writing the event code, it makes things clearer to introduce what a delegate is. .NET uses delegates to facilitate the event structure. You can think of a *delegate* as a class that can hold a reference to a method. Because delegates can only hold references to methods that match its signature, a delegate is sort of a type-safe function pointer.

Listing 11.5 shows the portions of code required for an event that has no parameters. The OnTimerEvent is a routine that was in the control before you added your event. It handles the timer event for the control that allows the control to flash its border.

LISTING 11.5   Event with No Parameters

```
public class NetLabel : System.WinForms.UserControl
{
  public event EventHandler TickTimer;
  protected virtual void OnTickTimer(EventArgs e)
  {
    if (TickTimer != null)
      TickTimer(this, e);
  }
  //code removed for brevity
  //this event fires when the timer expires
  private void OnTimerEvent(object source, EventArgs e)
  {
    OnTickTimer(EventArgs.Empty);
    //other code removed
  }
}
```

When looking at the code, you might wonder what purpose the OnTickTimer function serves. The code would work without it; in other words, you could "fire" the TickTimer event directly from the OnTimerEvent.

The OnTickTimer function is virtual and can be overridden. The event by itself cannot, so the OnTickTimer function is there to allow a control that is based on this control to override the event.

Let's put some data with this event and also use a private member to hold a reference to the event handler with a property function to set that private member. This is about as complicated as an event can get.

You have read a little about a delegate. The event you wrote in Listing 11.5 uses a delegate; it uses the default delegate for event handlers. On the other hand, Listing 11.6 uses a delegate that also has data or parameters and is written specifically for the event in the nLabel control.

Of course, Listing 11.6 is a partial listing from our complete sample control called netLabel. Because it is partial, it is missing some declarations for member variables that appear in the listing, and it is even missing the property procedures for those properties with which those member variables belong. This is done to focus you on the code that is required for the event.

LISTING 11.6   An Event with Data

```
namespace netLabel
{
  //removed using statements

  public delegate void TickTimerHandler(object sender, TickTimerEventArgs e);
  //this class defines that data that goes with the event
  public class TickTimerEventArgs : EventArgs
  {
    //define the member variables to hold the data
    private bool bCancel = false;
    private Color cBorderColor = System.Drawing.SystemColors.WindowFrame;
    //constructor
    public TickTimerEventArgs(bool bCancel, Color cBorderColor) {}
    //properties
    public bool Cancel
    {
      get
      {
        return bCancel;
      }
      set
      {
        bCancel = value;
      }
    }
    public Color BorderColor
```

LISTING 11.6   Continued

```
  {
    get
    {
      return cBorderColor;
    }
    set
    {
      cBorderColor=value;
    }
  }
}

public class NetLabel : System.WinForms.UserControl
{
  //code removed
  private TickTimerHandler  m_eTimer;
  //code removed
  //Timer Event
  [Description("Raised when the Timer message hits")]
  public event TickTimerHandler TickTimer
  {
    get
    {
      return m_eTimer;
    }
    set
    {
      m_eTimer = value;
    }
  }

  protected virtual void OnTimer(TickTimerEventArgs e)
  {
    if (m_eTimer != null)
      m_eTimer(this, e);
  }
  //code removed
  //this is an event in our control triggered by a timer that
  //we have set within the control's code.
  private void OnTimerEvent(object source, EventArgs e)
  {
    TickTimerEventArgs      etick = new TickTimerEventArgs(false,m_curflash);
    OnTimer(etick);
    if (!etick.Cancel)
    {
```

LISTING 11.6   Continued

```
        if (m_curflash==m_bordercolor)
        {
          m_curflash=m_flashcolor;
        }
        else
        {
          m_curflash=m_bordercolor;
        }
        Invalidate();
      }
    }
  }
}
```

The first thing that you do to support an event that requires data is declare a custom delegate. This is done outside the structure of the control's class.

Secondly, you need to create a class that will hold the data during the event. This class must be based on the EventArgs class. In Listing 11.6, you create the TickTimerEventArgs class. This class has a Cancel and a BorderColor property. Both are read and write. You also define a constructor that will define the values of these variables. Because these properties are read and write, they can be changed during the event by the event sink.

Next, you set up a handler property. In this case, you are using a private member variable of type TickTimerHandler. The m_eTimer private member is set though the TickTimer property.

After this, set up a routine to actually fire the event. In Listing 11.6, the OnTickTimer function handles this. Remember that this function is used to fire the event to facilitate a child class overriding the event. The event could actually be fired without this virtual function, but controls that use this control as a base class may need this virtual function to override the event.

Finally, you can actually use the event. Do this by creating a variable of type TickTimerEventArgs. You set the property values at the time you create the class. Then you call the OnTickTimer function to actually fire the event.

As you can see, handling events in C# is a bit more troublesome than in VB. In my opinion, it's a little too much work for a system that's supposed to be less code intensive.

Design Time Support

Instead of using property pages, .NET uses custom designers to provide design time setting of special properties. A designer controls the behavior of a component at design time. In .NET, a designer is just an object that is attached to a control at design time.

Custom designers allow much better flexibility than a set of property pages. They allow and encourage functionality that was possible in ActiveX controls only through ingenuity and even trickery. With a custom designer, these things become easier to do.

There are many things that can be done with a custom designer. This section will discuss the more common things and demonstrate how to accomplish a few of them.

Type Converter

The simplest kind of custom designer converts types. Intrinsic types have type converters provided for them already, so you should only need to write a designer if your type is a custom type. The TypeConverterAttribute must be applied to the property that will use the type converter.

Implementing a type converter is done by creating a class based on System.ComponentModel.TypeConverter. You override CanConvertFrom to provide the types that this converter will handle, and you also override ConvertFrom to do the actual conversion. Listing 11.7 shows the basics required for a custom type converter. This one is simply a string to number converter.

LISTING 11.7   Type Converter

```
namespace netLabel
{
  Using System;
  Using System.ComponentModel;
  public class TestConverter : TypeConverter
  {
    public override bool CanConvertFrom(ItypeDescriptorContext context, Type
sourceType)
    {
      if (sourceType == typeof(string))
        return true;
      return base.CanConvertFrom(context, sourceType);
    }
    public override object ConvertFrom(ItypeDescriptorContext context,
      object value, object[] arguments)
    {
      if (value is string)
      {
        string text = ((string)value).Trim();
        int convertedValue = int.Parse(text);
        return convertedValue;
      }
      return base.ConvertFrom(context, value, arguments);
```

LISTING 11.7 Continued

```
    }
  }
}
```

UI Type Editor

A UI type editor provides a graphical way for a programmer to choose a value for a property in your control. The color editor would be a good example of this type of custom designer.

The implementation of the type editor involves basing a class on a `System.Drawing.Design.UITypeEditor`. Then you override the `EditValue` method to set up properties and override the `GetEditStyle` to describe the support you will provide. Listing 11.8 shows the implementation for a border size property that uses a trackbar to adjust the size.

LISTING 11.8 UI Type Editor

```
namespace netLabel
{
  using System;
  using System.Collections;
  using System.Core;
  using System.ComponentModel;
  using System.Drawing;
  using System.Data;
  using System.WinForms;
  using System.ComponentModel.Design;
  using System.Diagnostics;
  using System.Drawing. Drawing2D;
  using System.Drawing.Design;
  using System.WinForms.ComponentModel;
  using System.WinForms.Design;
  public class BorderSizeEditor : UITypeEditor
  {
    private IWinFormsEditorService edSvc = null;

    public override object EditValue(ITypeDescriptorContext context,
      IServiceObjectProvider provider, object value)
    {
      if (context != null && context.Instance != null && provider != null)
      {
        edSvc = (IWinFormsEditorService)provider.GetServiceObject
          (typeof(IWinFormsEditorService));
        if (edSvc != null)
        {
```

LISTING 11.8   Continued

```
            TrackBar trackBar = new TrackBar();
            trackBar.ValueChanged += new EventHandler(this.ValueChanged);
            trackBar.ForeColor = Color.White;
            trackBar.Minimum = 0;
            trackBar.Maximum = 20;
            trackBar.Height = 23;
            bool asInt = true;
            if (value is int)
            {
              trackBar.Value = (int)value;
            }
            else if (value is byte)
            {
              asInt = false;
              trackBar.Value = (byte)value;
            }
            edSvc.DropDownControl(trackBar);
            if (asInt)
            {
              value = trackBar.Value;
            }
            else
            {
              value = (byte)trackBar.Value;
            }
          }
        }
        return value;
      }
    }
}

    //control's code removed for brevity
    //this is what the property that uses the designer would look like
    //BorderSize
    [
      Category("Appearance"),
      Editor(typeof(netLabel.BorderSizeEditor),typeof(UITypeEditor)),
      Description("Specifies the size of the border."),
      Browsable(true),
      Persistable(PersistableSupport.All),
      DefaultValue(1)
    ]
    public int BorderSize
```

LISTING 11.8   Continued

```
  {
    get
    {
      return m_bordersize;
    }
    set
    {
      m_bordersize = value;
      //Invalidate invokes the OnPaint method
      Invalidate();
    }
  }
}
```

As you can see from Listing 11.8, once you have the designer class, the property uses an attribute to "attach" the designer to a particular property.

Extender Provider

Extender providers add properties to other controls. In ActiveX controls, there was no good way to provide extended properties. A container (like Visual Basic) could provide extended properties for an ActiveX control, but it was not simple to do this from another control.

To build an extender provider, you must define a component that implements the System.ComponentModel.IExtenderProvider interface. This interface will typically be provided along with deriving your class from a "normal" control class, such as RichControl. You then override CanExtend and code it to return true for controls that you want to extend. Finally, you provide the properties you want to add to the other controls.

The properties provided for other controls are actually written as methods in the provider control. Listing 11.9 shows the bare essentials for a provider control. In this listing, you provide a control that can display text when the mouse moves over a control.

LISTING 11.9   Provider Control

```
namespace netLabel
{
  using System;
  using System.Collections;
  using System.ComponentModel;
  using System.ComponentModel.Design;
  using System.Drawing;
  using System.WinForms;
  using System.WinForms.Design;
```

LISTING 11.9   Continued

```
[
  ProvideProperty("FloatCaption"),
]
public class FloatCaption : RichControl, IExtenderProvider
{
  private Hashtable Captions;
  private Control currentControl;

  //here is where we tell the container what we extend
  bool IExtenderProvider.CanExtend(object target)
  {
    if (target is Control && !(target is FloatCaption))
    {
      return true;
    }
    return false;
  }

  //the constructor for our class
  public FloatCaption()
  {
    Captions = new Hashtable();
  }

  //the provided property
  [
    DefaultValue(""),
    ExtenderProperty(typeof(Control))
  ]
  public string GetFloatCaption(Control control)
  {
    string text = (string)Captions[control];
    if (text == null)
    {
      text = string.Empty;
    }
    return text;
  }

  public void SetFloatCaption(Control control, string value)
  {
    if (value == null)
    {
      value = string.Empty;
```

LISTING 11.9   Continued

```
        }
        if (value.Length == 0)
        {
          Captions.Remove(control);
          control.Enter -= new EventHandler(OnControlEnter);
          control.Leave -= new EventHandler(OnControlLeave);
        }
        else
        {
          Controls[control] = value;
          control.Enter += new EventHandler(OnControlEnter);
          control.Leave += new EventHandler(OnControlLeave);
        }
        if (control == activeControl)
        {
          Invalidate();
        }
      }

      //we use these two events to display our captions
      private void OnControlEnter(object sender, EventArgs e)
      {
        currentControl = (Control)sender;
        Invalidate();
      }

      private void OnControlLeave(object sender, EventArgs e)
      {
        if (sender == currentControl)
        {
          currentControl = null;
          Invalidate();
        }
      }

      //here we paint the captions
      protected override void OnPaint(PaintEventArgs pe)
      {
        base.OnPaint(pe);
        if (activeControl != null)
        {
          string text = (string)Captions[activeControl];
          if (text != null && text.Length > 0)
          {
```

LISTING **11.9**   Continued

```
            rect.Inflate(-2, -2);
            Brush brush = new SolidBrush(ForeColor);
            pe.Graphics.DrawString(text, Font, brush, rect);
            brush.Dispose();
        }
      }
    }
  }
}
```

Other Designer Features

A WinForms designer is based on `System.ComponentModel.Design.ComponentDesigner`. It implements the `IDesigner` and `IDesignerFilter` interfaces. You have read about several features of custom designers and have seen several examples of them already. There are several other features that a designer can provide, as shown in the following:

- A designer can add design-time drawing that is different than the code that is called at runtime. This can be desirable to allow a programmer to see and manipulate the control at design time.

- A designer can filter properties. This allows the designer to replace properties or add new properties or change the attributes.

- A designer can add specific commands at the context menu at design time. This can make commonly needed commands very convenient.

Custom designers are a welcome addition to the design capabilities of forms. As you see, more examples of this feature some very sophisticated designers should evolve.

Drawing

We could write an entire book on this topic. Drawing a control, whether it is an ActiveX control or a .NET control, can range from being rather simple to very complex. The thing that can throw you for a loop in .NET has to do with GDI+ drawing. GDI+ encapsulates the drawing routines in several classes.

Learning to draw your controls with the provided classes entails digging in and learning the features that are supplied through these classes. Doing so can be disconcerting and difficult. While the routines are not all that difficult to use (in fact, they are usually much simpler than C-based GDI code), there are a lot of them and they have lots of options.

Look at the code in Listing 11.10 for drawing a label control. Fairly simple, it draws a border and the text with the correct alignment.

11

LISTING 11.10   OnPaint Override

```
protected override void OnPaint(System.WinForms.PaintEventArgs sa)
{
  StringFormat style = new StringFormat();
  switch (m_alignment)
  {
    case enumAlignment.Left:
      style.Alignment=System.Drawing.StringAlignment.Near;
      break;
    case enumAlignment.Center:
      style.Alignment=System.Drawing.StringAlignment.Center;
      break;
    case enumAlignment.Right:
      style.Alignment=System.Drawing.StringAlignment.Far;
      break;
    default:
      style.Alignment=System.Drawing.StringAlignment.Near;
      break;
  }
  switch (m_valignment)
  {
    case enumVAlignment.Top:
      style.LineAlignment=System.Drawing.StringAlignment.Near;
      break;
    case enumVAlignment.Center:
      style.LineAlignment=System.Drawing.StringAlignment.Center;
      break;
    case enumVAlignment.Bottom:
      style.LineAlignment=System.Drawing.StringAlignment.Far;
      break;
    default:
      style.LineAlignment=System.Drawing.StringAlignment.Near;
      break;
  }

  sa.Graphics.DrawRectangle(new Pen(m_curflash,1),
      ClientRectangle.Top,
      ClientRectangle.Left,
      ClientRectangle.Width,
      ClientRectangle.Height);
  sa.Graphics.DrawString(Text,Font,new
SolidBrush(ForeColor),ClientRectangle,style);
}
```

There are several things to notice in the `OnPaint` override. First, the `PaintEventArgs` you are passed contains a graphics object on which you can draw. This object holds the `hdc` and all the routines to draw on that `hdc`.

You use your member variables, which hold the properties that were set in your control to influence where the text is drawn, creating and setting properties in a `Style` object. You use the `ClientRectangle`, provided by your base class, to position both your rectangle that you draw for your border and your text that you draw within that border.

Summary

In this chapter, you learned about .NET WinForm controls. This chapter should give you a good start in programming components in the newest technology available, C# - .NET. I certainly think that this is the future of component programming in Microsoft technologies.

You've been programming in a world of components for some time. If you haven't been doing so, now is the time to step up and make the change to components. If you have been doing so, .NET will make that process easier and more intuitive.

Definition of Terms

Abstraction   In object-oriented programming, the process of representing real world programming problems as objects.

Address   In C or C++, the location in memory of a value or object.

Aggregation   In COM, a way to reuse COM objects by holding a pointer to interfaces in other objects and exposing those pointers as your own interfaces.

ANSI (The American National Standards Institute)   An organization of American industry and business groups dedicated to the development of trade and communication standards. ANSI sets standards for C and other programming languages.

ANSI C   The American National Standards Institute's version of the C language, which specifies the formal syntax and semantics of the language, the standard libraries that are included, and the way in which the compiler is to translate the program.

ANSI Character Set   An 8-bit character set that contains the 7-bit ASCII standard character set as well as currency and mathematical symbols, accented characters, and other characters not normally found on the keyboard. Microsoft Windows version 3.1 and its applications use the ANSI character set internally.

ANSI String   A string comprised of ANSI characters, which are by definition 8-bit characters.

API (Application Programming Interface)   A function-based set of routines that a program uses to carry out some set of tasks.

ASCII   The dominant standard for coding information on computers and related equipment.

ASCII Character Set   A standard 7-bit code for representing characters—letters, digits, punctuation, and control instructions—with binary values. It is part of the American Standard Code for Information Interchange (ASCII).

ATL (Active Template Library)   A group of class libraries typically used for COM development with C++.

ActiveX   Specification for controls based on COM. ActiveX Controls are a successor to OLE Controls. The specification was changed at that time, but OLE Controls qualified as they were as ActiveX Controls.

AVI   Audio video interleaved. Denotes a type of streaming multimedia file that contains video along with the accompanying sound.

Base Class   In object-oriented programming, any class that is used as a base for a new class.

Binary   Refers to base-2 representation of information.

Binding   The process of associating the representation of an item (such as a variable name) with some descriptive information (such as an address or type). With objects, we can have early binding (by the compiler) or late binding (at runtime).

Callback Function   An application-defined function that is called by the system or some sub-system.

Caret   An insertion point for typed text. The visible component is a flashing line, block, or bitmap that marks the location at which inserted text will appear.

Class   A type that defines the interface of a particular kind of object. A class definition defines instance variables and methods and class variables and methods.

Client Area   That portion of a window used for output and interaction with the user.

CLSID   A universally unique identifier (UUID) that identifies a type of OLE object.

Code Page   A character set that can include numbers, punctuation marks, and other glyphs. Different languages and locales may use different code pages. For example, code page 1252 is used for American English and most European languages.

Collection   An object programming construct that can hold multiple references to other objects.

COM (Component Object Model)   An open architecture for cross-platform development of client/server applications based on object-oriented technology as agreed on by Digital Equipment Corporation and Microsoft Corporation.

Control   This word has several meanings and connotations, depending on the context in which it is used. This can refer to an ActiveX control, a 16-bit VBX control, a 16-bit C control, or a Windows control.

Delegation   In COM, a way to reuse other COM objects by exposing an interface that is the same as another object and implementing that interface by calling the methods in that other object. This is the way that Visual Basic 5 and 6 reused objects.

Descendant   In C++, a class that is derived from another class.

DTP   Date and Time Picker control.

Encapsulation   In object-oriented programming, the process of hiding the implementation within an object.

Far Pointer   A 32 bit pointer. In 16 bit, this is a pointer that can access any area of memory as opposed to a 16-bit pointer that is a near pointer. In 32 bit, all pointers are 32 bits and there is no need to distinguish between near and far pointers.

FIFO   First in first out. In message queues, this refers to the way that messages are serviced.

FTP (File Transfer Protocol)   This is an Internet protocol and uses TCP/IP to transfer files.

GDI (Graphics Device Interface)   The part of Windows that communicates between the program and device drivers.

Hexidecimal   Base-16 counting system using 0, 1, 2, 3, 4, 5, 6, 7, 8, 9, A, B, C, D, E, and F. This base is commonly used in computing because it conveniently represents a byte with two digits. A word or short would be 4 digits, a long 8 digits. For example, the largest unsigned word is 65,536 decimal, but simply FFFF in hex.

HTML (Hypertext Markup Language)   A markup language commonly used for Web pages.

HTTP (Hypertext Transfer Protocol)   The protocol commonly used by browsers and servers to transfer Web pages.

IDL   A standard language for specifying the interface for remote procedure calls.

IID   A globally unique identifier associated with an interface.

Implementation Inheritance   The type of inheritance associated with C++ classes. This type of inheritance happens most often with source code classes, and the descendant class inherits the functionality (implementation) of the base class.

Inheritance   The generic term applied to any object or class that gets its structure or functionality from another object or class.

Instance   Refers to the "in use" or running state of some object.

Instantiation   The act of creating an instance of some object.

Interface   In COM, a set of related functions that can be accessed through a common pointer.

JIT Compiler   Just-in-time compiler. Takes intermediate byte code and compiles when the code is needed to run. The .NET compilers are JIT compilers.

LCID   32-bit value that identifies the language and sub-language for a locale.

Localization   Process of translating screen text, help file and documentation into other languages. This also encompasses the process of making the program work under those locales.

Message pump   A loop that services the message queue with the `GetMessage`, `TranslateMessage`, and `DispatchMessage` functions.

MFC (Microsoft Foundation Classes)   An extensive set of class libraries for Visual C++.

OLE   A specification for transferring and sharing information between applications.

Pixel   The smallest unit that can be represented on a device.

Polymorphism   In object-oriented programming technology, this means that a particular function named the same can mean different things in different objects.

Pointer   In C or C++, a variable that holds an address as defined in this section.

Recursive   Ability of a function to call itself.

Reentrant   Code that will pick up an in-process task, complete a portion, and then exit. When the code is called again, it can continue the process.

Semaphore   In programming, an object that serializes access to a particular resource.

Subclassing   A technique that allows a program to intercept messages destined for a window's procedure and redirect them to a different procedure.

Twip   1/1440 of an inch.

UI (User Interface)   This refers to the things on the screen with which an end user will interact.

Unicode   A 16-bit character set. It is capable of encoding all known characters.

VBX   A custom control for the 16-bit world. Works in Visual Basic 3.0 and earlier.

A

DEFINITION OF
TERMS

Character Code Tables

Ctrl	Dec	Hex	Char	Code	Dec	Hex	Char	Dec	Hex	Char	Dec	Hex	Char
^@	0	00		NUL	32	20	sp	64	40	@	96	60	`
^A	1	01	☺	SOH	33	21	!	65	41	A	97	61	a
^B	2	02	☻	STX	34	22	"	66	42	B	98	62	b
^C	3	03	♥	ETX	35	23	#	67	43	C	99	63	c
^D	4	04	♦	EOT	36	24	$	68	44	D	100	64	d
^E	5	05	♣	ENQ	37	25	%	69	45	E	101	65	e
^F	6	06	♠	ACK	38	26	&	70	46	F	102	66	f
^G	7	07	•	BEL	39	27	'	71	47	G	103	67	g
^H	8	08	◘	BS	40	28	(	72	48	H	104	68	h
^I	9	09	○	HT	41	29	)	73	49	I	105	69	i
^J	10	0A	◙	LF	42	2A	*	74	4A	J	106	6A	j
^K	11	0B	♂	VT	43	2B	+	75	4B	K	107	6B	k
^L	12	0C	♀	FF	44	2C	,	76	4C	L	108	6C	l
^M	13	0D	♪	CR	45	2D	−	77	4D	M	109	6D	m
^N	14	0E	♫	SO	46	2E	.	78	4E	N	110	6E	n
^O	15	0F	☀	SI	47	2F	/	79	4F	O	111	6F	o
^P	16	10	►	SLE	48	30	0	80	50	P	112	70	p
^Q	17	11	◄	CS1	49	31	1	81	51	Q	113	71	q
^R	18	12	↕	DC2	50	32	2	82	52	R	114	72	r
^S	19	13	‼	DC3	51	33	3	83	53	S	115	73	t
^T	20	14	¶	DC4	52	34	4	84	54	T	116	74	t
^U	21	15	§	NAK	53	35	5	85	55	U	117	75	u
^V	22	16	▬	SYN	54	36	6	86	56	V	118	76	v
^W	23	17	↨	ETB	55	37	7	87	57	W	119	77	w
^X	24	18	↑	CAN	56	38	8	88	58	X	120	78	x
^Y	25	19	↓	EM	57	39	9	89	59	Y	121	79	y
^Z	26	1A	→	SUB	58	3A	:	90	5A	Z	122	7A	z
^[	27	1B	←	ESC	59	3B	;	91	5B	[	123	7B	{
^\	28	1C	∟	FS	60	3C	<	92	5C	\	124	7C	|
^]	29	1D	↔	GS	61	3D	=	93	5D	]	125	7D	}
^^	30	1E	▲	RS	62	3E	>	94	5E	^	126	7E	~
^_	31	1F	▼	US	63	3F	?	95	5F	_	127	7F	⌂

FIGURE B.1

ASCII character codes 0–127.

Dec	Hex	Char	Dec	Hex	Char	Dec	Hex	Char	Dec	Hex	Char
128	80	Ç	160	A0	á	192	C0	└	224	E0	α
129	81	ü	161	A1	í	193	C1	┴	225	E1	ß
130	82	é	162	A2	ó	194	C2	┬	226	E2	Γ
131	83	â	163	A3	ú	195	C3	├	227	E3	π
132	84	ä	164	A4	ñ	196	C4	─	228	E4	Σ
133	85	à	165	A5	Ñ	197	C5	┼	229	E5	σ
134	86	å	166	A6	ª	198	C6	╞	230	E6	µ
135	87	ç	167	A7	º	199	C7	╟	231	E7	τ
136	88	ê	168	A8	¿	200	C8	╚	232	E8	Φ
137	89	ë	169	A9	⌐	201	C9	╔	233	E9	Θ
138	8A	è	170	AA	¬	202	CA	╩	234	EA	Ω
139	8B	ï	171	AB	½	203	CB	╦	235	EB	δ
140	8C	î	172	AC	¼	204	CC	╠	236	EC	∞
141	8D	ì	173	AD	¡	205	CD	═	237	ED	ø
142	8E	Ä	174	AE	«	206	CE	╬	238	EE	∈
143	8F	Å	175	AF	»	207	CF	╧	239	EF	∩
144	90	É	176	B0	░	208	D0	╨	240	F0	≡
145	91	æ	177	B1	▒	209	D1	╤	241	F1	±
146	92	Æ	178	B2	▓	210	D2	╥	242	F2	≥
147	93	ô	179	B3	│	211	D3	╙	243	F3	≤
148	94	ö	180	B4	┤	212	D4	╘	244	F4	⌠
149	95	ò	181	B5	╡	213	D5	╒	245	F5	⌡
150	96	û	182	B6	╢	214	D6	╓	246	F6	÷
151	97	ù	183	B7	╖	215	D7	╫	247	F7	≈
152	98	ÿ	184	B8	╕	216	D8	╪	248	F8	°
153	99	Ö	185	B9	╣	217	D9	┘	249	F9	∙
154	9A	Ü	186	BA	║	218	DA	┌	250	FA	·
155	9B	¢	187	BB	╗	219	DB	█	251	FB	√
156	9C	£	188	BC	╝	220	DC	▄	252	FC	ⁿ
157	9D	¥	189	BD	╜	221	DD	▌	253	FD	²
158	9E	₧	190	BE	╛	222	DE	▐	254	FE	■
159	9F	ƒ	191	BF	┐	223	DF	▀	255	FF	

FIGURE B.2

ASCII character codes 128–255.

0		32		64	@	96	`	128	Ç	160	á	192	└	224	Ó
1	☺	33	!	65	A	97	a	129	ü	161	í	193	⊥	225	ß
2	☻	34	"	66	B	98	b	130	é	162	ó	194	T	226	Ô
3	♥	35	#	67	C	99	c	131	â	163	ú	195	├	227	Ò
4	♦	36	$	68	D	100	d	132	ä	164	ñ	196	—	228	õ
5	♣	37	%	69	E	101	e	133	à	165	Ñ	197	+	229	Õ
6	♠	38	&	70	F	102	f	134	å	166	ª	198	ã	230	µ
7	•	39	'	71	G	103	g	135	ç	167	º	199	Ã	231	þ
8	◘	40	(	72	H	104	h	136	ê	168	¿	200	╚	232	Þ
9	○	41	)	73	I	105	i	137	ë	169	®	201	╔	233	Ú
10	◙	42	*	74	J	106	j	138	è	170	¬	202	╩	234	Û
11	♂	43	+	75	K	107	k	139	ï	171	½	203	╦	235	Ù
12	♀	44	,	76	L	108	l	140	î	172	¼	204	╠	236	ý
13	♪	45	_	77	M	109	m	141	ì	173	¡	205	=	237	Ý
14	♫	46	.	78	N	110	n	142	Ä	174	«	206	╬	238	¯
15	☼	47	/	79	O	111	o	143	Å	175	»	207	¤	239	´
16	►	48	0	80	P	112	p	144	É	176	░	208	ð	240	-
17	◄	49	1	81	Q	113	q	145	æ	177	▒	209	Ð	241	±
18	↕	50	2	82	R	114	r	146	Æ	178	▓	210	Ê	242	=
19	‼	51	3	83	S	115	s	147	ô	179	│	211	Ë	243	¾
20	¶	52	4	84	T	116	t	148	ö	180	┤	212	È	244	¶
21	§	53	5	85	U	117	u	149	ò	181	Á	213	ı	245	§
22	▬	54	6	86	V	118	v	150	û	182	Â	214	Í	246	÷
23	↨	55	7	87	W	119	w	151	ù	183	À	215	Î	247	¸
24	↑	56	8	88	X	120	x	152	ÿ	184	©	216	Ï	248	°
25	↓	57	9	89	Y	121	y	153	Ö	185	╣	217	┘	249	¨
26	→	58	:	90	Z	122	z	154	Ü	186	║	218	┌	250	·
27	←	59	;	91	[	123	{	155	Ø	187	╗	219	█	251	¹
28	∟	60	<	92	\	124	¦	156	£	188	╝	220	▄	252	³
29	↔	61	=	93	]	125	}	157	Ø	189	¢	221	¦	253	²
30	▲	62	>	94	^	126	~	158	×	190	¥	222	Ì	254	■
31	▼	63	?	95	_	127	⌂	159	ƒ	191	┐	223	▀	255	

FIGURE B.3

ASCII multilingual character codes.

0 ■	32	64 @	96 `	128 ■	160	192 À	224 à
1 ■	33 !	65 A	97 a	129 ■	161 ¡	193 Á	225 á
2 ■	34 "	66 B	98 b	130 ,	162 ¢	194 Â	226 â
3 ■	35 #	67 C	99 c	131 ƒ	163 £	195 Ã	227 ã
4 ■	36 $	68 D	100 d	132 „	164 ¤	196 Ä	228 ä
5 ■	37 %	69 E	101 e	133 …	165 ¥	197 Å	229 å
6 ■	38 &	70 F	102 f	134 †	166 ¦	198 Æ	230 æ
7 ■	39 '	71 G	103 g	135 ‡	167 §	199 Ç	231 ç
8 ■	40 (	72 H	104 h	136 ^	168 ¨	200 È	232 è
9 ■	41)	73 I	105 i	137 ‰	169 ©	201 É	233 é
10 ■	42 *	74 J	106 j	138 Š	170 ª	202 Ê	234 ê
11 ■	43 +	75 K	107 k	139 ‹	171 «	203 Ë	235 ë
12 ■	44 ,	76 L	108 l	140 Œ	172 ¬	204 Ì	236 ì
13 ■	45 –	77 M	109 m	141 ■	173 –	205 Í	237 í
14 ■	46 .	78 N	110 n	142 ■	174 ®	206 Î	238 î
15 ■	47 /	79 O	111 o	143 ■	175 ‾	207 Ï	239 ï
16 ■	48 0	80 P	112 p	144 ■	176 °	208 Ð	240 ð
17 ■	49 1	81 Q	113 q	145 '	177 ±	209 Ñ	241 ñ
18 ■	50 2	82 R	114 r	146 '	178 ²	210 Ò	242 ò
19 ■	51 3	83 S	115 s	147 "	179 ³	211 Ó	243 ó
20 ■	52 4	84 T	116 t	148 "	180 ´	212 Ô	244 ô
21 ■	53 5	85 U	117 u	149 •	181 µ	213 Õ	245 õ
22 ■	54 6	86 V	118 v	150 –	182 ¶	214 Ö	246 ö
23 ■	55 7	87 W	119 w	151 —	183 ·	215 ×	247 ÷
24 ■	56 8	88 X	120 x	152 ~	184 ¸	216 Ø	248 ø
25 ■	57 9	89 Y	121 y	153 ™	185 ¹	217 Ù	249 ù
26 ■	58 :	90 Z	122 z	154 š	186 º	218 Ú	250 ú
27 ■	59 ;	91 [	123 {	155 ›	187 »	219 Û	251 û
28 ■	60 <	92 \	124 |	156 œ	188 ¼	220 Ü	252 ü
29 ■	61 =	93]	125 }	157 ■	189 ½	221 Ý	253 ý
30 ■	62 >	94 ^	126 ~	158 ■	190 ¾	222 Þ	254 þ
31 ■	63 ?	95 _	127 ■	159 Ÿ	191 ¿	223 ß	255 ÿ

FIGURE B.4

ANSI character codes.

C/C++ Keywords

List of C/C++ Keywords

KeyWord	Basic Use	Visual Basic Equivalent
__asm	In-line assembly	None
auto	Variable scope	None
bad_cast	Casting exception	None
bad_typeid	An exception to typeid operator	None
Bool	Variable type	Boolean
break	Loop, decision	exit for, exit do
Case	Decision	Case
catch	Structured exception handling	Catch (.NET only)
char	Variable type	String (sort of)
class	Class delaration	Class (.NET only)
Const	Variable modifier	None
const_cast	Removes attributes from a class	None
continue	Loop	Next
default	Decision construct	case else
delete	Frees memory	= Nothing (objects only)
do	Loop	do-loop
double	Variable type	Double
dynamic_cast	converts to type-id	None
else	Decision	Else
enum	Variable type	Enum
except On Error (all)	Exception handling	Except (.NET only)
explicit	Blocks implicit conversions	None
extern	Variable scope	Public (sort of)
false	Value 0 for bool	False
finally	Exception handling	Finally (.NET only) On Error (all)
float	Variable type	Single
for	Loop	For
friend	Allows access to private class members	Friend (.NET only)
goto	Jump	Goto
if	Decision	If

Continued

KeyWord	Basic Use	Visual Basic Equivalent
inline	Move the function to where it is called	None
int	Variable type	Long
long	Variable type	Long
mutable	Class member qualifier	None
namespace	Identifies a declarative region	None
new	Allocates memory	New (objects only)
operator	Overloads operators	None
private	Class member qualifier	Private
protected	Class member qualifier	Protected (.NET only)
public	Class member qualifier	Public
register	Variable scope	None
reinterpret_cast	Converts any pointer	None
return	Function return	None (kind of)
short	Variable type	integer
signed	Variable qualifier	None
sizeof	Variable size	len (sort of)
static	Variable scope	Static
static_cast	Converts to type-id	None
struct	User-defined type	Type
switch	Decision	Select Case
template	Parameterized classes or functions	None
this	Points to the current class	Me
throw	Creates an exception	Throw (.NET only) Error (all versions)
true	Value 1 for bool	True (-1 in Visual Basic)
try	Structured exception handling	Try (.NET only) On Error (all)
type_info	Stores type information	None
typedef	New variable type	None
typeid	Determines type at runtime	As Object (sort of)
typename	Used in template definitions	None
union	Type of structure	Simulate with types

Continued

KeyWord	Basic Use	Visual Basic Equivalent
unsigned	Variable qualifier	None
using	Works with name spaces	None
virtual	Overrideable function	Virtual (.NET only)
void	Empty return value	None, use Sub
volatile	Variable scope	None
while	Loop	While-wend

INDEX

SYMBOLS